THE COERCIVE ANIMAL

JAMES S. SERILLA

iUniverse, Inc.
NEW YORK   BLOOMINGTON

The Coercive Animal

iUniverse books may be ordered through booksellers or by contacting:

iUniverse
1663 Liberty Drive
Bloomington, IN 47403
www.iuniverse.com
1-800-Authors (1-800-288-4677)

Because of the dynamic nature of the Internet, any Web addresses or links contained in this book may have changed since publication and may no longer be valid.

ISBN: 978-1-4401-2431-0 (pbk)
ISBN: 978-1-4401-2432-7 (ebk)

Library of Congress Control Number: 2009923113

Printed in the United States of America

iUniverse rev. date: 3/31/2009

Also by James S. Serilla
An Essay on Thesisism:
An Accountability Method for Ideas and Morality

A New Moral Revolution.

There is a religious story about a woman named Eve who lived in the Garden of Eden. This story claims she went against the command of her God not to eat the apple of knowledge to good and evil. Nevertheless, she did, and her action threw humankind into darkness.

Here is a different interpretation. Eve did not eat the apple of knowledge to good and evil. She had eaten the apple of fantasy to good and evil. This story explains the start of when we moved the idea of reality obtained from our physical world to newly constructed ideas that contained no reality. We had the birth of arbitrary wills and the coercive animal. It was then that we lost sight of our Garden of Eden. This swept us from our firm footing and threw us into darkness.

Since then, we have had a rich history of human ideas. They have been rich in fancy and in grandeur. From that day we took the apple of false reality, we never have held our ideas to accountability. Science tried to return us to normalcy and to truth, but we have confined our rational vision carefully to the squint of an eye.

A Figure by Holbein, taken from L'Eloge de la Folie (Praise of Folly), by Erasme (Erasmus), 1731, Amsterdam, Chez. Francois L'Honoré (Personal Collection)

CONTENTS

Glossary 267
Bibliography 275

INTRODUCTION

During my junior year at University of Detroit, 1975, I spent a semester in the stacks searching and reading research papers on blind obedience to authority. Obedience to authority does not require a dominant person that coerces people to submission. Rather, obedience to authority resides in any one of us who will close our free will and give our personal responsibility to any authority figure. Because of this, we can have tyrants. We can have one person by virtue of perceived authority remove the individual personal responsibility across a mass of people and have them commit crimes without moral considerations.

During my lifetime, I have seen the coercive actions of human beings many times over. I have seen the coercive actions of bigotry, sexism, blind patriotism, communistic domination, capitalistic domination, and religious intolerance. I have seen wars in Korea, Vietnam, and Kosovo, Afghanistan and twice in Iraq. I have seen apartheid in South Africa and the slaughter of people across many nations. I know the history of World War I and II, the Civil War and the violent reconstruction afterward, the Mexican American War, the War of 1812, slavery, human indenture and so on we go with a coercive history as far back as records exists.

I am like most people. What I think to be true I think to be right. Nevertheless, what I think to be true and to be right when measured against the output of thought by humankind, I find contradictions. I find rationalizations for the existence of opposing conclusions. On one hand, we have the idea that some people are simply superior in intellect; and on the other hand, we have the idea that our existence is relative. Therefore, most people do not concern themselves when we have contradictory conclusions.

What I think to be true I think to be right. What you think to be true you think to be right. In these two lines rests the answer. I think. You think. We confuse reality with the action of thought. Our rational thought only requires our sense of it, and in that sense of it, we maintain our decision of truth measured solely within our minds.

We often define coercion as an arbitrary will forced on an individual. In turn, an arbitrary will forced on an individual then denies their freedom and liberty. However, what determines an arbitrary will from a non-arbitrary will? To determine arbitrary verses non-arbitrary will requires an assessment. An assessment requires a form of measurement against something.

We have been using religion and rational thought to make our determinations. Both operate within what "I think to be true I think to be right and what you think to be true you think to be right." Nevertheless, truth does not reside in our minds. What determines our truth resides outside of us. This means we must take ourselves out of the equation. In this book, *The Coercive Animal*, we find our source of measurement to determine arbitrary verses non-arbitrary will. We then can determine justified and unjustified coercion. When we measure our ideas under the correct source and know the difference, we can eliminate unjustified coercion and release our freedoms and liberties.

In *The Coercive Animal*, we examine in *Book One* our old measurement systems of rational and religious thought. We examine their deficiencies and demonstrate that they are systems of thought without accountability. We introduce the corrected system of thought through thesisism that brings us our needed accountability. In *Book Two*, we examine our historical and philosophical thought systems. In *Book Three*, we examine their affect on our view of government and capitalism today. In examining capitalism and not socialism, I am no way implying one over the other. Rather, it is my view that both derives from a singular and physically based expression of our human constitution. Both, when carried to extreme ends, result in suffering.

During the writing process, when I used references that were written in the Old English form, the Old English "f" was changed to our current use of "s." In all other instances, the quoted references are as found from the original source used. This includes old spellings, capitalizations and italics. Some authors quoted include source materials from both Old English and modern texts, dependent on the acquired publications. I did not take on the business of editing original sources to modern standards, as I am not qualified to; and as an antiquarian book collector, I find no discomfort in such early writings. For those that read the old writing and find discomfort, please accept my apologies. Because this publication is an examination of human thought under old systems, I presented as much of the original writing to sufficiently preserve and clearly demonstrate the intent of the original author.

Finally, truthfulness and honesty were virtues instilled into me during my formative years. From my youth onward, I had a simple maxim that I carried with me throughout my life. It went like this. I have to accept the truth of things no matter how unpleasant or undesirable it may be. Without my understanding or knowledge, this stance opened my free will to accept truth with minimal distortion. I can make this claim because my source of measurement of truth does not reside in me. My open free will measured against our creation and creator—physical existence. Over the course of my life, I have learned that truth is not cold or harsh. It is enlightening and freeing. It brings us clarity to our condition and our needed interactions. Before us resides our source to infinite wisdom. Truth takes away our fears and reveals our common cause and direction, and how to reach our balanced and justified happiness.

BOOK ONE
THESISISM—RATIONAL THOUGHT WITH ACCOUNTABILITY

Defined Coercion Leads to the Release of Freedom and Liberty

1. *When we discover how to separate arbitrary coercion from non-arbitrary coercion, we will reduce our suffering, promote harmony and improve the condition of humankind.* We should seek this quality of life and move that quality of life forward for future generations. Nevertheless, we currently justify our actions from a cobweb of ideas procured over a long history of thought. None of our historical or current thought systems that we have can provide physical evidence to distinguish arbitrary coercion from non-arbitrary coercion. This means that any assertion we make to what is coercion and what is not coercion are only human decrees. If we reflect for a moment, we can find many historical decrees we have today that we have placed together in arbitrary ways.

2. *Here is a small inventory of these old and accepted pronouncements.* We have the conviction held by many people that we ought to operate to our individual self-interests. This individual self-interest idea has its origin in our philosophical declaration of individual pursuit of happiness. We have our religious decree that a higher authority has given this planet and its creatures as property to individual human beings. This higher authority being also has given selected human beings special understanding over other people concerning its commands. We have ideas justified by reason and rational thought with no requirement to stay connected to our physical realities. Instead, reason and rational thought connects to our unreliable mental environment with a blurry measurement against bases, motives and good sense. We have governments that allow people to evaluate the value of their self-interest against their own self-interest. We have the cause and effect idea

1

from science that we have applied against human social activity. When it fails, people offer it as proof that we cannot apply reason and rational thought to human activity. We have economic ideology procure this and state that human economic activity is beyond human comprehension. What economic behaviors we cannot comprehend we can leave to an invisible force for moral guidance. We have human decrees from philosophy, religion and economics that people, when left alone, will do more good than bad. We have systems of thought from economic and philosophic theory, as well as government and religious systems of thought that stand on an undefined idea that we should have no arbitrary will placed against any individual. Arbitrary wills comes from the coercive animal and denies us our freedom and liberty. Nevertheless, no one has removed the claim of arbitrary will against the wills of their own application.

3. *What all this means is that coercion, defined as an arbitrary will that is forced on an individual, derives from a long history of ideas pooled together by rational thought sensing its position mixed with divine guidance ideas.* We have no historical system of thought that can make a distinction between an arbitrary and a non-arbitrary will applied against another. Until we can, no one can claim that his or her rules operate with justified coercion or unjustified narrow self-interest. What this means is that our religions, our secular groups, our governments and our economic rules of the game operate with arbitrary rules, as we cannot make them accountable under religious or rational thought.

4. *There is a two-fold reason why arbitrary systems of thought continue. Reason 1:* We have a moral void in our human society throughout our earth that leaves us without any recourse except to act in our non-evaluative and narrow self-interest. If we do not, we can have the physical consequence of being homelessness, hungry and more. When we have a majority of behavioral actions with no solid moral foundation that occurs around each individual, we operate largely in the survival mode. We have many people that ignore suffering, and even many that view suffering of others as justification to their privileged position. This last statement involves ideas that led people to view themselves as superior and above others over *all manners of existence.* The random position of birth could surround people with ideas of superiority or inferiority dependent on their position in society. The random position of birth where people are provided with individualistic superior abilities, such as understanding mathematics, ability to dance and so on, may lead some people to think they are superior to people in all ways. We have religions that teach we should love and care for the suffering. We also have religions that teach the importance of money, wealth and their exemption to moral obligations because their God has decided who is to live in paradise on earth and who

2

is to suffer on earth. Many believe their God had given them success and privilege, and in this, their God had given others poverty and suffering. They view themselves justified to exempt themselves to any moral code of conduct because their God determined the state of our human suffering and they were not to interfere with the will of their God. We also have the philosophy of moral relativism, faith-based economics and subgroups of individuals that determine government policies. They too bring arbitrary ideas to exempt themselves from a required moral code of conduct. Therefore, on closer examination, we discover that we operate without clear moral guidance in all areas, be it in religion, secularism, government or economics.

5. *Reason 2:* When people operate in survival mode, they seek power for protection and security in position. People seek this power and position without any comprehension or clear understanding to our moral code of conduct between human beings. Since no clear moral code of conduct exists, this led us to the use of coercion. When we apply coercion and we claimed it as justified, we cannot know its accuracy, as we had determined it by our historical and arbitrary systems of thought. Arbitrary coercion then led us to reduce and even eliminate freedom and liberty. I have made an absolute statement that we currently operate under arbitrary thought systems that end in a survival and power acquisition mode. This is a broadband statement. This means that in the large picture, this is what is happening. Any one of us can animate in the narrowband and provide specific situations that do not support my statement. Nevertheless, in a collective since, be it by the actions of all individuals, and the power and weight of given individual actions to individuals, we operate under this mode. The idea that it may be better here and now than before does not eliminate the realities of the collective sense, nor does it justify not progressing forward. Until our physically based balance to moral conduct reaches a certain point, we are required to be in a state of progression. One objective of this book is to assist humankind toward accurate moral positions based on physical evidence that leads to the improvement of the quality of life for all human beings.

6. *We have based our historical view of coercion on decrees. Part 1a:* We have a rich history of philosophers, theologians and economists. They have provided their positions that deal with these specific topics. They often inadvertently contribute to the sustaining of coercion and our basic survival mode. There are volumes after volumes of mental animations by people over thousands of years. Our philosophers often focused on human happiness as being our ultimate end. John Locke moved the idea of individual pursuit of happiness as the highest aspirations of humankind into the minds of landowners, the precursors to modern capitalists. Theologians moved the idea of human pursuit of happiness to mean the pursuit of their God. In

doing so, they decreed that property ownership was ordained and given to humankind by the authority of their creator. This authority was higher and absolute; and therefore, not questionable. Friedrich Nietzsche created the idea of his ideal man. He allowed people to animate that some people, perhaps themselves, were greater in all aspects of existence than other human beings were. Immanuel Kant made a broadband statement to his categorical imperative, but did not connect to our physical world. He allowed for the idea that ideas sprang forward from a greater and otherworldly source. We had David Hume, who announced that reason and rational thought could not understand nor comprehend the complexity of actions by all individuals in our society. We had Adam Smith, a contemporary and friend of David Hume, pick up this idea of no human ability to bring accountability to social understanding and applied it to economic activity. We will see that all this decreed thought from history continues to affect us today.

7. *We have based our historical view of coercion on decrees. Part 1b:* We have our modern capitalists that took their cue from their viewed father of finances, Adam Smith. Adam Smith took the idea from David Hume that no individual could comprehend all things and moved it into economics when he made his famous "invisible hand" statement. This statement, though publish in 1776, has a continued affect on our thought and has contributed to our dismissal of any long-term consequences of our economic behaviors. The modern extended order of capitalism often refers to this "invisible hand" when others confront their self-interest with resistance. Anything that resists against their "invisible hand" they often follow with the cry of coercion via arbitrary will, which in turn violates their decreed freedom and liberty. Please allow me to present the statement by Adam Smith.

> As every individual, therefore, endeavours as much as he can both to employ his capital in the support of domestic industry, and so to direct that industry that its produce may be of the greatest value; every individual necessarily labours to render the annual revenue of the society as great as he can. He generally, indeed, neither intends to promote the public interest, nor knows how much he is promoting it. By preferring the support of domestic to that of foreign industry, he intends only his own security; and by directing that industry in such a manner as its produce may be of the greatest value, he intends only his own gain, and he is in this, as in many other cases, led by an invisible hand to promote an end which was no part of his intention. Nor is it always the worse for the society that it was no part of it. By pursuing his own interest he frequently promotes that of the society more effectually than when he really intends to promote it. I have

never known much good done by those who affected to trade for the public good. It is an affectation, indeed, not very common among merchants, and very few words need be employed in dissuading them from it. (1, Book IV, Chapter II, p335)

8. *We have our modern capitalist taking cue to their ideas from their viewed father of finances, Adam Smith. Part 1c:* People in recent history, like Milton Friedman and Friedrich A. Hayek, took the idea from David Hume that we could not apply reason and rational thought and applied it to economics. The "invisible hand" idea by Adam Smith and the position on reason and rational thought by David Hume became a two-ended pointer that validated each other. Their conclusions had us placing faith in the "invisible hand." If everyone was working in his or her self-interests, somehow that translated into we were all working toward a common self-interest of a greater good. Hayek wrote of freedom as being free of coercion by the arbitrary will of others to follow the "invisible hand." Hayek wrote, "Our faith in freedom does not rest on the foreseeable results in particular circumstances but on the belief that it will, on balance, release more forces for the good than for the bad." (2, p31) We now had a belief that unevaluated freedom would lead us by a John Locke "general consensus" to good.[1] This allowed actions to be without evaluation as to whether they were good or bad actions. This could only allow power to move its self-interest, independent of whether it was a good or bad self-interest, forward and over top of people. Faith in freedom meant accepting all actions without any requirement to accountability and questioning self-created authorities.

9. *We have based our historical view of coercion on decrees. Part 2:* What Milton Friedman and Friedrich A. Hayek left us with was a faith-based form of capitalism. It also meant we had an unaccountable system of thought and worse yet, an unaccountable system of action. These Chicago-based men transferred our moral obligations between each of us to their economic rules of the game. We had justifications to self-interest actions with no physical evidence based on the following ideas presented as decrees:

- Our ultimate end was decreed to be our personally desired and individualistic pursuit of happiness.

- We had decreed that each individual had the god-given right to own all things on this planet and in this universe.

---

1 The "general consensus" idea from John Locke is discussed in full in the chapter, *John Locke and the Big Give Away.*

- We had decreed that each individual had a god-given right to any individual self-interest and to use our planet resources as they perceived in their self-interest manner.

- We had decreed ideas that some people were superior over all areas of existence.

- We had decreed that economic actions were individuals in pursuit of happiness that involved self-interest actions and this moved humankind to good in a greater degree than bad.

- We had decreed that since no one individual could comprehend all individual actions, we could not identify freedom and liberty, but could only restrict coercion.

- We had decreed by use of rational thought that this coercion was anything that violated the rules of the game developed by the extended order of capitalism.

10. *We have based our historical view of coercion on decrees. Part 3:* The problem with this historical thought was that we based it on a human egocentric view. All our past ideas were ideas measured toward our own internal existence. Our pursuit-of-happiness idea made the relational measurement to our ideas and actions to be against our own human mind. Happiness leads us to personal desires. There is nothing wrong with wanting happiness. Nevertheless, if we were in a constant state of happiness we would be carried away to the funny farm. Happiness is an excited state that eventually comes to saturation and then to a natural attenuation. We cannot maintain a state of constant happiness.[2] To measure ideas and actions against the obtainment of happiness meant we were measuring the value, worth and moral character of these ideas against an arbitrary source, individual and personal desires that varied from person to person. We have arguments that claim the end is in the *pursuit*. This ignores the relationship between pursuit and happiness. The actual ultimate end of pursuit by itself is action. Therefore, we are back to liberty and freedom. With the idea of happiness attached to pursuit, we place ourselves into action in our physical world by measurement against the non-physical existence of our experience of happiness. Without physical connections, we can animate anything we want without any relationship to reality or moral code obligations. Our historical philosophy becomes arbitrary.

---

2 This statement is broadband. Some people may be known as a constantly happy person. Whether any individual is or can be in a constant state of happiness is not the source to the statement, but rather to the collective and normalized population of people.

If our beginning of philosophical inquiry was flawed, all our human history of thought collapses. Our ideas of gods fail like our egocentric view of our pursuit of happiness as an ultimate end for humankind. We had developed god-ideas relational to our specific existence in states of historical ignorance. When we animate in our human mind various god-ideas and the pursuit of happiness without accountability, we pool these ideas together and arrive to ideas of a god giving the earth as a gift. This arbitrarily justifies individuals with economic and political position to engage in coercion by the use of this false-reality to their ends. We made our moral ideas relational to our human mental existence.

11. *We have based our historical view of coercion on decrees. Part 4:* How can we stop coercive indenturing and manipulating of people to human created systems when we are free to animate reality to anything we want with our minds? If we can attach reality to any idea, we can decree anything we want. We cannot understand and identify coercion under these conditions. It is not that reason and rational thought collapses under the weight of large civilizations. It always has been a collapsed system of thought, as reason and rational thought itself is not an accountable system. Reason and rational thought applied to social actions resulted in erroneous combinations of decreed ideas, such as our pursuit of happiness and liberty both being universal in nature. We also have erroneous combinations of decreed rational and divine ideas, such as our pursuit of happiness and a god giving us ownership of all things. Like theological ideas, reason and rational thought could move without accountability and come to conflicting conclusions. The enlightenment of rational thought moved us from a fundamental disconnection to reality to a partial or even a weak connection to reality. In rational thought, we are only required to think it or sense it to be right. The enlightenment period, with the exception of perhaps Thomas Paine, was an enlightenment that moved from one unaccountable system of thought to a different unaccountable system of thought.

12. *To understand and identify coercion requires that we stay connected to our physical existence.* This is our first step. To understand what coercion is, and how we can release ourselves to freedom, liberty, and our ultimate end in life, we must stop our egocentric view. We must move conceptually our mental existence from revolving around us to perceive that we are relational to physical existence. We need to get out of ourselves and see that we are the products of our physical existence, both in design and in our thought. Our thinking and understanding can be relational to physical existence, or it can be lost to the chaos of our own human mind. We can know our creator—our physical existence—or we can separate from the truth of existence and live mentally in all kinds of manufactured ideas broken from physical existence. We can

maintain the idea of reality with real things or we can attach the idea of reality to anything we desire despite any misalignment with reality. To understand what coercion is, what freedom and liberty is, what our humankind ultimate end is, we must not measure reality against our mental chaos. Instead, we must measure reality against our incoming physical existence. This starts with how physical existence inputs us. To obtain our moral code of conduct, we must measure against the reality of our human physical existence for guidance. Physical existence has determined our conduct between one another. Physical existence has determined it by how it had created us. We use our human physical construction as our connections to reality. From this physical reality, we can provide physical evidence to our moral code of conduct. We find our code of conduct between us in the physical structure of what makes a human being a human being across all human beings.

13. *Once we break our ideas from the chaos of the human mind and measure our ideas against our physical existence to maintain a relational understanding to reality, we can begin to understand our moral obligations.* Although David Hume may be correct that no one individual can comprehend the individual actions of all individuals, we can create a tool to bring moral measurement. When each individual has this tool, we begin to have individual moral action engaged by each individual. When each individual uses our physical existence as our reality measurement, we move our proposed faith in the "invisible hand" away from its inherent chaotic swings. We amend our ideas based in false reality to stable and accurate reality-based ideas. In our simple reality loop, we can remove the manipulation that comes with the faith and "general consensus" ideas, and ground the interference that comes from created false-reality ideas. This greatly reduces the noise of false-reality mental animations to human thought. In our simple reality loop, we include one reality, physical existence. No one person could ever claim any ultimate authority since physical existence is the same for all of us. Now we can begin to understand when we have an arbitrary will and a non-arbitrary will of a person or subgroups of persons. We can begin to understand what coercion is and what moral obligation is. We can make the arbitrary rules of the game given by the extended order of capitalism required to be accountable to moral obligations. No one individual or a subset of individuals by their personal desires could decree their arbitrary will onto others. We are commonly obligated to our creator and creation, which is our physical existence.

14. *When we maintained our connections to physical existence, we have the foundation of thesisism.* Our ideas with attached reality must measure against physical existence. Thesisism stands on this base. Our human physical construction resulted from physical existence. We connect our moral obligations to this physical existence. In understanding this, we discover a

tool to social understanding. It not only shows us what coercion is or is not, which in turn releases freedom and liberty to all human beings, it tells us when we are dealing with minority rights and individual rights. It shows us clearly and measurably how, where and when we are not conducting ourselves morally. It then exposes coercive power, to which we can begin to work against. When we work toward moral actions that measure to our physical realities, which includes our government and economic behaviors, this leads us to responsibility at all levels. It takes away evangelical and insect style capitalism, as well as immoral self-interest actions of government and individuals. It provides us an understanding about our required relationship with our physical existence and the balance that we need to maintain.

15. *Our simple reality loop of thesisism has a commonality to all individual human beings.* Despite not knowing all individual actions, it can work because it has a common measurement source between every individual. Our needed constant was not the human mind, but our common physical existence. We have a common physical reality without the interference of human beings except for those that chose to act immorally. The actions of these people become exposed and their actions would not be defendable. If the majority of people chose to act immorally, they could by choice or by ignorance. Education is critical to any civilization and to its long-term survival. Faith-based education, be it religious or economic, can only lead to suffering, as they do not connect to our physical realities. Reality-based education is education with accountability. This accountability can lead to the removal of suffering, to increased harmony and to the improved condition of humankind.

16. *We can begin to outline and present thesisism.* In *Book One*, we will learn how to move our ideas so they measure against our physical world. We will learn what ideas are, where they reside, and how we can manipulate them. We will learn the difference between our physical existence and our experiential existence. We will discover that our human mental animating abilities have physical characteristics that can bend us away from our truth or bring us directly to truth. When we bring in our physical-world realities without the interference from a framed-reference, our free will is open to truth.[3] We do not alter our understandings by attaching the idea of reality to non-reality ideas. We will discover through an open free will that physical existence determines our code of conduct. We will discover that morality measures against our physical human characteristics. We will discover how we can or cannot move our actions in our physical world relationally to our physical realities. When we understand these measured actions, we know when people attempt to manipulate people by moving ideas between broadband and narrowband ideas. This movement can manipulate and disenfranchise

---

3 Framed-reference and free will are fully discussed in their specific chapters.

people to their given rights and provide individuals ways to subvert their moral obligations. We could have further disenfranchisement accomplished by manipulating the true physical boundaries of ideas to our actions. This happens when people present ideas as being universally possible in action when they are limited in possible actions.

17. *Thesisism can provide physical evidence to distinguish between an arbitrary will and a non-arbitrary will.* We need our understanding to fit our physical existence. It is simple. It is also difficult. It is difficult because we must shift our thought in its basic state. Nevertheless, once you have it, you will have a tool to understand the realities around you. You will understand these realities because they are simply there for you to see. You will understand them because you will experience them first hand. Reality does not come from books or people telling you what truth is or is not. Therefore, our physical connections with thesisism are simply a way to measure back to our physical realities. We can stay tuned to our realities and move toward a fulfilling course of action for humankind. With our tool of thesisism, we can control coercion and release our freedoms and liberties.

Is Our Use of Reason Accountable?

1. *When we engage in the use of reason, do we measure our reason against our physical world or our human mind?* Our science operates under a specific system of thought that requires them to measure their ideas with the use of reason. Science associates itself with examination of our physical world. In hard science, we require the examination of ideas to measure against the physical world. We have progressed because we have built accuracy between our understanding of the physical world and the reality of the physical world. Nevertheless, as a presented method, do we have within the definition of reason a requirement to connect to the physical world?

2. *What is our definition of reason?* Because the idea is broadband, we have different ideas of reason animated in the minds of human beings. To discuss the idea of reason, we have to work through various ideas of reason. We need to narrowband the idea of reason into its various accepted forms. Once we do this, we can then analyze the definition to see if we are measuring reason against the physical world or against the chaos of the human mind.

3. *One narrowband idea of reason we have is that it is the bases for our actions, our decisions, feelings or beliefs.* We have no statement in the narrowband definition presented that reason has to connect to the physical world. Our bases could just as easily connect to non-reality ideas. We can have people justify the murder of people on the bases that they think differently to their thinking. When we define reason as measuring against the bases, we do

not have a requirement for accountability because our bases may reside in the human mind and not relational to our physical world. We could have the bases to justify defending ourselves, even to the point of having to kill someone in our defense. Our base for this justification is that our physical existence is threatened. Our base here in our reasoning was that we measured against a physical reality. When we do not require the bases for our reasoning to measure against physical reality, we can end with our use of reason with accountability and unaccountability. We have left the idea of reason open to the chaos of the human mind.

4. *One narrowband idea of reason we have is that it is the motive for our actions, our decisions, feelings or beliefs.* Again, we have no statement or requirement that we connect our reasoning to the physical world. By the actual use of the word motive, we placed it into the human mind. Motives involve internal drives. We have placed reason into an adhesive mindset[4] where people can randomly attach any sliver or master idea to ideas. We refer to what was the motive as the reason for it. It is the why, but no accountably to truth is ever required to follow.

5. *One narrowband idea of reason we have is that we have an underlying fact or cause that provides a logical sense to any idea.* Whether this definition connects to physical existence or not depends on the idea of fact or cause by the user. If we require a fact to connect to our physical world and the cause of the action to connect to the physical world, we can say that reason connects to the physical world. We have a narrowband definition that is aligning with hard science. Science works in the why. In the why we get our fact and cause. Notice that the why connection to the idea of reason works for science. Nevertheless, when we apply this why to all ideas, we have a breakdown.

6. *The reason for this break down is due to the different existences the why resides in.* We can follow the two different paths that hard science and social science takes with the reasoning of ideas. We can create the following flow of action:

- Fact → Event → Cause → Why.

An example of hard science would be:

- Fact (A released ball drops) → Event (A falling ball) → Cause (Gravity) → Why (Because gravity exists in physical existence).

An example of social science would be:

---

4 The term *adhesive mindset* is not a term used in thesisism. The thesisist term is *adhesive framed-reference*. Because the later term is not defined until the chapter titled *Framed-Reference*, the term *adhesive mindset* adequately reflects the meaning to the uninitiated reader. The term "*adhesive framed-reference*" is also defined in the glossary.

- Fact (A person looks or thinks differently.) → Event (Murder) → Cause (False-reality ideas) → Why (Because false-reality ideas exists in human thought).

Now we have a mismatch of reason between science and social thought. One connects to the physical world while the other does not. Nevertheless, they both gave their why. In the cause and effect ideas of science, physical existence is a uniform and unchanging existence. By its own nature, physical existence is a singular source and directly associated with reality. Physical existence cannot attach false-reality to itself. Our human thought does not have uniformity when we allow ourselves to attach reality to non-reality ideas. We have one additional movement in the human mind that physical existence does not have. With social ideas, we have Fact → Event → Cause → Why-1 → Why-2. We then have:

- Fact (A person looks or thinks differently.) → Event (Murder) → Cause (False-reality ideas) → Why-1 (Because false-reality ideas exists in human thought) → Why-2 (False reality exists because of an unaccountable system of thought).

Notice that the *why* in science is stable as it rests in physical existence. Notice too that the *why-2* of social actions is only stable when our thought system rests in maintaining its relationship with physical existence. Once we break from our physical existence and allow the attachment of reality to non-reality ideas, we end with unstable actions as it rests in the chaos of our minds.

7. *When we move from hard science of our physical world to our human thought existence, human thought existence can begin with false-reality facts.* False-reality facts are actually non-reality ideas, as they do not exist in the physical world. Our use of reason under why-1 can only be reason if a system of thought with accountability existed for all ideas. Ideas are not restricted to scientific ones that measure physical existence with physical existence, but include ideas that measure human action against humankind. The move of fact and cause from science to human activity breaks from physical existence. We must maintain a required alignment to physical existence if accountability to ideas is to remain. Otherwise, we break from our physical world and easily begin to make statements of facts, presented as ideas with reality, when they are really non-reality ideas. Once we start with non-reality ideas, our logical sense has no reality-based logical sense. Simply, when we use reason for social ideas without an accountability method, we begin to measure against the chaos of the human mind.

8. *One narrowband idea of reason is to think logically.* We have no statement of required accountability. Because we have no requirement to maintain reality measured against reality, we can move logical outcomes to non-reality ideas.

We can move these non-reality ideas in a logical form in relation to their false ideas. You could start with the idea that witches exist. You could follow with the idea that these witches hate water. We could then use logic to conclude that a reasonable action would be to dunk a suspected witch into water. We have no reality or truth required to the logical reasoning.

9. *One narrowband idea of reason is that it operates within the realm of good sense and practicality.* We have to ask ourselves the following. What do we measure our good sense against? We have human beings in history that reasoned it made good sense to sacrifice children to manufactured ideas about otherworldly authorities. We have people that reasoned it made good sense to murder anyone branded as a witch. We have people that reasoned it was practical to murder millions of people in gas chambers. Our measurement of ideas under an arbitrary idea of good sense and practicality allows us to go to any non-reality idea as long as we deem it to have good sense and practicality. We lost our physical reality and allowed people to measure to their preconceptions, reality-based or non-reality-based.

10. *One narrowband idea of reason is the use of faculty reason.* Faculty reason is simply the capacity to think. We human beings are mental animators and we can move our sliver ideas around with ease.[5] Our sliver ideas have arrived to us via our physical existence. When we move these sliver ideas around without maintaining our measurement of them back to physical existence, we end with chaos in the human mind. This happens because we allow the sliver idea of reality to attach to non-reality ideas. We now have our use of reason measured against any created non-reality reality. Our non-reality reality only resides in our minds. The idea of faculty reason can even create a greater divide between reality and non-reality. It gives us the idea that thought is internal only. It ignores our original inputs from physical existence. The idea of reality, which arrives from the experience of our physical world, we defaulted to good sense, practicality, providing our bases, motives or our logical follow in faculty reason. It encourages thought of any sort. Faculty reason defaults people to measure their ideas against themselves or other human minds. We have started ourselves to think in a void without any measurement against the physical world. We have chosen chaos with our human ideas.

11. *When we tie the idea of human sense to our impulses, such as sex and vices, this leads us to a conception of reason away from connecting to the physical world.* Allow me to present a piece of writing from 1713. The title of the work was *The Art of Self-Government, in a Moral Essay.* A passage went as follows, "and break those Fetters wherewith the rational part is bound up; to restore the Man to that State that God made and intended he should live in;

---

5 Sliver ideas are the individual components to our ideas. Sliver ideas are fully discussed in the chapter, *Thought Existence: How Ideas Work.*

that the Soul might govern the Body, and the reasonable Will the Appetite; so that he might live as a rational Creature, and act as one that is moved upon future Hopes and Fears, and not upon present Enjoyments without respect to the fatal Consequences thereof." (3, p8-9) This example provides us a historical view where we tied a narrowband idea of our senses to the vices of humankind. Notice they had our minds controlling our body as our intended state. They had the idea of soul paired with the idea of reason. It was through this soul-based use of reason that they had us becoming rational creatures. A soul-based use of reason meant we thought relationally to our mind only. This use of reason and rational thought certainly falls under its definition. Again, we dropped our physical world from our relationship with reality. We cannot control our body by mind only. We can only control our body with our mind engaged relationally to physical existence. If we look at Diagram 2 and 3, we see that we have ignored physical existence. Some may protest against my claim that reason and rational thought are unaccountable and declare fault in this use of the idea of sense. Nevertheless, the complaint does not change our broadband definition of reason and rational thought. One technique to amputate physical existence from reason and rational thought was to tie it to *vices* from our senses.

12. *We cannot remove our required physical connection to reason because of vices and vicious actions.* This author further wrote, "For, if the Man were but brought to himself, and to the use of his Understanding, Virtue and Piety would find as ready Entertainment as Vice now doth. He would then exercise his Reason, instead of Sense, and consider the end of vicious Actions; the present Enjoyment and future Reward would be brought into Balance, and Hell and Heaven consider'd as well as Earth." (3, p9) The answer to stop vicious actions was not to remove our physical connection to reality. We need our physical reality to measure actions to determine if they violate thesis[6] (physically based) morality. We cannot evaluate to a "Balance" when we measure against the chaos of our human minds only. This stops and eliminates the relational aspects of our external reality and our thought integrity. These words by this eighteenth century author demonstrate the mysticism impregnated in our view of reason and rational thought that continues to exists today.

13. *One narrowband idea of reason is that it is the capacity for rational thought.* When we do not require our rational thought to connect to the physical world, it becomes an unaccountable system of thought. To say reason is the capacity for rational thought is to say reason requires an ability

---

6 Thesis-morality is morality that connects to physical existence. The physical connections from physical existence determine our code of conduct. Thesis-morality is discussed in the chapter titled, *"Morality Connected to Physical Existence."*

to engage in reason. This contributes nothing, and certainly does not require any relationship between reality and physical existence.

14. *We must measure reason against the physical world.* We are missing an important piece of the definition that would narrowband it to a form with accountability. Our missing part of the broadband definition of reason is that we must measure *all* our ideas against the physical world. Since we do not have this requirement, thesisism and reason are not the same. Because thesisism requires the connections to the physical to maintain, thesisism has accountability where reason in its broadband sense does not have the requirement to accountability. Hard science may have maintained the required physical connection, but reason in its broadband definition lost this requirement to social actions. We need to understand this limitation of reason and acknowledge its unaccountability.

Is Our Use of Rational Thought Accountable?

1. *Do we measure our rational thought against the physical world?* When we apply the word "rational" to the word "thought," we find that rational thought nearly equates to reason. We often refer to the word "rational" as agreeable to reason or reasonable. We often refer to the "act of thought" with the word "rational" as having or exercising reason. We often endow rational thought with the faculty of reason or having reasoning powers. Despite these definitions, we never mention any requirement to measure our ideas against our physical world. Under this, our rational thought defaults to the same arguments given above on the character of reason.

2. *One narrowband definition of rational thought is that it involves good judgments.* What are we measuring our good judgment against? We can use any system of thought and claim good judgment in terms of how it relates to that system. Slave owners bought and sold people measured against the good judgment of the surrounding economic system. We see claimed good judgment by one religion while others viewed it as bad judgment. With human centered systems of thought, we cannot distinguish good judgment from bad judgment because we have measured our ideas against the chaos of the human mind. We have only one requirement with good judgment. We only need to *deem* ourselves sane and lucid. How can we determine this if we measure our ideas against our own human mind? Nevertheless, we do have one aspect to the various definitions given for the word rational that brings us a bit closer to thesisism.

3. *One of our narrowband definitions of rational thought is that we reference against our senses.* We often refer to rational thought as sensible or in good sense. If we use the word sense in its pure form, and not include human

thought or emotional reactions, we have a potential to line up with thesisism and our requirement to stay measured against the physical world. This is because our sensory existence is our player to our physical world. What we bring in with this player is the input of our physical existence. If we maintain our connections to physical existence, we bring accountability to all ideas. If we allow ourselves to move our sliver idea of reality around without maintaining the required connection to reality, we end with unaccountability and chaos. The use of sensible and in good sense becomes useless once we drop our accountability method and begin to animate sensible and in good sense to ideas with our misplaced sliver idea of reality. Sacrificing children to manufactured ideas about a higher consciousness made good sense in that non-reality. Although deadly false, it is rational to the false idea. It does not matter if the traditional users of reason and rational thought wish to deny this. Unless we require ourselves to keep the sliver idea of reality measured against our physical reality, they are as unaccountable as religious thought. Friedrich Nietzsche did not measure his ideas against physical existence with a complete grasp. He acquired and created non-reality ideas as reality. He created within himself an adhesive mindset that bent his perceptions so that he could not see the full physical aspects of human beings. He ignored our equal aspects while he focused on our differences. Under the use of rational thought, he created his *higher men* idea that began to violate our moral code of conduct to our equal aspects.

4. *Our historical thought is in doubt.* We need to review our historical thought under thesisism. If we currently operate reason and rational thought without accountability, it is likely that our history of thought contains errors of magnitude. We would have compounded all these errors with further errors. Our review of human thought through history is the purpose of *Book Two* and *Book Three*. Once we have outlined thesisism, we can begin to measure our ideas with accountability. We will review our history and find how well we matched to our reality. From what we find, we can evaluate ourselves today and begin to move to a real-world civilization where we can eliminate coercion and liberate our freedom and liberty.

Is Our Use of Religious Thought Accountable?

1. *Religion does not connect their fundamental ideas to the physical world.* Religions claim that they know the *otherworldly*. Otherworldly refers to an existence that is beyond our physical existence. By their own definition, they do not connect their ideas to the physical world. No religion has shown this otherworldly that can satisfy any conclusive and physically based (thesis) idea requirements. The idea of intelligent design only shows the order in the

physical world and not any otherworldly component. Therefore, if we have no physical connections to an otherworldly conscious designer, and the core ideas themselves are not of the physical world, then all their ideas become non-reality ideas, except those by accident or necessity.

2. *A core component of religion is the requirement to suspend maintaining the accountability position of the sliver idea of reality.* This suspension derives from their requirement to accept their ideas as reality by the method of faith. The faith idea requires a person to place the sliver idea of reality into manufactured ideas. While pretending the manufactured ideas are real, their faith idea states to notch out the idea that they are pretending. This application of applying the sliver idea of reality to non-reality ideas while suspending the truth of this misalignment is manipulative, destructive and only leads us to chaotic swings in human mental animations of false-reality ideas. It allows false justifications to illegitimate coercion and leads to our reduction of freedom and liberty.

3. *The religious system of thought needs an adhesive framed-reference to maintain their ideas.* In *Book One*, the section on *Framed-Reference* defines the idea of an adhesive framed-reference. For the moment, an adhesive framed-reference involves the attachment of preconceived ideas to incoming perception. To maintain a religious manufactured system of thought requires us to create a strong form of adhesive framed-reference to bend all ideas to conform to this system of thought. Our adhesive framed-reference would be required because we do not connect our ideas to the physical world. When reality challenges our preconceived manufactured ideas, to maintain them, we must make them conform. Since these preconceived ideas are ideas based in non-reality to which we can animate in the human mind without any requirement to accountability to reality, many different systems of thought arise. Unlike thesisism, where we measure against the physical world, which is the same for every human being, our unaccountable systems of thought fractures into many different forms of thought systems. This leads us to animations that others are different to us when they are in reality equal to us. When we misplace our sliver idea of reality within our thought existence, this misplacement can transfer to false ideas about our differences in our physical or thought existence. We can have people animate they are greater in areas where we are equal in physical existence. Our mental animations without proper attachment to physical reality can lead to murder and suffering of many people. People apply incorrect moral equations. We have based our equations not in physical existence, but in human created equations. We apply our evaluation with an ill-conceived manufactured and immoral equation. In doing this, we often apply coercion as we try to force the thought existence of others to become ours.

4. *Preconceived false-reality ideas lead to dogmas, domination and static systems of thought.* We can maintain our accepted false-reality ideas only if we adhere to a preconceived framed-reference. This framed-reference is adhesive to any incoming idea that counters our false reality. It captures conflicting ideas and bends them to desired false reality. We certainly can and ought to have our personal desires. Nevertheless, when we are seeking truth and our proper code of conduct, we must remove any human intervention and allow our view of reality to be without distortion. We all can hope for a better world. We can obtain it if we evaluate to our physical reality. If we start with a hope of a better world through preconceived false-reality ideas, we move away from our desired end. If we start with a hope of a better world through preconceived false-reality ideas from an unaccountable form of rational thought, again we move away from our desired end. We need to measure our ideas against physical existence. Instead, we measure our ideas against preconceived ideas, be them reality or false reality. Because our reality will always contradict our false-reality, we engage in forms of indoctrination and rule with strict adherence. Since our religions require an adhesive framed-reference to bend incoming ideas to a false reality, the development of a vengeful god works to force idea acceptance. Because of this, no questioning or human progression can occur.

5. *Religion tries to create ourselves to an end.* Each religion provides us a doctrine to measure our actions. They provide us a model we try to aspire to obtain. How successful and unsuccessful they have been, we have seen over the past millenniums. This means that one aspect of religion was our attempt to create ourselves to an end.

6. *To what end do we want to create ourselves.* Different religions led us to different ideas about what *end* do we want to create ourselves to. We had the *end* idea of salvation, nirvana and enlightenment. Nevertheless, can we create ourselves and to what end? Oddly, we can turn to an atheist to demonstrate how we can create ourselves. Part of the philosophy of Jean-Paul Sartre was the idea of in-itself-for-itself. We generally interpret this as a human being trying to be god. From this we ask, what is trying to be god mean? He wrote in *Being and Nothingness*, "But hitherto although possibles could be chosen and rejected ad libitum, the theme which made the unity of all choices of possibles was the value or the ideal presence of the en causa sui. What will become of freedom if it turns its back upon this value?" (4, p797)

7. *Sartre took in ideas of "the cause of itself," which led us to more non-reality ideas.* We know that en causa sui means a being that is the cause of itself. The problem Sartre was dealing with was how to make personal responsibility the cause of itself. Nevertheless, if we had an alleged desire to be a god and that meant to be a being that was the cause of itself, then we had a broadband

interpretation to deal with first. For example, if we say we want to be a being that literally creates itself from nothing, obviously we have a manufactured idea with no connection to physical existence, as no human, when in a state of non-existence, could consciously create his, her or its self.

8. *Perhaps the idea of creating oneself by Sartre involved ideas after initial creation.* If we talk about beings that can modify themselves by engaging in actions to achieve an end in mind after initial creation, perhaps then we are a being that could create or modify ourselves. From a thesisist point of view, it holds, but only in part. We can have two ideas about how a being can create itself, one by connecting relationally to the physical world and the other by connecting relationally to false-reality ideas. If we want to engage in the later, then we should look at our free will model in Diagram 8. We can create a harsh framed-reference and interject interference from personally held false-reality desires to bend incoming reality. However, if we want the former, then free will is opening us to the truth to existence. We recognize the needed accountability to ideas. We open a clear space for our thought and reactive existences to understand the information that the physical world provides to us. From this, we learn about ourselves. We learn about our equality with other people. We learn about our unequal aspects as well. When we do this, we *free* ourselves from our mental chaos. We can measure our ideas and engage in our code of conduct appropriately. It provides us understanding and certainty. It takes away the sense of the unknown, uneasiness, self-doubt and all other uncertainties from you. No person could dictate a doctrine or make an authority, be it a human-made, higher-consciousness idea, or the consciousness of other human beings that arbitrarily places their will above yours. We obtain balance to our community and ourselves. We will be stable because we work off the same set of conditions, our physical world.

9. *The idea of creating oneself after initial creation holds as an idea relationally to our physical world.* Therefore, trying to be a being that creates itself is exactly what our physical world is doing to us. Religion has the correct idea that our lives are works in motion. Nevertheless, the question becomes how are we to do this and to what end? We ought not to attempt to make ourselves into a god, the original creator of existence. Nor we ought to allow ourselves to be made by the arbitrary will of others by false-reality doctrine. They could manipulate us to use their arbitrary will onto others. Our rational thinkers are also correct that we must develop ourselves with education. Here too, we ought not to allow ourselves to be made by the arbitrary will of others with false-reality doctrine. We should respond to the non-conscious action of our physical existence as it brings us to our end of creating ourselves. Physical existence is our creator and our source of truth. We need to continue creating ourselves relationally to our creation by our creator, physical existence. We

then can treat one another properly and develop real-world civilization. We can grow ourselves planted in the physical world.

10. *Thesisism differs from religion as a social system.* Religion typically places a god first, then our human existence, and then our physical existence. This distant god beyond our physical existence speaks to certain human beings. They then tell others about their experience. Thesisism places our human existence and physical existence together. Our creator is our physical existence in action. We are the result of physical existence in action. Our thought existence is the product of our physical existence in action. We are not three separate entities as religion presents. We are relationally one.

Human Survival with our Creator, Physical Existence

1. *Our survival is connected to our physical world.* Deist Susannah Newcome wrote, "And as there are no innate Ideas of a God, so likewise we can have no Proof of such a Being *a priori*: and if there is really such a Being, we can only come to a Knowledge of his Existence, from a Consideration of Existence of Things." (5, p9) We can come to know our creator and creation from our consideration of physical existence. Physical existence is the source to our knowledge of our creator, as physical existence is our creator. Truth and reality does not come to us from within our minds. The reality of our existence comes to us by our senses and in our maintenance of this reality. We must maintain this relationship to our ideas. Nevertheless, we currently ignore our physical existence when we move the idea of reality around in our minds to our ideas of morality and justice. For us to have accountability of thought, we must stay connected to our physical existence and our reality. It is then that we can progress. Volney wrote, "Let man study these laws, let him understand his own nature, and the nature of the beings that surround him, and he will know the springs of his destiny, the causes of his evils, and the remedies to be applied." (6, p34)

2. *Our concept of reason and rational thought must incorporate this maintenance of incoming reality to our ideas.* Seneca wrote, "PHILOSOPHY is divided into *Moral, Natural* and *Rational:* The *First* concerns our *Manners*; the *Second* searches the Works of *Nature*; and the *Third* furnishes us with Propriety of *Words*, and *Arguments*, and the Faculty of *Distinguishing* that we may not be impos'd upon with Tricks and Fallacies. The *Causes* of things fall under *Natural Philosophy*; *Arguments*, under *Rational*; and *Actions*, under *Moral. Moral Philosophy* is again divided into Matter of *Justice*, which arises for the Estimation of Things, and Men, and into *Affections* and *Actions*, and a Failing in any one of these, disorders all the rest." (7, p119) His three aspects of *morality, nature* and *rational thinking* were correct in every way except one.

The relationship between nature and rational was not defined in a way to make human ideas accountable. We have to define our words and arguments to nature. The "Faculty of Distinguishing" was never defined other than a vague reference to nature. What Seneca did was what all other rational philosophers had done in history. They had a rational *sense* that physical existence was the *bases* for understanding. We simply needed to *sense* and *base* off physical existence. That was the missing piece, as simple as it is. With this understanding, we can begin to align ourselves to the realities to which we live in. Let us start with the simple basics.

3. *It is a wonderful spring morning.* Around me are mesquite trees young in their leaves. They are light, bright and held by the dark darting lines of their branches. The palo verde trees hold tiny yellow specks of sun-colored flower pedals. They cover the trees like a cap of warm and brilliant bubbles. The birds move with excitement and with song surrounded by the youthful life growing around them. The quail chortle while they look for safe places to nest. Spring is the time of rebirth and it reminds us of the beauty of the physical world.

4. *Physical existence is our ecosystem.* Physical existence surrounds us. No matter where we are, this is true. Physical existence is the ocean to which we live and swim. Under the right conditions, it is where we breathe and nourish. It is what we are to know.

5. *Physical existence is our creator.* Physical existence creates us from the action of the physical material under its natural law. Physical existence is our source to determine how we must act to survive. It is our foundation of development and growth. It created our bodies and minds. It maintains our life. It also sources us information in how we are to conduct our lives.

6. *Our physical existence is without consciousness.* The action of physical material to which we find ourselves immersed in operates under its physical laws. Each action of physical existence moves to its next action dependent on the previous action. This movement is without consciousness, as it never deviates from its prescribed laws of intermixture. Even in deep levels of existence, in quantum or string theory, where unusual actions may occur, it continues to bring either a consistency in the actions or a consistency in the inconsistency of the actions, and not actions that display a conscious manipulation.

7. *Our mental existence revolves around our physical existence.* Each of us encapsulates a consciousness, like the yellow sun bubbles of the palo verde tree. We grow within it as light and bright leaves. We express ourselves like the excited spring song of birds. We are made from physical existence and we grow according to its laws.

8. *Physical existence gave us our life and our mental life.* It was through our physical existence that we evolved into the species we are today. Physical existence gave us our capacity to think—to reason, to solve problems and to create new ideas. It was from physical existence that our thought existence arrived. By the action of physical existence, it created an existence that was separate from physical existence, yet dependent on it, for its expression. Our thoughts, feelings and senses were given life from the movement of physical actions that created the physical structure of our minds.

9. *We have an intellectual capacity that requires development of a system of thought to function in our environment.* Different systems of thought as well as their level of development determine the capability held by that capacity. Our different systems of thought can undergo an evolution. This evolution has its unique characteristics as it resides in a difference existence than physical existence. We pass it not genetically, but pass it culturally. Unlike genetic evolution where physical existence determines its placement, we can evaluate our thought systems to determine how well they serve us. It is under this evaluation that we must entertain the idea that our intellectual abilities need scrutinizing to find the best evaluative system of thought to meet and line up with the realities to which we live in.

10. *Humankind must behave differently from other species.* We have seen many other species gain dominance to their environment. They thrived until they exhausted all their resources, at which time they became extinct or severely diminished. The action of our physical existence provided intelligence to species for short-term survival. This is true because our physical existence operates without consciousness. Since physical existence is without consciousness, it only responds to immediate actions. It needs many different events for an organism to evolve a consciousness that could operate with long-term understanding. Our question is—do we have this advancement?

11. *Our human mind has limitations.* Our physical existence engages in its unconscious actions. In doing so, it results in its expression of logic, and not in a human expression of logic. Our human logic involves our consciousness and our ideas within it. When we evaluate the accountability position of any idea within our consciousness, we have to evaluate it against something. When we use our internal mind as the source to where we can place our idea of reality, we end with chaos. When we use our physical existence as the source to where we can place our idea of reality, we end with accountability and stability. Our human mind under the action of thought operates in a different existence than that of physical existence. Since conscious thought did not create the human mind, nature did not structure us for an inevitable form of reasoning with accountability, but for survival in a physical existence without any end in mind. Nevertheless, one of the unconscious artifacts

with the action of the physical was to map the physical world and respond with survival behaviors. Because this was an unconscious development, this mapping to survival led to two human being characteristics.

12. *Characteristic one, the development of mental animation:* Physical existence resulted in animal form structures that assisted survival by mapping the physical world. Along with this mapping of the physical world came an evaluative format. From the results of this evaluative format came survival responses. The structures to which we achieved this evaluative format involved the development of a brain to hold and manipulate ideas. Our ideas are not singular entities. They are stored as a cluster of several sliver ideas that make a master idea. Because of this characteristic, we can acquire sliver ideas and shuffle them around to create new master ideas. These new master ideas operate independent to our physical existence. Now we have by the unconscious action of the motion of physical existence an artifact that led to two different outcomes to human survival.

13. *Outcome 1:* We could rearrange our sliver and master ideas to enhance correct evaluations that boost our survival in physical existence. We can demonstrate this with the narrowband example of finding fruit to eat. By mapping and developing ideas of location to know where to return combined with ideas of different seasons over time, we can have movement of these ideas in sliver or master form to create a new master idea to know when to return. This adds to our survival ability. Note that all of this was reality-based. This enhanced survival came about by maintaining our connection to our physical reality. It also contained some elements of ideas that required moderate thinking in terms of time.

14. *Outcome 2:* We could rearrange our sliver and master ideas to deteriorate our correct evaluations and diminish our survival in physical existence. We can demonstrate this with the same narrowband example. By mapping and developing ideas of location to food and when to go for the food, if the food was gone, or destroyed by natural causes, humans could move sliver and master ideas in a way that they think an invisible entity was unhappy with them. We could begin to move our sliver and master ideas in a random fashion without connections to our physical world. One random move we made in our historical human past included human sacrifice to invisible entities. We could move our acquired sliver idea of fear from our experienced reactive response of fear to this invisible entity as well. This outcome of our mental animation ability led us to deterioration.

15. *The affect of these two options evaluated:* Because we have these two options available to our thinking, our capability to engage in moderate to long term survival has become connected to our ability to think in ways of survival that incorporate moderate to long term interest. We need to break

the typical cycle of other diminutive-thinking animals. Our survival for the long-term requires not only physical-world actions, but also our development of an evaluative system of thought that brings in long-term understanding of the physical world to which we live in. We must understand that there are times where short-term self-interest leads to the destruction of or hardships for our future generations. We need to tap into our relationship with our physical existence. When we consider self-interest, we must consider it under short to long-term self-interests and in relation to the individual and across all individuals. We then have individual self-interest and all-individuals self-interest applied to any proposed self-interest.

16. *The progressed evolution of thinking animals*: Since our action of physical existence is unconscious, the options it provides us, as cognitive animals, are that we survive well, survive poorly, or become extinct. If we develop a reality-based system of thought, we may continue to survive, and survive well. If we continue with our non-reality-based and unaccountable systems of thought, we will become extinct, or survive poorly.

17. *Characteristic two, short-term verses long-term:* Since our creator is an unconscious action, living Beings result with short-term survival. Its actions are in reaction to immediate cause and effect. From our human point of view, this resulted in development of animals where their reactions to needs were short-term. Any development of physically created mental animating minds that engaged in long-term actions or understandings was an unconscious creation. When physical existence created a thinking organism like this, it was by the unconscious convergence of numerous physical requirements and balances that allowed this type of mind to develop.

18. *We need human thinking with long-term understanding to survive as a species.* Since we can animate ideas in an unaccountable and accountable form, we have developed both a technological society of significant advancement while at the same time we continue to kill, enslave and coerce one another. Along with our technological advancements come additional stresses and conflict with long-term survival. We do not respond to the balance needed for our earth to sustain life. We do not consider the long-term affects when we diminish and deplete our natural resources. If our survival occurs just under the threshold of extinction, the quality of human existence becomes a poor existence. Under this, we have a lot of suffering. When we have human or animal suffering, it involves a living being with consciousness or awareness of that suffering. Any human created actions that leads to suffering without physically based justifications is immoral action.

19. *We have different requirements between actions from physical existence and actions from systems of human thought.* Physical existence is without consciousness or awareness. It operates under its code of conduct, which is

the action of the physical material. When we have earthquakes or tsunamis, it was occurrence without conscious action. Our human actions operate under its own code of conduct, which derives from our human thought and the movement of our ideas. This movement of ideas involves sliver and master ideas. We are required, as conscious beings, to operate our code of conduct measured against the physical world. We are required because we are physical beings and the equations for our code of conduct between us reside in the physical. This is our moral source to discover our required code of conduct. When we maintained reality to real-world physical existence, we led ourselves to our understanding of science. It will be our maintenance of reality where we can find the balance to our physical existence to maintain our survival within it. Our relational balance to our physical environment leads us to our human code of conduct between us and to all other living creatures and physical structures. Our physically based code of conduct requires us to maintain our balance of moral actions. Our balance of moral action leads us to quality survival in terms of a balanced happiness and fulfillment of life experiences. This is our beginning to eliminating unjustified coercion.

20. *We must study and understand ideas so that we can maintain a system of accountable thought with them.* We must accept ideas under their terms, not ours. Various philosophers have seen the importance of understanding the structure of ideas. John Locke understood that the study of ideas was our beginning to understanding ourselves. He wrote in his *Essay on Human Understanding*, "I must here in the Entrance beg Pardon of my Reader, for the frequent Use of the Word *Idea*, which he will find in the following Treatise. It being that Term, which, I think, serves best to stand for whatsoever is the Object of the Understanding, when a Man thinks." (8, I.i.8) Hume wrote at the beginning of his book, *A Treatise on Human Nature*, "By *ideas* I mean the faint images of these in thinking and reasoning; such as, for instance, are all the perceptions excited by the present discourse, excepting only, those which arise from sight and touch, and excepting the immediate pleasure or uneasiness it may occasion." (9, p5) Isaac Watts at the beginning of his book, *Logick: Or, The Right Use of Reason in the Enquiry after Truth*, started by defining ideas as, "An *Idea* is generally defined a *Representation of a Thing in the Mind*; it is a Representation of something that we have *seen, felt, heard* etc. or *been conscious of*." (10, p8) Isaac Watts, like David Hume and John Locke, started their treatises on the subject of defining ideas because without understanding ideas, and how they work, we cannot begin to bring accountability to them.

21. *Perhaps we have been using a false standard of measurement with our ideas.* Sigmund Freud wrote, "It is impossible to escape the impression that people commonly use false standards of measurement." (11, p10) Have we been using a false standard of measurement to our ideas, and if so, how long?

Have we been living in our physical world, or have we been trying to escape it? Nevertheless, we are of the physical world. We are made of it and we flow through it like fish in water. We breathe it. We eat it. It enters and leaves our bodies constantly. Why then do we ignore the entering of it by our senses into our minds? Physical existence is not just outside of us; it has a relationship in us as well.

22. *Our relationship with physical existence and our thought existence is the true extension of our creator.* Freud also wrote, "It is asking a great deal of a man, who has learnt to regulate his everyday affairs in accordance with the rules of experience and with due regard to reality, that he should entrust precisely what affects him most nearly to the care of an authority which claims as its prerogative freedom from all the rules of rational thought." (12, p233) We have a relationship with physical existence that sets up our need for rules of experience. Even reason and rational thought involves the acceptance of intellectual nihilists to which we lose our relational actions with physical existence. Freud wrote about the intellectual nihilists, "It is true that they start out from science, but they succeed in forcing it to cut the ground from under its own feet, to commit suicide, as it were; they make it dispose of itself by getting it to refute its own premises." (12, p240) Reason and rational thought does not have a requirement to stay connected to physical existence. In allowing this, we can animate anything and falsely attach the sliver idea of reality to it. Freud recognized our relational need for rules of experience. He wrote, "This correspondence with the real external world we call truth." (12, p233)

23. *We can see this evolving physical relationship in how our words evolve over time, giving us evidence of how human beings move sliver ideas.* The education Friedrich Nietzsche received was in classical philology, considered a science, but a science of reviewing ancient texts and submitting a critical analysis. (13, p35) This included the study of language that focused on precision in meaning and following its changes over time. Friedrich Nietzsche understood the movement of sliver ideas and their subsequent affect. Nietzsche stated, "these two words 'bad' and 'evil,' how great a difference do they mark...." He showed us how an idea like "bad" with the attachment of an idea about a higher-consciousness authority operating in a non-existent spiritual world could change the idea of "bad" and create the word "evil." (14, p22) The word "evil" could bring with it many manufactured ideas of justice, and manufactured-based justifications to commit atrocities against our counterparts, be it men, women or children. These ideas without connections to the physical world could animate a surgeon saving the life of a human being as an act of evil. A person of one thought existence could animate the helping action of a person that held a different thought existence than they as an act of evil. A

person with false-reality ideas that broke our moral equality could animate people of a different race or a different sexual orientation as evil, because the idea of "evil" broke the connections to the physical world. A person could animate any random, unjustified and unaccountable idea with the idea of reality attached to the idea of evil.

24. *The closer we maintain our connections to physical existence, the better our reality aligns.* The idea of "bad" contains within it a more compassionate outlook, which is, it does not carry the action of a vengeful swung hammer as the word "evil" does. The application of justice, reality-based or non-reality-based, that comes from "bad" comes from a human being, whereas, the application of justice, reality-based or non-reality-based, that comes from "evil" comes from a human being that wishes to act as a God. In this respect, Nietzsche was correct. The person that holds the idea of "evil" can be more of a brute.

25. *Freud recognized the fundamental principle that reality and thought existence had a relationship.* Our sensory existence is the player to the physical world around us. Our sensory existence is then our source to our reality. We bring that information in and when we later animate new ideas with the movement of sliver ideas, how we maintain the sliver idea of reality determines whether we are animating with accountability or without accountability. Freud wrote of the "reality principle." However, he presented it as a developmental separation where we learn to differentiate ourselves from the physical world. He wrote, "One comes to learn a procedure by which, through a deliberate direction of one's sensory activities and through suitable muscular action, one can differentiate between what is internal—what belongs to the ego—and what is external—what emanates from the outer world." (11, p14-15) He beautifully expressed the learning process where we as infants begin to distinguish between the physical world and ourselves. He followed with, "In this way one makes the first step towards the introduction of the reality principle which is to dominate future development." (11, p15) What we human beings forget to do is maintain accountability to the sliver idea of reality in our future development.

26. *Freud recognized that in time our thought existence could begin to animate independently to physical existence.* Freud wrote, "Originally the ego includes everything, later it separates off an external world from itself. Our present ego-feeling is, therefore, only a shrunken residue of a much more inclusive—indeed, an all-embracing—feeling which corresponded to a more intimate bond between the ego and the world about it." (11, p15) What Freud described was actually the most fundamental problem with humankind. Instead of separating off from the external world where we now animate as a separate entity, we need to maintain the relational aspects of the

27

external world and our mental life. This separation allows the religious feeling of infinity or the "oceanic feeling," as Freud referred to it, to create a separate animation room without any requirements to maintain the accountability position of the sliver idea of reality.

27. *We can develop a system of thought to assure ideas are accountable.* First, we remove the human being as the source of accountability to ideas. We do this by not measuring the idea against the backdrop of the human mind. We take ourselves out of the equation to any given idea. Second, we bring in the realities that present themselves to us. This reality is our physical existence. This physical existence has a prescribed code of conduct in relation to itself. This code of conduct is not human-made. The meaning of physical existence is to move in its prescribed laws to the subsequent set of actions. Since we are not only living in physical existence, but created from it, it is our only reality. Reality is in relation to our reality of physical existence and the forms that it creates to which we measure our ideas against, as any idea not in relation to this reality is a non-reality idea. This is how we maintain our accountability. A non-reality idea is not from our physical world. Therefore, it becomes an unaccountable idea to the truth of existence.

28. *We can bring accountability to ideas.* Since we know that our physical existence is our truth to existence, we can measure against it. By measuring our ideas against our physical existence, we can bring an evaluative system of thought to determine its relational position. This provides us a system of thought that can bring accountability to any given idea.

29. *We can bring accountability to ideas related to our moral code of conduct.* Since all ideas are accountable, we can even bring accountability to ideas of morality. Our moral code of conduct derives from physical existence and is relational between all of physical existence and us. This code of conduct involves all physical entities, be they human beings, animals or physical structures. Our moral code of conduct between human beings derives from our physical existence and relates to our human physical makeup that the action of the physical has made.

30. *The name of this system of thought is thesisism.* Since measuring ideas against the backdrop of our physical existence involves evaluations of its relational aspects, any idea given is open to discussion by all people. Therefore, all ideas given as reality or truth are thesis presentations. If we are interested in truth and reality, which includes the correct moral code of conduct, we seek ideas that stand up to thesis presentation and discussions. This means that ideas that stand as thesis is a movement toward our reality and truth. Because of this, we call this system of thought thesisism.

31. *Thesisism is important.* Thesisism is important to our discussion about long-term survival. If we are to break the historical and behavioral actions of

species that dominate their environment until they deplete all their resources, followed by their extinction or extreme suffering, we need a good and solid system of thought that matches our technological advancement. Survival in the long-term can only occur when we can identify non-justified coercion by how it violates our physical realities. Once we use a system of thought that measures against the physical world, we can recognize unjust human coercion and we can release our freedom and liberty. Only when we tune to our reality can we make our long-term decisions so that our future children can not only survive, but also live with a quality of life.

Thought Existence: How Ideas Work

1. *Thought existence is the animation of our ideas.* Thought existence is an area where we can animate our acquired ideas and arrange ideas into any form. It is our post-sensory existence and post-reactive (emotional) existence. When we remove physical existence, our sensory existence and our reactive (emotional) existence from all that we experience, we have left ourselves with only thought existence. Our thought existence in action involves only ideas.

2. *We must view the physical origin of ideas under their terms and not ours.* To bring accountability to ideas, we must first understand their existence and actions. Our ideas do not spontaneously spring forward from non-existence. In their individual pieces, we do not derive our ideas from en causa sui, a self-created existence that arrived by *a priori* impregnation or *a priori* generation from something else other than physical existence. In fact, we have no ideas that exist in *a priori*. Our ideas result from the action of the physical world. We have both the physical actions of our thought and the physical actions of physical existence that input to our sensory and reactive existence. Our sensory and reactive inputs contribute to our thought existence. They too are our original source to all ideas.

3. *The natural development of our human brain involved mapping our physical world.* Our brain developed by the non-conscious action of the physical material of the universe and involved a stimulus-response relationship in its interactions with physical existence. As we developed in complexity, our brain became increasingly more sophisticated in its capacity to map and learn from the sensory input it received from its physical world.

4. *John Locke had a sense of the relationship between physical existence and thought existence.* He wrote,

> If it be the Motions of its Parts on which its Thinking depends, all the Thoughts there must be unavoidably accidental, and limited, since all the Particles that by Motion cause Thought, being each of them in

itself without any Thought, cannot regulate its own Motions, much less be regulated by the Thought of the whole, since that Thought is not the Cause of Motion, (for then it must be antecedent to it, and so without it) but the Consequence of it, whereby Freedom, Power, Choice, and all rational and wise Thinking or Acting, will be quite taken away: So that such a Thinking Being will be no better nor wiser, than pure blind *Matter*, since to resolve all into the accidental unguided Motions of blind *Matter*, or into Thought depending on unguided Motions of blind *Matter*, is the same Thing; not to mention the Narrowness of such Thoughts and Knowledge that must depend on the Motions of such Parts. (15, IV.x.17)

5. *It is the relational interaction between physical existence and our thought existence through our various senses that brings us our actions.* If we as an adult lost our senses and reactive (emotional) responses, we would live a life of thought existence only. We would only be able to live in what was experienced in our acquired ideas. We could acquire the individual pieces of an idea and reconstruct them back to the originally experienced idea. We also could acquire the individual pieces of an idea and arrange them differently or mixed them with other ideas. For sake of clarity, we are talking about a normal operating mind.[7] Our actions of thought follow their prescribed motions. When we use our senses, we follow the interactions between physical existence and our thought existence. If I am talking to you, I am not carrying a conversation with my wife as she is elsewhere. Physical existence moves the relational aspects of our thought existence through sensory existence. When John Locke above wrote, "no better nor wiser," it involved the combination of previous experience and the capability of that particular brain.

6. *It is the movement of the physical that results in ideas.* The physical world carries information of its existence by the movement of physical actions. This includes wavelengths of light, sound and other sensory information that our senses respond to by their existence and reception. These various informational actions result in physical stimulation of *intermediaries* that provides information to the physical brain. This movement into the brain generates actions in physical existence that result in awareness. John Locke understood this with his "since all the Particles that by Motion cause Thought" statement above.

---

7 We are removing sensory and reactive existences for comparison purposes to demonstrate core functionality. How a human mind operates under extreme conditions of isolation between various fractions of the human mind, although a valid area of study, does not concern us on this present subject.

7. *The intermediaries are our senses.* Our five senses input us information from our physical existence. The reactions of our senses to the physical environment transmit information to our brain. It is through our five senses that awareness arises. Awareness arises from the movement of physical existence within our mind.

8. *Our awareness comes from our physically created mental grid.* Our awareness comes to life by physical-world impressions on our internal mapping of space and motion to create and mimic the various forms of existence to which our senses interact. Within our brain, we have a mental grid. We have been limited to the non-conscious structuring of our brain by our physical world in what it has and only can result in making. My thesis presentation of "mental grid" is a broadband presentation and is open to challenge. I base this theorized-manufactured idea[8] on the form and structure that we have expressed in our thought existence.

9. *Our mental grid is blank at birth.* We have no inherent ideas that exist prior to any intermediary action. Any claim of *a priori* ideas only derives from the prescribed mechanism of our evaluative structure contained within our brain. None of our ideas can spring forward to awareness that had no original interaction with physical existence. An example would be the sucking action of a baby. The development of our brain to prescribed action is not equal to ideas. This action is not from conscious thought or awareness until after its natural trigger of physically related actions. John Locke alluded to this when he wrote, "In time, the Mind comes to reflect its own *Operations*, about the *Ideas* got by *Sensation*, and thereby stores it self with a new Set of *Ideas*, which I call *Ideas* of *Reflection*. ... All those sublime Thoughts which tower above the Clouds, and reach as high as Heaven it self, take their Rise and Footing here...." (8, II.i.24)

10. *Our ideas of shape and form derive from our internal mapping abilities.* As an infant, the child works to develop an internal reflection of the external physical world. In the state of infancy, the sensory inputs initially develop ideas of shape and form. It is not that we know *a priori* of shapes and forms, but derive the idea of them when we have experiences in physical existence that measured against the map wall of our mind. Arguments of predisposed ideas or predisposed understandings of space and time are a misunderstanding. Understanding only arrives after the experience of it as inputted from our physical world. This grid only provides us the opportunity for understanding, but we cannot come to understanding until sensory experience begins.

---

8 Theorized-manufactured ideas are ideas that have partial, weak or various connections to physical existence and therefore can have other possibilities, known or unknown. See chapter titled, *How We Categorize Ideas* and the *Glossary*.

11. *Our map wall allows us to develop awareness that we then move to ideas.* We have an internal physical construction where we can create in awareness a representation of physical existence around us. Our inputted sensory existence can move from our map wall to awareness and then to ideas in thought existence. Our inputted reactive (emotional) responses also can move from our map wall to awareness and then to ideas in thought existence. As adults, when we experience inputs from physical existence, we frequently retrieve old known ideas to develop and understand basic forms to this new experience. For example, if we saw an orange for the first time as an adult, we obtain several ideas pulled together to make an orange. The mind of this adult already knows shapes and shapes in three dimensions. We can attach the previously acquired sliver idea of circular shape to the idea of orange. We acquired these types of sliver ideas early in childhood. We may have or not have experienced its color. However, we have other sliver ideas that attach. Its texture, size and other attributes converge to make a bundle of sliver ideas into a master idea. This bundling is also a skill we acquire in early childhood. We can show a visual representation of how sliver ideas are involved in making a master idea in Diagram 7.

12. *Historically, our problem was our not measuring against physical reality.* For example, John Locke wrote, "If it shall be demanded then, *When a Man begins to have any ideas?* I think, the true Answer is, When he first has any *Sensation* ... 'Tis about these Impressions made on our Senses by outward Objects, that the Mind seems first to employ it self in such Operations as we call *Perception, Remembering, Consideration, Reasoning,* &c." (8, II.i.23) He linked ideas with sensation from "outward objects" that showed he understood there was a connection between ideas and the physical world. He even placed "reasoning" within this "when he first has any sensation." Part of the problem with historical philosophy was to attempt to answer the human adult mind without clear acknowledgment of the early childhood development of the human mind. Our "when he first has any sensation" may indeed develop to perception, but this first sensation to perception occurred during infancy and not during adulthood. Remembering, consideration and reasoning are far beyond our first sensations and their developmental purpose. An infant is not equal to an adult in physical existence. The statement by John Locke was too broadband and made an unacceptable leap. In doing this, he broke the needed physical-world connections to our sliver idea origins and gave them over to the mental animation of the adult human mind without its original footing.

13. *Ideas are not singular entities, but consist of a bundle of sliver ideas.* Our ideas arrive from the physical world and we assimilate them within our brain. In the adult, this assimilation does not involve holding an idea as a singular

entity. We place ideas together from many individual ideas. They are pooled together to make a master idea.

14. *A bundle of sliver ideas creates the master idea.* When all the individual components converge, we have the master idea that arrived from the original experience of it. We cannot treat the master idea as a singular entity. Since our master idea is made of a bundle of sliver ideas, various master idea characteristics can follow. In our normal discourse in inter-human relationships, our master ideas may be narrowband or broadband in structure. Our identifying these two characteristics is crucial in knowing if two or more people are animating the same master idea while they engage in discourse.

15. *Idea categorization is always in relation to the master idea.* Our individual sliver ideas, as singular entities, can be master ideas. This means that a master idea is simply a collection of sliver ideas, even if the collection is only one sliver idea. Our master ideas are when they are the main idea. For general consideration, our master ideas usually involve a collection of sliver ideas. Our sliver idea becomes a sliver idea when we make it a part of a collection of ideas that pool together to make a main idea.

16. *The narrowband idea has its signature.* We have ideas that we term narrowband. When we bring to our consciousness an idea that has a relatively few sliver ideas or a set of sliver ideas that significantly overlaps itself with other ideas or significantly overlaps itself relationally to other master ideas within oneself or with others, we have a narrowband idea. When we pull up the same or nearly the same set of sliver ideas to a master idea between ourselves, we achieve a high level of correlation. When we engage in discourse between people, we have a higher precision of accuracy between people during our discussion. We can then begin to confer agreements and consensus between ourselves. We have a visual demonstration in Diagram 6.

17. *The broadband idea has its signature.* We have ideas that we term broadband. When we bring to our consciousness an idea that has a set of sliver ideas, it may result in many different potential master ideas between people or within the same person. We then have a broadband idea. We have two aspects to our broadband ideas that we must understand. One is the relationship of a broadband idea to a single person and the other is in relation to the collection of all individuals.

18. *The broadband idea can be broad or narrow to an individual.* We could have different sets of relatively small sets of sliver ideas creating a master idea in any singular individual. Those sets of sliver ideas could be relational similar or dissimilar with others in the population. We need the exchange of discourse to move and change sliver ideas to reach common understanding. We could have two people talk about an idea that they assume is the same between them, but in fact each contains a different set of sliver ideas that misalign

understanding and conceptualization of the master idea in discourse. Our broadband idea by its nature of having various bundling of sliver ideas creates variations between people. Our overlap of sliver ideas to each master idea can become non-existence or vary greatly. We often see this between people of different cultures or life experiences.

19. *Another attribute of broadband ideas is that each person may contain several master ideas under one idea.* We could have a large number of sliver ideas to a general idea that could lead us to several different master ideas. We each could evoke a different master idea that was to whatever specific perceived circumstances our immediate environmental situation provided. Our specific circumstances would work to trigger up a subset of sliver ideas that would direct us toward one specific master idea. In this instance, we would be in discourse while engaging in different master ideas, but we would not be aware of the non-matching ideas. We would converse as if we were talking about the same idea. However, if our discourse was that each of us had moved to the same set of sliver ideas, we would have come to the same master idea and our discourse would be with mutually understood ideas. Before discussion, we need to confirm between ourselves if our ideas indeed align with each held idea between us. For an example of a large pool of sliver ideas that could lead to several different master ideas, please refer to Diagram 6.

20. *It is critical that our language correlate between us for proper discussion to occur.* When we engage in discourse between one another, we must recognize broadband ideas and move to assure we are animating the same set of sliver ideas to a master idea, otherwise fruitless discourse will result. We must understand this aspect of ideas in relation to our language. This is an important element in bringing accountability to given ideas. John Locke understood this, although he did not articulate it this way. He wrote,

> First, *They suppose their Words to be marks of the Ideas in the Minds also of other Men, with whom they communicate:* for else they should talk in vain, and could not be understood, if the Sounds they applied to one *Idea,* were such, as by the Hearer, were applied to another, which is to speak two Languages. But in this, Men stand not usually to examine, whether the *Idea* they and those they Discourse with have in their Minds, be the same: But think it enough, that they use the Word, as they imagine, in the common Acceptation of that Language; in which they suppose, that the *Idea,* they make it a Sign of, is precisely the same, to which the Understanding Men of that Country apply that Name. (15, III.ii.4)

People have realized that for good conversation to occur, we must animate the same subset of sliver ideas to master ideas during our discourse; otherwise, it all becomes foolish. It is important that we narrowband our ideas so we can create fruitful conversation.

21. *We have had philosophers use broadband verses narrowband ideas to confuse us.* Jean-Paul Sartre is one such philosopher. Here is an example. "if my consciousness were not consciousness of being consciousness of the table, it would then be consciousness of that table without consciousness of being so." (4, p11) How does his sentence bring any understanding? His broadband presentation promotes confusion in that it allows the trigger of numerous different master ideas to the same word. When we use broadband presentations for narrowband ideas, it can only lead to misunderstanding or conceal true meaning. It can also be a trick to present yourself as if you are deep and smart when you are just playing games. Here Sartre was folding back broadband words unto themselves to make a jumbled statement. Since he used the word "consciousness" in the broadband, we can create a formula. We can make C equals consciousness and T equals being consciousness of the table. We can then create the following formula Sartre has given us. "If C is not equal to T, C would then be C equals C plus T minus T." Nevertheless, we mental animators will attempt to plug in all sorts of variations to the formula that Sartre has given us and to try to make sense of it. When we reduced it to a formula, we can see it says nothing. Ten equals ten plus forty minus forty. My goodness, ten equal ten!

22. *We can rewrite his sentence by taking his broadband presentation and apply narrowband ideas.* Owing to the horrid use of the broadband word consciousness, many narrowband versions to the word can occur. This means we could make numerous rewrites of his sentence. If we attempt to make it have sense and clarity, here is my version. "If my human mind were not conscious of being aware of the table, my human mind would then be aware of that table without conscious of being so." First, in Sartre's sentence, the word "it" referred back to the first use of the word "consciousness." We have taken his broadband word "consciousness" and pulled out different narrowband ideas. Here I used narrowband ideas of our human mind, being conscious and awareness. Awareness is the action of experience. Consciousness is a sustained form of awareness.[9] We can have awareness *and* being conscious of the table, as when we have awareness of the table sustained, we are being conscious of the table. We can have awareness *and* being conscious of consciousness. We can sustain our awareness of consciousness as well. I use the terms *being conscious* and *consciousness* the same, except as follows. *Being conscious* is the state of action to specific awareness whereas *consciousness* is a general statement to the state of action of any awareness. This means that *being conscious* is a limited idea, as we tie it to an action from a specific awareness. This also means that

---

9 See the section on *Awareness and Consciousness* or the *Glossary*.

consciousness is a universal idea, as we do not tie it to specific action. This also makes it broadband, as it can entail many different narrowband ideas. When we use the universal form of consciousness, we have to be careful that we do not confuse it with our physical mind. Our human brain is a structure capable of outputting awareness and consciousness, but the human brain itself is not a consciousness.

23. *Since the first use of the word "consciousness" in the sentence by Sartre was the universal idea form, he inadvertently referenced the physical structure of the human mind.* We cannot have a physical structure aware of action. The action can be aware of the physical structure. In his not referencing physical existence, he left people in an endless loop of C equal C plus T minus T of infinite variations. In our rewrite, we have the physical human mind, which we can represent as H. The difference between awareness and consciousness is that consciousness is awareness sustained. This translates to consciousness equals awareness with sustain in time (C = A+S). Awareness is without sustain in time (A = C-S). When H is in action, it is either C or A. By using narrowband ideas, I provided these formulas. The rewrite then translates to, "If H is in action, it is either C or A. If H is C minus S, then H is A." In simple words, if we do not have awareness in a sustained mode, we have awareness. It does not say much, but it is now clear.

24. *These narrowband aspects hid inside the broadband word "consciousness" that Sartre used.* In the rewrite, we see that Sartre attempted his first use of the word consciousness in relation not to its physical self, but to undefined awareness, A or A+S. This is significant because awareness and consciousness do not mean the same thing. This example from Sartre displayed well how we can use large pools of sliver ideas in broadband ways to obscure meaning. His use of the word consciousness had so many potential bundles of sliver ideas to master ideas that it became a useless statement. Nevertheless, people argue endlessly in misperceived but desired deep thought. We must understand the difference between deep thought and chasing mental tails. Although his sentence sounded nice and clever, it obscured his meaning. Once we dug out from his obscured presentation and aligned our narrowband ideas, we even found he could be correct. Nevertheless, it depended on which set of sliver ideas one pulls from his broadband presentation. We have to invoke our language element to bring accountability to ideas. In this example, we see that he allowed the word consciousness to be broadband and that it included the physical aspects of the human brain to be consciousness as well as different types of mental activity.

25. *Thought existence is separate from physical existence.* We can now see the importance to distinguish between physical existence and thought existence. If we do not, we can mix the two different narrowband ideas together as we

have seen with Sartre. Thought existence is distinct from physical existence. The movement of the physical material in our brain can result in thought. Our thought is a separate existence to physical existence in that it resides in its action. If we abstractly remove all physical existence from our human thought during its actions, we could think of it as leaving ideas only. Therefore, thought existence is our domain of ideas. We must treat it as a unique existence.

26. *We can now begin to understand how ideas work.* We have the relationship between physical existence and our thought existence. Our ideas involve a collection of sliver ideas that bundle together to make our master idea. We have to be conscious of this bundling of sliver ideas to the master idea within ourselves to outside ourselves to determine master ideas that are narrowband. We then can begin to see how they relate to the master idea of another person. We have to be aware that for discussions to have value, we have to align our sliver ideas to our master ideas that we consider the same.

How We Categorize Ideas

1. *The original physical source of ideas becomes our backdrop of accountability.* If we obtain our ideas by the physical interactions between the physical world and ourselves, how we measure against physical existence determines our position of accountability. Our sliver idea of reality stays to its original source. If we chose to measure against ourselves, we lose our accountability. This is because we can attach our sliver idea of reality to any animated and rearranged idea. Therefore, to have ideas that are accountable, we must measure our sensory interactions and ideas against physical existence. We must breakdown the parts of actions that occur in our physical world to our result of ideas in our minds to maintain our accountability. We not only collect from physical existence sliver ideas to a master idea, we can move our sliver ideas into new positions to create new master ideas independent to our physical world.

2. *Our capacity to mentally animate ideas and move sliver ideas creates a set of categories.* If we could not move our sliver ideas, then we would maintain a reality-based system of thought. Nevertheless, this would lock us into having reaction only to our physical surroundings, as we could only know and respond to ideas in original experienced form. We would be severely limited in our capacity to create new and novel situations. It is, perhaps, the capacity and the degree to which we can move sliver ideas into new and novel positions that provides us the separation between other animals and ourselves on this planet. With our mental animation capability, the question becomes, what types of ideas do we create?

3. *The category of any idea is its relationship with physical existence.* We can first ask does our master idea connect to our physical world or not. If we have

connections to the physical world in a complete sense, the idea becomes thesis. If we have no connections at all, we have a manufactured idea. Therefore, to start, we have two categories, one thesis and one manufactured. We have identified two categories of ideas that reside on the two ends of a spectrum.

4. *Our two ends of idea accountability are pure in nature.* A thesis idea in pure form maintains a complete connection to our physical world. All sliver ideas to the master idea relate back to the original experience in physical existence. A manufactured idea in pure form separates our master idea from physical existence. When we remove or add sliver ideas so that the master idea no longer aligns with physical existence, then the connection to physical existence for the master idea becomes broken. This creates our two categories. Our categories are relational to the master idea. Diagram 7 provides a visual representation of the difference between ideas that are pure or manufactured.

5. *One category we term pure-thesis ideas.* Our pure-thesis ideas arrive as a collection of sliver ideas to a master idea by maintenance of the original collection of sliver ideas from physical existence. If we had seen an orange or an apple, all the physical interactions that occurred to create the collection of sliver ideas we maintain intact. When we retrieve pure-thesis master ideas, all the original sliver ideas that made the master ideas have a root or a connection to the physical world around us common to the original source. We never added or removed a sliver idea from the master idea. By this one to one connection, we can classify it as a pure-thesis idea because it has a complete set of links to our physical existence. Our physical-world relation is not just to the individual sliver ideas but also to the collection. Our level of probability is one-hundred percent by our actual experience of it in physical existence.

6. *Previous philosophers have understood pure-thesis ideas.* Nevertheless, they did not understand the requirement to maintain the connections to physical existence, nor did they understand that one sliver idea attached to pure-thesis ideas is the sliver idea of reality. This sliver idea of reality we learn at infancy. In early childhood, when we begin to animate ideas, we humorously teach our children to misplace the sliver idea of reality to non-real things. We find it funny and cute when they misunderstand reality. By our dropping the understanding of the sliver idea of reality to pure-thesis ideas, we are allowing ourselves to begin to animate unaccountable ideas. Nevertheless, in our history we have understood the importance of pure-thesis ideas. John Locke wrote, "These *simple Ideas*, when offered to the Mind, *the Understanding can no more refuse to have, nor alter,* when they are imprinted, nor blot them out, and make new ones itself, than a Mirror can refuse, alter, or obliterate the Images or *Ideas*, which the Objects set before it do therein produce." (8, II.i.25) He presented his simple ideas as absolute. However, he did not seem

to understand that this *absolute* he observed was that they had a fully vested connection to the reality of our physical existence. He allowed, as with other historical philosophers, to ponder our second category of ideas, manufactured ideas, without any relational requirements to our physical existence.

7. *Our second category we term pure-manufactured ideas.* Our pure-manufactured ideas arrive as a collection of sliver ideas to a master idea by rearrangement of the sliver ideas into a new form that does not maintain in our physical world. If we think of an orange, change its color to purple, add flashing green lights on it, we have a new master idea that does not link to the physical world in its collective sense. This idea can only exist in our thought existence. Although the various sliver ideas arrived from the physical world, the arrangement of the sliver ideas did not, nor do they align with any existing reality known. We had experienced the idea of shape, in this instance roundness, the color purple, flashing green lights and so on, from our physical world. We animated in our minds these acquired sliver ideas and created a new set of sliver ideas to a master idea. Since this *set of sliver ideas* did not arrive from our physical world, we have created a pure-manufactured idea. Its level of probability is zero as no master idea experience of it in the physical world has occurred and we acknowledged it came from pure mental rearrangement into a new non-reality form. Diagram 7 provides a demonstration between pure-thesis and pure-manufactured ideas.

8. *We have two categories of ideas that exist between the categories of pure-thesis and pure-manufactured ideas.* If we have a complete maintenance with our physical world and a complete break from our physical world, can we have categories between the two? Here I chose to break into two more categories. My choices of these two categories are the first pass to understand thesisism between pure and manufactured ideas. I am confident that future thinkers can bring refinement and clarity where my limited abilities and resources fail. Nevertheless, this is a start. I know we can create a category termed *conclusive-thesis ideas* and a category termed *theorized-manufactured ideas.* Each category has a relationship between our physical world and the ideas presented.

9. *Our second category in thesis ideas is conclusive-thesis ideas.* Our conclusive-thesis idea involves the collection of sliver ideas that when collected together the master idea maintains its physical connections to the ideas. However, we have a collection of sliver ideas that leads to a master idea we cannot otherwise experience by direct and complete input from sensory existence. An example would be that we can experience evolution in its present state of actions, but we derive its actions in the past by physically connected evidence. In doing this, we are maintaining our connections to the physical world. Another example is mathematics. We start at an early age understanding that when we have five apples and we get five more, we have ten apples. We can

strip away the sliver ideas of apples and think in terms of space. As we develop complex equations, we strive to find evidence that they work. We can work in mathematical models based on the correlation of mathematics and our physical existence. There arrives a time when an idea moves to this conclusive-thesis idea category when only one conclusion can be contemplated, or all other possible conclusions have very low probability. We can make this movement to this category by a consensus of many thesisists on the idea. All our ideas, including pure-thesis ideas, we as thesisists always leave open to challenge. The difference in "consensus" here with the "general consensus" from John Locke is that the measurement of the idea and its consensus is dependant on the physical world and not the arbitrary *sensing* against the human mind against any human created false reality.

10. *Our second category in manufactured ideas is theorized-manufactured ideas.* Our theorized-manufactured ideas involve a collection of sliver ideas that when collected together have a partial connection to physical existence, or we have several connections to physical existence to conflicting master ideas. We have at least two or more conclusions with physical existence connections that we can entertain. This category is a wide category. We could have ideas that come close to conclusive-thesis ideas or ideas that come near pure-manufactured ideas. Our relationship of sliver ideas and how close they come to either of the two pure types of ideas we can express in terms of probability. We can access a likely probability in our evaluation to whatever physical connections are present. As long as our collection of sliver ideas have more than one master idea that brings probability levels of uncertainty, we always categorize these ideas as theorized-manufactured ideas.

11. *Therefore, we have four categories of ideas that we hold.* The four categories of ideas within our thought existence are pure-thesis, conclusive-thesis, theorized-manufactured and pure-manufactured ideas. Each category has a relationship back to our physical world. In the occurrence of our pure-manufactured ideas, the relationship is that we do not have any connection back to our physical world.

12. *It is the category of manufactured ideas that our reason and rational thought failed to acknowledge properly.* For example, John Locke wrote, "*First then, I say, That when the Truth of our Ideas is judged of, by the Conformity they have to the Ideas which other Men have, and commonly signify by the same Name, they may be any of them false. But yet simple Ideas are least of all liable to be so mistaken. Because a Man by his senses, and every Day's Observation, may easily satisfy himself what the simple Ideas are...*" (8, II.xxxii.9) Instead of placing physical existence as the center, or our measure to which we determine, he placed human beings as the center. His *thesis* ideas were not determined by their connection to physical existence, but instead defaulted to

"*conformity ... other men have.*" His reason and rational thought had human beings determining truth. When you have human beings determining truth, then the statement by John Locke becomes problematic as we begin to develop manufactured ideas without accountability. It was problematic because physical existence determines accountability while John Locke had human beings deciding accountability. It does show he understood mental animation and original thesis ideas. Nevertheless, he did not bring any accountability method to them. He worked in a form of manufactured accountability determined by human beings. When we drop the measurement of our sliver idea of reality against our physical existence, we amputate accountability from reason and rational thought. Under this view, we have been living in a prolonged Dark Age. Our historical moments of enlightenment have been unsuccessful attempts.

13. *John Locke understood that our human mind undergoes rearrangement of ideas and that we can create true ideas and false ideas.* John Locke wrote,

> Though what has been said in the foregoing Chapter, to distinguish real from imaginary Knowledge, might suffice here, in answer to this Doubt, to distinguish *real Truth* from *chimerical*, or (if you please) *barely nominal*, they depending both on the same Foundation; yet it may not be amiss here again to consider, that though our Words signify nothing but our *Ideas*, yet being designed by them to signify Things, the *Truth* they contain, when put into Propositions, will be only *Verbal*, when they stand for *Ideas* in the Mind, that have not an Agreement with the Reality of Things. And therefore Truth, as well as Knowledge, may well come under the Distinction of *Verbal* and *Real*; that being only *verbal Truth*, wherein Terms are joined according to the Agreement or Disagreement of the *Ideas* they stand for, without regarding whether our *Ideas* are such as really have, or are capable of having an existence in Nature. But then it is they contain *real Truth*, when these Signs are joined, as our *Ideas* agree; and when our *Ideas* are such as we know are capable of having an Existence in Nature: which in Substances we cannot know, but by knowing that such have existed. (15, IV.v.8)

This statement shows his understanding that there was at least two different types of ideas, pure-thesis and pure-manufactured ideas. He even acknowledged there was a third with his throw in of "(if you please) *barely nominal*." This third was our conclusive-thesis ideas and theorized-manufactured ideas. This also showed his confusion in understanding the difference between the reality of physical existence and the reality of thought existence. Our purple orange with flashing green lights has no reality in physical existence, but it does have

41

a reality in thought existence. Nevertheless, the reality of thought existence does not relate to truth. Truth resides outside of human mental animation. Since he made claim early in his book that sensation was the original source to ideas, I find it peculiar that he did not follow its continued relationship with ideas.

14. *Our idea of reality is a sliver idea.* One sliver idea we have to acknowledge and properly categorize is the sliver idea of reality. When we experience our physical world, we obtain the idea of real existence. This is a sliver idea that we can move to any other idea if we wanted to do so. It is no different as when we had our idea of the fruit orange, and we removed the sliver idea of the color orange from the idea of the fruit and replaced it with the sliver idea of the color purple. Our four categories to bring accountability always have this sliver idea of reality in its proper place. We maintain our accountability position when we place our sliver idea of reality with a master idea that has physical reality. Our physical world is our only reality with footing. When we express our ideas and maintain our connections to the physical world, we have our truth of reality and not a created human false reality. This is important to understand as we can corrupt coercion and lose our freedom and liberty.

15. *The improper movement of our sliver idea of reality can create unaccountable systems of thought.* If we do not maintain the idea of reality connected to our physical world, but attach it to our thought existence, we end in chaos. Human systems of thought that allow the idea of reality to be suspended or attached to manufactured ideas are unaccountable systems of thought. This can only lead us to the mental animation of anything. When we allow ourselves to misplace the sliver idea of reality, we can only create groups of people that require indoctrination to their set of unaccountable ideas.

16. *John Locke provided us an excellent example of how in our use of reason and rational thought we had dropped the requirement that we maintain our sliver idea of reality with physical existence.* John Locke wrote, "When the Understanding is once stored with these simple *Ideas*, it has the Power to repeat, compare, and unite them, even to an almost infinite Variety, and so can make at Pleasure new complex Ideas."(8, II.ii.2) Here we have evidence he understood mental animation and the movement of ideas. Nevertheless, he gave no accountability to our sliver idea of reality when his shuffling of simple to complex ideas occurred. He simply said that when we move around our simple ideas they create complex ideas. He did not define simple ideas as a collection of sliver ideas. He did not explain how we could move around our individual simple ideas into complex ones. He stayed in a gross understanding that ideas were in clumps that moved around. He did not clearly separate

sensory existence with thought existence. He allowed unaccountability to maintain between thesis and manufactured ideas. We know how to separate thesis and manufactured ideas. Real existence would have to connect to the physical world. Unfortunately, in his view of verbal existence stated in paragraph 13, he gave it completely to thought existence. His thought existence consists of ideas without distinction, even to "make at pleasure new complex ideas." Verbal existence and truthful ideas has a relationship back to physical existence. Verbal existence and ideas may or may not have a relationship back to physical existence. We see how he dropped our sliver idea of reality from our simple ideas to the mental animation of our complex ideas.

17. *Unaccountable ideas require coercive human authorities.* Under unaccountable systems of thought, our mental animations become the property of human animation. Individual human animations lead us to specific human authorities that dictate their individual thought and how they deliver it to other people. Since their measurement is against the human mind and it is subject to many interpretations that do not align with the realities of our physical world, it is not in the power seekers interests to allow each individual to perceive and evaluate the physical world as independent human beings. Thesisism allows each individual to evaluate the physical world. This creates our commonality whereas unaccountable systems of thought create false-reality individualism that needs to coerce to create a community to an arbitrary individual or a sub-group of individuals. This is so because when people evaluate to our physical realities, the given ideas would not align. Power mongers require people to move our evaluation of physical existence to their manufactured existence. This means we begin to measure our ideas not against our creator and creation, but against other human thought existences. The ultimate authority becomes the human being with a peculiar thought existence. The only way we can transfer individual thought existence is by written or spoken word. A large difference between thesisism and false-reality systems of thought is that we point to our common physical world. We need not to coerce against anyone. All we have to do is look at our reality given to us by our creation in physical existence.

18. *Unaccountable systems of thought lead to human suffering.* Self-appointed human authorities from an unaccountable system of thought can lead to misuse of people and power. Authors of unaccountable systems of thought teach people to forgo their evaluative abilities and to give their code of conduct to the direction of others. This can lead to authorities that misuse people and power and lead us to suffering. Our foregoing to authorities is evident with religious thought. It is less evident with reason and rational thought for social ideas. Nevertheless, the unaccountable system of thought

impregnated in reason and rational thought gives us individual ultimate authorities as well.

19. *Accountable ideas require our physical existence to be our authority.* Under a system of thought with accountability, we measure our mental animations against physical existence. Physical existence is our creator. Physical existence is the same for all humankind. This measurement not only results in a stable and consistent understanding of our creator, but also in how we are to conduct ourselves in it. We gain our control of coercion. We, the coercive animal, can change ourselves to measure against the physical world and release our freedom and liberty.

20. *The accountability of thesisism brings justice to all.* Our accountability system, since it connects to our physical world, eliminates self-interest motivations of individuals that seek power and domination. Our accountability system is open to everyone equally and to the same conclusive ends. It involves the equations of justice measured against our same physical existence. This eliminates arbitrary coercion and creates a self-correcting system to our proper code of conduct. It moves us in opposition to manipulations made by human animation that lead us to injustice. It does not require knowledge of all things, only the individual actions of each person. This is the "invisible hand" of Adam Smith. However, unlike Adam Smith and the members of the extended order of capitalism where they procure a faith position in this "invisible hand," thesisism brings in a reality-based and yet small tool that plugs into the actions of all people. This reality-based tool in turn brings an order with accountability to the "invisible hand" of the extended order of capitalism and to all other human actions.

Experiential Existence
Section 1: Experiential Existence

1. *When we remove all of physical existence during the action of human mental activity, this leaves us experiential existence.* All our thoughts, feelings and perceptions rely on our physical world and our physical brain. If we seize existence over a moment in time and remove all physical material, we leave ourselves with the output of experience and results that came from the action of the physical material. This action of the physical creates an existence we call experiential existence. This existence is a separate, but dependent existence on our physical existence.

2. *Our experiential existence is relational to physical existence.* We have a relationship between our experiential existence and our physical mental structure. This relationship resides in the physical action when our minds

function. This aspect results in our awareness and our consciousness. We have an additional relationship we grossly ignore. We have a relationship between what our sensory inputs acquire from our physical world to create our experience of our physical world. Our relationship with the external world and to its actual internal manipulations to our brain arrives as a singular action to each sense, but our minds assess it by deconstructive action into sliver ideas that we then pull back together to match the best we can to the original inputted reality. Reality is singular experience and a singular sliver idea. Our ideas and memories are reconstructed sliver ideas bundled and invoked in parallel to attempt to match the original incoming source.

3. *For our experiential existence to come into existence, an order of the physical material must come together to form a mental structure.* In living beings, we refer to this mental structure as the brain. Each living being has its own nature to the construction and capacity of this brain. Since we are examining human ideas, we are examining the construction and capacity of the human brain. Our experiential existence that we outline here is to human experiential existence. How we match or do not match with other species is a valid area of study. It is not the scope of this examination.

4. *For experiential existence to come into existence, our brain must be in the action of operating.* When we have physical action and physical movement in our brain, we have experiential existence result into existence. Without action, it ceases. Our experiential existence is a separate existence to our physical existence that is dependent on the existence of physical material in a specific form. In the specific form termed human, we engaged in its natural actions.

5. *In addition to the development and creation of our experiential existence, we develop a continued interaction with physical existence with our sensory inputs.* By the structure of human mental creation, we have between our brain and our physical world an interaction that contributes to our experiential existence. Our interactions with our physical world result in separate types of experiential existences. The subtypes of experiential existence are sensory, reactive and thought existence. In addition, experiential existence has two characteristics to its condition, one being awareness and one being consciousness.

Section 2: Sensory Existence

6. *Sensory existence is our player and the original input of information between our mental existence and physical existence.* Our sight, sound, taste, feel, and smell provide a physical interaction between our human brain and physical existence. The interaction we have between physical existence and our brain creates our sensory experience. For example, our vision derives from the physical wavelengths of light that strikes our receptors to form physical

reactions into our brain. The action of this physical existence creates our player to our physical world. If we have interrupted or physically damaged our sensory input, then our subtype of experiential existence ceases to exist.

7. *Sensory existence is our intermediary between physical existence and our thought and reactive existences.* Our sensory existence plays its responses to the interactions between our physical world and our human brain. During the evolution of the physical material into human brains, we had the creation of sensory existence that fed thought and reactive existences. How our thought and reactive existences bring in this information and uses it is determined by the existing physical construction of our mind and our life experiences. Over time, as experience and the occurrence of mental animation builds, we have potential interception of incoming sensory existence in how we could perceive it. We can see in Diagram 2 our sensory interplay between physical existence, thought existence and reactive existence.

8. *Philosophers quickly amputate our connection to physical existence that arrives through our sensory existence.* Our sensory existence provides inputs from our physical existence. Nevertheless, we immediately drop this relationship and animate human mental existence solely as if our experiential existence exists only. This non-relational thought system centers only within itself. Jean-Paul Sartre is an example of this, as he wrote centered on consciousness. In his model, he wrote about the idea of absence. "The object does not refer to being as to a signification; it would be impossible, for example, to define being as a *presence* since *absence* too discloses being, since not to be *there* means still to be."(4, p8) What Sartre did was to confuse the external source sensory existence with our internal thought existence. Since he measured his idea against the human mind, he dropped the relational aspects of physical existence. His "object" was something external, be it an orange or to use one of his references, nausea. Our experience of this allowed the creation of memory and the idea of it now resides in thought existence. Our acquired ideas have many sliver ideas to make the master idea. The absence idea in thought existence is the absence of most sliver ideas, leaving the most basic form or structure. Therefore, we have a three-stage process to create an absence idea. There is the original perception. There is the idea of it created in thought existence. Then there is the removal of all sliver ideas down to its form and structure, leaving its impression. A metaphor could be that an absent idea is a footprint in the sand of our mind. In the end, his absence idea as having being is so because of our original source in physical existence. Therefore, his absence idea is not actually an absent idea.

9. *Sartre ignored the original interactions between physical existence and thought existence, and animated solely relational to thought existence.* In fact, all ideas have absence ideas by their mere interaction with us. In the sliver idea

form, all ideas have an original perceived idea somewhere in physical existence. We have our presence of object in physical existence that interacts with our sensory existence and by its physical actions moves into thought existence. The idea of absence and it having being involves only thought existence. His idea had no relational aspects to physical existence. If we do not consider the sliver idea of reality, the absence idea is strictly a manufactured idea that only exists in the human mind. If we relate the absence idea to physical existence, the object from original sensory interface may or may not exist in the original percept form. If the object no longer exists, the absence idea does not apply because we know the material of physical existence changes. Under this, we begin to see the silliness of Sartre in his ignoring physical existence. Sartre is only one of many philosophers and rational thinkers that amputated physical existence and the reality connection we need to maintain alignment to truth.

Section 3: Thought Existence

10. *Thought existence minus physical existence, sensory existence and reactive existence leaves our ideas.* Thought existence procures our sensory existence and transforms that experience into ideas. It uses the physical interplay of the experience from our physical world, which gives us our *pure-thesis ideas in sliver and master form,* and immerses them into our previous experiences. By our ability to retrieve previous experiences and hold them as ideas, thought existence has the capability to animate and hold in consciousness previous experiences in idea form. By our ability to mingle sliver ideas with other sliver ideas, thought existence has the capability to animate and hold in consciousness ideas that no longer align with any original experience in physical existence.

11. *We can create ideas in thought existence from any sensory existence form of input.* Our ideas can arrive from auditory, visual, feel, taste and smell. All these origins from sensory input can be part of the full idea. An experience of the fruit orange, for example, can result in the idea of an orange. That idea contains visual components, such as roundness, color, the visual word orange and more. It contains auditory components, such as the auditory word orange. It may contain the feel of texture and the smell of the fruit.

12. *Ideas are many sliver ideas collected together to make a master idea.* When we have the idea of the fruit orange, it holds many sliver ideas that converge to make the master idea of the fruit. We have the sliver idea of round, which we experienced by our seeing the orange. We also have our experiences through life to round objects. Because of this, we can acquire and understand the idea of orange easier. The sliver idea of color too comes from

our current experience of it and our having experienced this color previously during our lives. This adds to our ability to obtain easily the experience of an orange and remembering it. Our abilities to remember an orange, and the accuracy to remembering it, depend on how well we pull these sliver ideas together. If we have previous experiences in the sliver components of the object, we remember easier. This may be why we can experience a new object, be it an orange or something else, and remember it while we may have initial difficulty in remembering the name. The name would be new and without any sliver idea history, at least, no history in its total context.

13. *Imbedded in the idea of ideas we have two characteristics that need to be determined.* Any time we have two people talking about an idea, we need to assure that each person holds the same idea in their thought existence. Anytime we state an idea, we have a response of sliver ideas that pool together to make the master idea. How well we pool our sliver ideas together across people reflects its characteristic. We can have with a collection of sliver ideas to a master idea a bandwidth. The bandwidth of any master idea may be very small to very large.

14. *One end of this continuum we term narrowband ideas.* When we have two or more people bring up an idea and their sliver idea components to the master idea are nearly or purely similar, we have the characteristic of a narrowband idea. We can use our idea of the fruit, orange. By our common thesis experience of this fruit, the idea of an orange when conversed between people would be identical or nearly identical. Any variations we would have would be in relation to the experience of each person. If we had people that only saw and knew small oranges, they would think oranges as small. If we had people that only saw and knew large oranges, they would think oranges as large. If we had people that saw and knew various sizes of oranges, they would have this characteristic added to their master idea.

15. *The other end of this continuum we term broadband ideas.* When we have two or more people bring up an idea, and their sliver idea components vary such that each one elicits a different master idea, or each one can elicit several potential master ideas to the same idea, we have the characteristic of a broadband idea. When we have an idea that can elicit several different master ideas even to the same individual, we need to take the time to define our master ideas to assure that each person in discussion is indeed discussing the same idea. When we state an idea that people ought to treat people well, most of us would agree. Nevertheless, which sliver ideas we would pool together to the idea that we should treat people well would vary significantly. Some people may bring up the idea of treating people politely. Other people may bring up the idea of health and education for all people. Some people may

only include people that are similar to them and not to all other people across our species.

16. *Since this is a continuum, we have different levels between narrowband and broadband ideas.* Our narrowband and broadband ideas are not distinct categories. The level or number of different potential master ideas across people can vary. If we only refer to orange, without the idea of fruit, we can have the master idea of a fruit or simply the color. Our most important understanding to narrowband and broadband ideas is that we must align our idea between us to engage in useful discourse.

17. *Our physical world exists in parallel.* Our experience of physical events is serial in nature, as it is the movement through time. Nevertheless, our physical existence moving through time is parallel to our existence and our experience of existence. Since sensory existence inputs our ideas, which operates in parallel, we understand our ideas during thought in parallel, as we can pool the sliver ideas together to our original experience and to the master idea in its original parallel nature.

18. *Our master ideas are the parallel experience of sliver ideas.* The interaction between our physical world and our sensory existence involve the parallel connections of sensory input to our physical world. This parallel input of sensory existence results in sliver ideas that give us master ideas. When we experience them in our thoughts, they are the parallel reconstruction of sensory experience to our physical world. Our discussion in this paragraph so far concerns the narrowband idea of pure-thesis ideas. If we animate the idea of ideas in the broadband, we can bring in interactions that involve our human mind only. When we break the relationship of the sensory experience back to our physical world, we partake in a different narrowband idea of ideas. When our break from physical existence is a complete break, we are dealing with the narrowband idea of pure-manufactured ideas. Master ideas are the parallel experience of sliver ideas. We can animate master ideas in our minds without any statement to their connections or lack of connections back to physical existence.

19. *Our articulation of master ideas under language, written or spoken, cannot be a parallel presentation of the idea.* It is impossible, because of the physical restraints to our human structure, to articulate a master idea in parallel to others. Our own mental construction restricts the transfer of our internal parallel understandings in an outward serial form. Our written and spoken language is for most part a serial output of our internal parallel understandings of our master ideas.

20. *We can convey in some forms of communications our master and sliver ideas in parallel.* Our visual representation of art, posters and more could portray some master or sliver ideas in parallel. Our movies could convey some

master or sliver ideas in parallel. Even these forms of communications we end with people using language for discussion. Because we have this aspect to our prime form of communications, which is verbal and written language, serial communications dominates human communications.

21. *Our serial communications has advantages and disadvantages.* An advantage of serial communications is that we begin to layout our sliver ideas one by one. This is our method to assure we are thinking the same master idea. It is a way to verify with others that our collection of sliver ideas indeed aligns with the master ideas each person holds. The disadvantage is that it requires us to take time, and to give a dedication to the verification. As our complexity of ideas grows, so does our time and dedication.

22. *We can retrieve our sliver ideas and rearrange them into new forms of master ideas.* When we engage in mental animation of ideas, we bring up a collection of sliver ideas to a master idea. We can also rearrange, add or subtract sliver ideas to create new master ideas. Because we can reconstruct sliver ideas into new forms, we can change the relationship between physical existence and the master idea.

23. *We can animate our reconstructed bundle of sliver ideas to a master idea that no longer matches with physical existence.* When we have a pure-thesis idea, we can match the set of sliver ideas back to the physical world. However, when we reconstruct a new set of sliver ideas, we can break the connections back to our physical world in its set. The word "set" here refers to the collection of sliver ideas. We can have sliver ideas, owing to previous animations, that have attached a set of sliver ideas that does not have any connections to the physical world. Therefore, any set of sliver ideas we may have created to a master idea may have a combination of sliver ideas that relate individually back to physical existence, and yet, in the combination bundled is a manufactured master idea with no connections back to physical existence. Under this understanding, we now see why we begin to create different classifications of ideas.

24. *Our pure-manufactured ideas break completely away from our physical world.* When we pool together a collection of sliver ideas to a master idea and that master idea does not have a physical counter part in its complete form, the master idea becomes a manufactured idea. When we have an arrangement of sliver ideas that does not have any probability to exist in our physical world, it is a pure-manufactured idea. When we rearrange our sliver ideas to make an orange purple and to have flashing green lights, we have no connection to physical existence with the set of sliver ideas. Someone could make a representative model, but it is then only a physical representation of a pure-manufactured idea. The original source of the idea of reality does not follow our attaching the sliver idea of reality to this purple orange. If genetically we were to create a purple orange with flashing green lights, then

we could attach the sliver idea of reality to it when this entity comes into physical existence. Nevertheless, we cannot attach the sliver idea of reality to any human created reality in thought existence that we may or could bring into existence by human manipulation until we had brought that idea into physical existence.

25. *Our different classifications of ideas are in relation to the interaction of physical existence.* As we go through life, and as our species evolve, our relational exchange between the physical world and us may change as it changes and as we understand it more. Therefore, thesisism cannot and does not start as a statement of completion. Thesisism is a dynamic system of thought that requires us to be in a state of constant evaluation with our physical existence and the maintenance of that relationship between our ideas in our thought existence and with our physical reality. This is how we build our understanding of the reality and truth around us.

26. *When we match a collection of sliver ideas to physical existence that brings a syllogism or a categorical preposition, we then can arrive to a conclusive-thesis idea.* When we pool and rearrange our sliver ideas together, we can often develop ideas that bring an understanding of our physical world in its more complex form. The original intent of rational thought, I contend, was to monitor the rearrangement of our sliver ideas relationally to physical existence. I point to natural law in general as evidence of this position. Ideas of how our universe works, how we came into existence by evolution over time, and many other ideas requires matching the collection of sliver ideas that brings us to a one-conclusion idea. If we want rational thought with accountability, all ideas underneath our complex master ideas must contain evaluations to physical existence. In our science, we create experiments to experience our physical world in a form of actions to pure-thesis ideas. When we maintain our required connections to the physical, we can construct ideas deemed as having a reality. When we as a group collect evaluations to a certain idea, we can pool together ideas deemed as pure or near pure and come to a conclusive determination. This conclusive determination is solely for whether we can assign the sliver idea of reality. We call these ideas conclusive-thesis ideas, as we can support them by their connections to the physical world. When we allow the sliver idea of reality to attach to an idea, it must be with physically based (thesis-based) justifications.

27. *When we have theorized-manufactured ideas, we do not have a complete match to our physical world.* Because we can rearrange many sliver ideas as well as pooling together other ideas in a master idea form, we can create many complex ideas. How well they all connect or stay connected to the physical world determines position. When we have ideas where we cannot demonstrate the needed connections or can only provide some connections

to our physical existence, we end with ideas that have uncertainty to their full relation to physical existence. We could have ideas that have incomplete connections to our physical existence. Our incomplete connections may vary from a few to many. Further, our complex ideas could have several ideas behind it. Each sub-master idea to the complex idea has its relational position to physical existence. When we have uncertainty whether the idea connects or does not connect to our physical existence, different potential realities may exist. Under these conditions, we must categorize them as theorized-manufactured ideas. Therefore, a theorized-manufactured idea is different to the pure-manufactured idea, as it has some form of connection to physical existence, even if it is weak.

28. *Our theorized-manufactured ideas can have a large probability range.* Our number of physically related connections to an idea may vary greatly from many to perhaps only one. Across all possibilities, we can determine our probability by the nature of the connections to physical existence or the lack of connections to physical existence. We can have the idea that aliens from other worlds live with us and claim we have a connection to physical existence. Because we exist, we have developed travel into space, and with the size of our universe, the idea that intelligent beings outside our earth exist has a fair probability. However, our original idea that they are here lacks physical connections to the realities that we experience. We have no connections to physical existence that supports this idea. Our physical existence demonstrates that the existence of other beings in the universe does have a probability, as we had come to existence. Our probability level to this last theorized-manufactured idea is good. The idea that other beings engage in space travel and they have frequented our planet does not align to physical existence as it has been presenting itself. Our probability level to this theorized-manufactured idea is very low, if not even zero. We have a good argument to place this idea into our pure-manufactured idea category because the claims provided are through human accounts under written or spoken language. Diagram 1a, 1b and 2 provides us a visual account of idea categorization.

29. *Our idea of reality is an idea as well.* Reality is a sliver idea. We acquire this idea from our experience of it. Nevertheless, our philosophical and religious idea of reality is too broadband. We can have two realities. One reality is the reality of physical existence. The other reality is our experiential existence. These two realities are not the same. The reality of physical existence is stable and infinite to our experience. The reality of experiential existence is simply sensory input of physical existence, reactive coloring of emotion as well as arrangement and rearrangement of acquired sliver and master idea events in action. Experiential existence is unstable and finite to our experience. When

we as thesisists speak of the sliver idea of reality, it is *always* in relation to physical existence.

30. *When we have arguments that reality may not exist or we cannot prove reality, this argument ignores our experience of physical existence.* Our experience of interactions outside of our mental experience is our reality. The idea that a tree we see may not really exist ignores our interactive aspects to this reality. Ideas of a *pure* reality are attempts to identify reality with our senses removed. Whether reality exists in some other form outside of our capacity to experience does not change the requirement of our interaction with it. We have a result in our experiential existence derived from physical existence to which we must learn our interaction and relationship to this on going result between physical existence and experiential existence.

31. *Our sliver idea of reality can inappropriately move in our mental animation.* The idea of reality is an idea in itself. It is one idea that we can move as a sliver idea and to which we can attach or not attach to any master idea. Our ability to apply probabilities to any theorized-manufactured ideas is a measurement against the idea of reality. Our idea of reality is in relation to the physical world and the physical world is the source to which we measure our truth. To maintain our understanding and relationship to reality and truth, we must measure our ideas against this physical world.

32. *Our sliver idea of reality is not limited to science, but to all ideas.* When we measure our ideas against our reality, we should not limit it to science, but apply it to all ideas that we have. Our physical existence is our source of structure to understand the truth to all things. It provides us information beyond how this physical material operates. It provides us information about us physically. It is in our physical construction that we learn how to conduct ourselves. This means we can and need to measure our ideas against the physical world. We can know the accuracy of any idea in its set of sliver ideas in how it relates back to our physical world. Our science ought not to simply be the study of cause and effect. Our scientific ideas have thesisism built into it, as they connect back to the physical. Without this, we could not engage in our science of cause and effect experimentation with any accountability. Thesisism moves beyond the cause and effect of science. This means we maintain accountably with physical existence to our ideas that do not involve cause and effect.

33. *Our ideas of morality involve our behavioral conduct with one another.* Because our behavioral conduct involves mental animation of thought existence and not our physical existence, our ideas to morality connect not to the *movement* of physical material that we find in the study of science, but to the *result* of our physical existence to the construction of the human being and all life-forms. We do not have physical existence in the cause and effect

under these ideas. Rather, we have thought existence in the cause and effect. Our thought existence involves our acquisition of life experiences and the development and implementation of a reality or false-reality based thought system that develops comparative equations to behavior. The physical existence of non-life operates under cause and effect. The physical existence of human life operates within our thought existence. Because of this, we have to change our cause and effect idea to our life existence and comparative equations. Under thesisism, our life existence is relational to physical existence and our comparative equations derive from physical existence.

34. *Our ideas of morality must measure against our reality.* Because our ideas of morality are ideas, and all sliver ideas arrive from physical existence, we can measure our ideas of morality against our physical existence. We can determine our moral code of conduct between people and our planet earth by the examination of the physical connections between the physical world and us. When we examine the physical connections between people, we can determine our moral code of conduct between ourselves.

35. *Our ideas of morality between people and our planet we measure against physical existence.* We can determine our moral code of conduct that is between our planet and ourselves. We do so by maintaining the balance to the physical material that maintains the livability of our planet earth to our species. When we act morality and maintain the balance of our earth as required by physical existence, we maintain a moral relationship between our earth and ourselves. When we break this moral relationship, it affects all human being and all animal species. We can only maintain this moral relationship when we are able to transfer our physical realities to our human experiential existence. When we move ourselves from non-realized capability to actually having conscious understanding, we personally and socially reach our highest potential. Our moral relationship to our earth comes from our obligations to one another under thesis-morality. Thesis-morality is morality that connects to our physical world.

36. *We measure our ideas of morality between people and our physical world.* We determine our moral code of conduct by our human physical structure. Physical existence has given us our human physical structure. How we determine our moral code of conduct, our behavioral obligations between us is by assessing the physical makeup of human beings.

37. *Our moral expression as determined by our physical existence has two expressions.* All human morality has physical connections. When we have ideas that have physical connections, we call them thesis ideas. Therefore, thesis-morality is morality that connections to our physical world. Although we have one physical existence, our human structure has two expressions. We will see in the section titled *Morality Connected to Physical Existence* that

our thesis-morality results from two different characteristics in the physical structure of human beings.

Section 4: Reactive Existence

38. *Our reactive existence is experiential existence minus physical existence, sensory existence and thought existence, which leaves us our reactive experiences.* We have reactive responses result from sensory input. From our early evolution, we have interacted with our environment with engaged evaluative responses without language.[10] Our human brains have evaluative interpretations to sensory input that moves us to reactive responses. Our reactive response has a singularity to its character. One example of our reactive response is the fight-flight response. We have others such as love, hate, joy and anger. In the end, our reactive experience to sensory input evokes a color of feeling.

39 *Our reactive existence has both internal and external sources.* We have internal sources to reactive existence, such as our sexual impulses, hunger impulses and other reactive responses that are due to physical world changes within our brain and our bodies. We have external sources to reactive existence that we derive from sensory existence. We could involve only one, or a combination or all five of our external source senses. Our external sources play into our senses and involve a non-conscious evaluation of the sensory input. Whereas, our internal sources to reactive existence can play directly to our mind to provide stimuli. Here we have a chemical interaction that moves us toward our external search for satisfaction. Under this, we could consider our own brain an additional sensory input.

40. *Our reactive experiences become ideas in thought existence.* When we experience a reactive response, we obtain an idea of it in our thought existence. When we remember the idea of the reactive experience, we pull together a set of sliver ideas to the original experience. When we bring up an idea experienced from a reactive experience, we can invoke a reactive response to different experiential degrees. Our reactive responses can and do turn into ideas that can then feedback to have a reactive reaction not from physical existence, but triggered from thought existence. This mean we have again the

---

10 Ideas are the representations experienced from physical existence, arranged, and rearranged into many different master ideas. It is important to understand that although reactive existence developed before language and thought existence, in later stages of evolution thought existence arose with ideas (memory) of experience that in turn led to language. Therefore, pre-language reactive existence can involve thought existence similar to sensory existence. Thought existence then is the recipient of both sensory and reactive existences that transform into ideas. Language is an expression of these ideas.

need to bring accountability to our reactive existence as it too can be broken from physical existence and result in a reactive response to something that has no reality attached.

41. *Our output of a reactive response is reactive coloring.* When we experience a reactive response in our experiential existence, it is that of feel. Like color, where our brain interprets the wavelength of the light and it in turn colors our world, our reactive feel, by the inputs of the reactive responses, we interpret it and create a coloring of feel.

42. *Once we move the reactive experience to an idea, it too can be a master idea with sliver ideas that we can move or remove from any idea.* When we have reactive experiences, it contributes to thought existence in the creation of the idea of the reactive experience. We now have an idea that we can manipulate the same as all other ideas. We can evoke the idea of any reactive experience and have it contribute to any experiencing reactive response. It could even trigger a reactive response and experience. This means that we can have ideas from our reactive experiences under reconstruction break away from our physical world and not align with any current experience. They can contribute and add to any reactive coloring to any person. Therefore, we can have manufactured reactive responses and experiences as well.

43. *Our reactive responses can occur without sensory input if the areas of the brain responsible for the reactive coloring are somehow artificially simulated.* We have other possible ways to evoke reactive coloring. It may be by the introduction of drugs, by a chemical imbalance or by physical disease.

Section 5: Our Historical Experiential Existence with Physical Existence Ignored

44. *Our sensory existence is our source that leads us into thought and reactive existence.* When we have the input of sensory existence that results in our thought existence and reactive existence, we begin to see the interactions that can contribute to ideas. Our thought existence and reactive existence can and do interact. Each of our three existences requires the action of the physical material in our brain during its operation. Our original or prime source of thought existence and reactive existence comes from the input of our sensory existence. Whether we obtain it from our vision of seeing the physical world or our experiencing pain in our bodies, all sources of our sensory existence feeds into our thought and reactive existences.

45. *Immanuel Kant separated sensory existence with thought existence, and then ignored the relational aspects between the two.* Immanuel Kant in his book, *Fundamental Principles of the Metaphysics of Morality*, stated in his preface, "All rational knowledge is either material or formal."(16, p1) First, rational

knowledge is simply human knowledge. The position of Kant was that material knowledge "considers some object," whereas his formal knowledge "is concerned only with the form of understanding and of the reason itself ... without distinction of its objects." (16, p1) This does not fit our physical world, as material knowledge is our sensory inputs and our formal knowledge is our mental animations. Kant gave no relational requirement to our sliver idea of reality. The obvious difference between this statement of Kant and thesisism is that he viewed his formal as independent of objects. He animated our thought existence as not having any original and relational connection to the physical world. This ignored the accountability aspects of thesisism under our seven elements to truth. Additionally, with the view held by Kant on material knowledge, he actually placed its knowledge into the physical world rather than within our own thought existence. He had not stated it as such, but the effect of his thinking this idea as true did just that. To understand his mistake we have to ask where the source to our ideas resides.

46. *Our physical existence is our source to ideas.* Were do our ideas reside? Our ideas reside in our thought existence and how they relate to physical existence determines accountability. We can animate ideas in our thought existence to break our physical-world connections, but we can trace the source of each original sliver idea to any master idea back to physical existence. The material knowledge idea by Kant was our pure-thesis ideas, conclusive-thesis ideas and perhaps theorized-manufactured ideas of high probability. His formal knowledge heavily involved theorized-manufactured ideas and pure-manufactured ideas, which in turn had weakened pure-thesis and conclusive-thesis ideas. I say this *based* on his distinction of objects to material objects and his without distinction of objects to reason. This sets up and reinforces the traditional system of rational thought without accountability. We can say this because he animated his ideas without any original source to our ideas, and in doing, he eliminated our accountability system. This was important because later he tried to put the truth of existence and morality into his formal knowledge category. He considered this *a priori* knowledge. This meant that he viewed ideas as if they were independent to our physical world, and even more than that, not coming from our physical world. Interpretations of Kant vary greatly. Some claim the *a priori* knowledge of Kant simply meant that we had some ideas constructed physically into our minds, thus existed prior to experience. This implies to some the existence of conscious actions and they animate the idea that this provides evidence of a conscious and self-existent being. Some of the problems with philosophers like Kant, Sartre and others, are that they too suffer the wild oscillations in interpretations to their rational thought that religious thought experiences.

47. *John Locke confused sensory existence with reactive existence.* John Locke wrote in his, *An Essay on Human Understanding*, "we find, that their names lead our thoughts to the mind, and no further. When we speak of *Justice*, or *Gratitude*, we frame to our selves no Imagination of anything existing, which we would conceive; but our Thoughts terminate in the abstract *Ideas* of those Vertues, and look not farther; as they do, when we speak of a *Horse*, or *Iron*, whose Specifick *Ideas* we consider not, as barely in the Mind, but as in things themselves, which afford the original Patterns of those *Ideas*." (15, III.v.12) First, in his example, we have his use of sensory existence, reactive existence and our capacity to evaluate-to-balance.[11] His horse, or iron, has its origination from our physical existence. They are also pure-thesis ideas. They have a direct connection to physical existence, and they arrive via our sensory existence. They, by their nature, can come to the visual aspects of our mental life. We derive "gratitude" not from sensory existence as a distinct object, but from an evaluate-to-balance from experienced sensory existence to our reactive existence. The experience of this can and does become translated into an idea. We can think back to it just like our horse or iron, but instead of coloring a visual representation, we color out a reactive representation. Therefore, when Locke says, "we frame to ourselves no imagination of anything existing," this is not true. It exists, but not in our visual account. Its existence is in the physical as we are physical creatures and gratitude felt is the evaluation of physical actions that occurred. It, like justice, plays to our sense of balance. The problem is this. The interpretations to the physical actions that occurred we measure in our experiential existence, as gratitude and justice involve evaluation. This means, without thesisism we can measure our sense of balance against reality or false reality.

48. *Jean-Paul Sartre treated sensory existence in terms of internal existence only.* One of the first presentations of Sartre in his book, *Being and Nothingness*, was the *phenomenon of being*. He wrote, "Thus there must be for it a *phenomenon of being*, an appearance of being, capable of description as such." (4, p7) He provided examples of *boredom* and *nausea*. Already we have a shifting away from thesisism, but in a subtle way. I contend that the *phenomenon of being* by Sartre was sensory existence. Instead of recognizing this, and pulling ourselves closer to the physical world, Sartre maintained the philosophical tradition of trying to think of the human mind as a brain without sensory input and thus ignoring sensory existence. Philosophers have

---

11 Evaluate-to-balance is a term used in thesisism. It refers to the natural ordering that occurs by the physical structure of the normal and healthy human mind. It is the evolutionary construction to evaluate our physical environment to make our decisions and movements. Evaluate-to-balance is the core stimulus-response mechanism that has been built on since the rise of life.

only viewed the human mind in terms of our mental animation capability. They have ignored the physical world input. These examples of *boredom* and *nausea* given were attempts to place his view of phenomenon of being as an internal source only. He had amputated all external world inputs. However, what was the source to his presented examples of *boredom* and *nausea*? Our physical body! Instead of saying *of seeing a tree, the physical light bouncing off the tree and into our eyes*, he was saying *the feel of boredom from lack of physical stimulation* or *the feel of nausea due to physical interactions creating imbalances and disruptions to ones body*. His choice to use internal feelings as a source of *phenomenon of being* is suspicious, as it easily allowed him to not deal with the source of his *phenomenon of being*.

49. *If we do not maintain our measurement against our physical world, we begin to endanger our species' survival.* Our mental animations of the acquired physical experience in sliver idea form can lead us to the creation of ideas that do not exist in reality. Our reality is our physical world. Our internal reality is human created reality. We can and do direct ourselves to manufactured ideas that contribute to manufactured reactive responses and experiences, and to manufactured ideas about our physical world. Unless we maintain our connections to the physical world, we start to separate ourselves from the truth and reality of the world around us. Because we can separate our thought existence from physical reality, we can place ourselves into jeopardy to our long-term survival as a species. We have a long history of thought existence separating from physical reality and it has demonstrated the suffering we can inflict on one another because of it. This infliction results from unjustified coercion through unaccountable systems of thought.

50. *Our experiential existence consists of the three existences just outlined.* Our sensory, thought and reactive existences together make up experiential existence. Our sensory existence feeds into thought and reactive existences. Our thought and reactive existence in turn can interact between each other and can create different possible animations. They may connect to the physical world or they may begin or completely break away from our physical world. We can begin to affect our sensory input by the development of our framed-reference. We will discuss framed-reference in the chapter titled *Framed-Reference*. Before then, we need to distinguish between awareness and consciousness that resides in our experiential existence.

Awareness and Consciousness

1. *When we have our experiential existence occurring, we have two potential aspects to its character.* We refer to these two forms of activity as awareness and consciousness. Because they are the center of our existence, we often

study them. We often subjugate awareness to a lesser role. We often viewed it as the subconscious. Our awareness is conditional for consciousness. They are the same in form. The difference between them is a small difference. It is in the difference that consciousness possesses that has tempted not only our theologians, but also our philosophers and even scientists to make our conscious mind the center of existence. We view our mind as the thinking machine and begin to measure our ideas against our own consciousness. We even measure reason and rational thought against the diffuse idea that we measure against our conscious capacity to think logically.

2. *Our awareness is the play of experiential existence without a future or a past.* When we have awareness, it is our activity in its original and non-holding form. It is our one-to-one time ratio to the physical activity leading to awareness. Our awareness operates only in the present. When we operate our car and stop at a red light without being conscious of it, we have awareness in operation. When we enter a place and begin to feel uneasy and we begin to consciously assess the physical surrounding where we find a threat, be it a tiger in the bush or an unsavorily character in the shadows, we had awareness in operation before consciousness.

3. *The activity of sensory existence in the present is awareness.* When we are awake, our senses are in operation at any given moment. When we are heavily in thought and not attentive to our visual inputs, our visual inputs continue to occur and awareness continues to operate. When we watch the activity around us with conscious attention, we continue to feel the hot or cold weather around us. We may reach for or remove a coat without conscious experience. We nevertheless have physically triggered inputs from our touch that inputs awareness into our experiential existence. When we operate under these conditions, we have awareness operating in the present without the hold of consciousness. This non-conscious experience maintains with us.

4. *The activity of both thought and reactive existence in the present is awareness.* When we are awake, our thought and reactive existence can operate in the present. Our feed of sensory existence and even thought existence to our reactive existence can bring us reactive activity in the present only. Our feed of sensory existence and even reactive existence can bring us the activity of thought existence that operates in the present only. We do not need conscious thought for thinking, reacting or sensing to bring us behavioral actions. We frequently drive a car and realize we had been driving with minimal and even non-existing conscious thought. Children tend to show us the difference. Bruyère wrote, "Children think not of what's past, nor what's to come; but enjoy the present time, which few of us do." (17, p223)

5. *Since our awareness operates in the present only, our reaction time is quick.* We often use awareness to react in dangerous times. If we operate in

awareness only, we react in the present. If suddenly someone were to swing a club at our head, we could react in the present without taking the time for conscious thought. Awareness will react quickly. If we were to stop to think consciously that someone has swung a club at our head and concluded we needed to defend ourselves, and then tried to decide the best course of action, the club would have been on our head several times at that point of conscious thought. We will soon see where conscious thought has its advantages.

6. *Our consciousness is the play of experiential existence with a future and past.* Our awareness is our experiential existence operating in the present. Our consciousness is selected awareness that we, as well as other animals, chose to hold in a static state. This static state of our consciousness brings a brief hold in a moment of time. During this moment of time, we have the present, but now we also have a past and a future. How long this duration of time for each moment of hold is, I do not know. Nevertheless, when we engage in this hold, this duration brings us our consciousness.

7. *Since our consciousness operates in the past, present and future, our reaction time is slow.* Consciousness taps into awareness and holds the present state briefly. This has advantages in specific situations. When confronted with a dangerous situation that is not immediately looming, we can then by conscious action work out better solutions. Historically, hunting may have contributed to the rise of our consciousness because of its advantage in obtained success.

8. *Our consciousness in experiential existence is the activity of played input, evaluative actions and sliver and master ideas with a hold of time.* Our thought, reactive and sensory existences make for experiential existence. Our consciousness is the hold of these existences over a given time. This hold only involves our selected awareness over these three existences. In thought existence, we can pull together sliver and master ideas and animate these ideas in awareness and in consciousness. Our ideas that come to our consciousness are ideas in awareness held over a period to any given set of sliver ideas to any master idea.

9. *Our consciousness has a bandwidth that is less than our awareness.* We have a limited amount or span of consciousness bandwidth. This bandwidth is smaller than awareness. We can move it across all three sub-groups of experiential existence. We can move it under one sensory group completely or divisionally shared between sensory, reactive and thought existences. We cannot have more than awareness, as consciousness is awareness in a different state. Our consciousness is less than awareness as our brain can only suspend within its limitations.

10. *Sartre implied a difference between awareness and consciousness.* Sartre presented several ideas of *beings* that we hold within our mind. One *being* he

presented was consciousness. He wrote, "consciousness is a being such that in its being, its being is in question in so far as this being implies a being other than itself."(4, p24) We do bring into our consciousness our awareness. Therefore, consciousness indeed implies a being other than itself as Sartre expressed. In this regard, Sartre was correct when thinking of consciousness as nothingness, as it was nothing new. Sartre added to this with "Consciousness is in fact a project of founding itself." (4, p789) We should not confuse the word founding with finding itself, such as discovering itself; rather it is establishing itself. Again, he was right; it comes into existence by illumination of what is already there.

11. *The complexity of our human mind in terms of awareness and consciousness goes beyond the undertaking of this book.* For our purpose on the subject of thesisism and to our examination of the coercive animal, we do not need a fuller understanding here. All we need to understand is that we can have ideas in our conscious mind and we can have ideas that are not in our conscious mind that continues to contain awareness.

Framed-Reference

1. *Our thought existence operates differently from our other experiential existences.* Our thought existence is unique because in addition to consciousness selecting awareness, we can search and pull up storied ideas to consciousness. We can influence our reactive existence, and we can alter true meaning to our incoming sensory existence. We have an interactive element to its performance.

2. *Our thought existence and reactive existence is structurally different from our sensory existence.* Our thought existence and reactive existence operates within the physical construction of the human mind, whereas physical nature inputs to our sensory existence. All of our inputs from sensory existence to our thought or reactive existences we obtain by the physical movement of interactions from our external world. In addition, our reactive response to internal bodily function is nevertheless external world interaction. The physical structure to our thought and reactive existence has a physical characteristic of spatial area. Since physical material has a spatial aspect, we have an action that goes to point A to point B. How we place and order our memories, whether they are ideas or reactive coloring to specific environmental conditions, creates a hierarchy of initial to later responses. Because of these set triggered locations, we have an order to which we compare ideas. This we call framed-reference.

3. *The nature of our physical structure is not relational to the physical length of specific mental pathways.* Our framed-reference comes about by the placement

of valued ideas against lesser-valued ideas. The importance we place on a held idea, physically determines the strength of synaptic connections. Because of our previous interactions with our physical environment and by our spoken or written transference of master ideas, as we receive ideas from physical existence, our frame reference can contribute to the attachment of sliver ideas to maintain a personal desired view.

4. *We can have a framed-reference that is free flowing or that is adhesive.* Both of our two different types take in the original physical-world experience and they both affect the validity of any final evaluation. They both contribute to the accuracy or inaccuracy of the original physical-world experience. Our framed-reference is important because its state or position on the incoming original experience can influence all subsequent mental animation. The accuracy or inaccuracy of our experience will determine the accuracy or inaccuracy of the systems of thought we create. Without an accurate experience of the physical world, we cannot come to any system of accountability.

5. *When we have a framed-reference that is free flowing, we allow the original physical-world experience to maintain its accuracy.* The reason why we can maintain accuracy is that we bring in the original physical-world experience without any attachment of sliver ideas from any preconceived ideas of reality. We maintain the experience to its truest source, our physical world, as it allows us to have an accurate understanding of our physical world. Because we are free to accurate acceptance of physical reality, we are in a state of free will. A framed-reference that is free flowing allows us to achieve a state of free will. The two are almost identical with the only difference being that a framed-reference with free flow allows free will to exist. We define a framed-reference that is free flowing as a free-flow framed-reference.

6. *Diagram 8 provides us a visual representation why a free-flow framed-reference is the mechanism to achieve free will.* Since we have an accurate acceptance with our free-flow framed-reference, we can know the true existence of reality. When we know our true physical existence, we can learn to adapt and adjust to it in an accurate way. Our free will can only occur when we have a free flow of physical reality to our being. Therefore, under this condition, we have a free-flow framed-reference. This not only includes our adaptation by science, but to our ideas of social structures as well.

7. *When we have a framed-reference that is adhesive, it distorts our reality from any original experience to our physical world.* The reason why it does is that we bring in the original experience of the physical world and filter it through preconceived ideas where we attach sliver and even master ideas to the experience. When we do this, we not only create manufactured ideas, we change the reality of our incoming sensory existence. When we have a framed-reference that is adhesive, it denies us to achieve a state of free will.

63

We define a framed-reference that is adhesive as an adhesive framed-reference. If our alterations do not connect to physical existence or if they have only partial connections to physical existence, then we break from reality. We have separated ourselves from our original creation and creator, the physical world. The tragedy is that all subsequent mental animations of ideas are manufactured ideas as well. We are no longer in a state of free will. We have placed ourselves into a state of non-free will. We have bound and shackled ourselves to the chaos of our minds. We no longer have an ability to know our physical reality accurately and this places us into unaccountable systems of thought. Our denied state of free will can and does result in many different unaccountable systems of thought that leads us to violations of thesis-morality. This then leads us to false-reality coercion to create suffering for our species as well as fall out to other species.

8. *Our reactive existence can flood our framed-reference.* When our emotions overwhelm us, our framed-reference becomes highly adhesive. We create in ourselves an adhesive framed-reference that is reactive-based. This presented idea, the reactive-based form of adhesive framed-reference, is broadband. In the narrowband, the activity and results may be good or bad depending on each narrowband situation. We could have the reactive response of fear flood our framed-reference with such adhesion we paralyze with fear. We could also flood our framed-reference to run and not think about anything else but running. Our outcome depends on the specific situation if not moving or running was the best option. Our best option may have been to maintain a free-flow framed-reference that allowed us to input the physical world to evaluate with consciousness. When we need to have careful deliberations of our environment in how we are to conduct ourselves with our planet and with one another, an adhesive framed-reference can only lead us away from what we need to know. When we have an adhesive framed-reference that is either reactive-based or idea-based or both, we can contribute to unjustified coercion.

9. *When we measure our ideas against personal desires, we are measuring with an adhesive framed-reference.* Our discussion of personal desires involves a narrowband form of this idea. We are only discussing these personal desire ideas when they become an adhesion to our framed-reference and move us away from physical reality. Our personal desires can be powerful motivators. They can give us emotional support during bad times. They can motivate us to action. Our motivated action can be good or bad. Nevertheless, when we have desires that are contrary to physical reality, we are not open to accept reality. When we are attempting to perceive reality and determine our code of conduct, we have to set aside any ideas framed with anticipated or predetermined master ideas with the attached sliver idea of reality. If we do

not, we can manipulate the incoming reality by rearrangement of sliver ideas intercepted by the personally desired master ideas. When we find ourselves in need of truth, under this narrowband situation we need to drop any adhesive framed-reference and open our free will with a free-flow framed-reference. When we hold preconceived ideas of what and how we want our existence to be, we are placing physical experience through a mental filter filled with sliver and master ideas. We can build an adhesive framed-reference so that any idea experienced or discussed cannot freely move in its truth position without the manipulation and adjustments of attached sliver and master ideas to these personal desires. Freud touched on this. In psychoanalysis, hypercathexis was another way of saying strong desires. It was his way of referring to our framed-reference; especially a strong form of an adhesive framed-reference. Freud wrote, "It is like a demonstration of the theorem that all knowledge has its origin in external perception. When a hypercathexis of the process of thinking takes place, thoughts are actually perceived—as if they came from without—and are consequently held to be true." (18, p16)

10. *We have historically created for ourselves an adhesive framed-reference that has allowed an amalgamation of false and unrelated ideas to pool together to make social constructions.* It was through our adhesive framed-reference that we have many of our mainstream ideas today. We have ideas that a deity gave the earth to people. We have ideas that this deity even selected who received his gifts. We have accepted without accountability the idea that self-appointed higher people have a god-given right to pursue their self-interest without any need for comprehension of their actions. We have the common idea that pursuit of happiness is not to be question by any individual but left to faith. We have a common idea that no one can question our pursuit of happiness and our acceptance of unaccountable systems. We have the idea that if anyone does, it is a form of coercion and an assault on the life, liberty and freedom of people. Each of these ideas resides in our adhesive framed-reference where they attach and move any incoming information toward our own personal desires. How we are to get around this so we can bring control to the coercive animal is to understand and engage in free will.

Free Will and Freedom

1. *When we conduct ourselves in relation to the evaluations gathered from our exercise of free will, we have freedom and liberty.* Our freedom and liberty involves our free movement in relation to our physical existence justified by that physical existence. Therefore, in order to know our physical existence to obtain our justifications to our movements, we must operate with free will. Free will is without any adhesive framed-reference that would skew our

incoming reality by the attachment of master and sliver ideas to change this incoming reality. It allows our experiential existence to experience reality to its truest form. Free will is possible when we achieve a free-flow framed-reference.

2. *Our free-flow framed-reference allows our physical-world inputs to remain accurate.* When we require incoming ideas from our physical world to maintain their required connections to the physical world, we set aside our adhesive framed-reference. This is true whether it involves our direct experience from our senses or involves our indirect experience from our senses of oral, visual and written language. Our free-flow framed-reference provides us free will to know what proper or improper behavior is because we have reality properly positioned. See Diagram 8 for a modeled representation of a free-flow framed-reference.

3. *Our adhesive framed-reference allows our physical-world inputs to be altered by existing internal false realities, resulting in further inaccuracies.* When we do not require our incoming ideas from our physical world to maintain their required connections to the physical world, we lose accountability to our sliver idea of reality that comes with the original physical-world experience. This is true whether it involves our direct experience from our senses or involves our indirect experience from our senses of oral, visual and written language. This can only result in the mixing of non-reality-based ideas with reality-based ideas without properly accounting for the movement of the sliver idea of reality. Our adhesive framed-reference cannot provide us free will, as we are in a relationship with ourselves only, and not ourselves in relation to physical reality. See Diagram 8 for a modeled representation of an adhesive framed-reference.

4. *When we have a free-flow framed-reference, we allow proper evaluation and accountability to ideas.* When we have accurate reality reach our evaluative abilities, we can measure back to construct the true reality to which we live in. We build our accountability to ideas when we maintain thesis-based reality within our thought existence. If we have an adhesive framed-reference, we inappropriately, inaccurately and deceptively alter the ideas to manufacture false reality. Here we do not measure back to physical reality, but to our mental reality. Our thought existence can measure against our mental animations of any sort. We can only lead ourselves to grossly inaccurate views of our physical existence and lead ourselves to many types of thought perversions. Thought perversions are the creation of manufactured realities. A free-flow framed-reference only uses thesis-based reality; where as, an adhesive framed-reference mixes both thesis-based and manufactured-based realities.

5. *When we have a free-flow framed-reference, it allows us to evaluate to a balance properly.* During our free-flow framed-reference, our evaluate-to-

balance brings in our physical world and it allows us evaluations without preconceived impinging forces. When we have a free will, we allow ourselves to engage in our internal physical structure to balance the physical-world experience. This allows us to understand our reality. We then know how to respond physically and behaviorally because we have our thesis-based justifications provided to us by physical existence.

6. *Once we have our physical-world evaluation, we have to accept thesis-based justifications for action or for non-action.* When we have our understanding of physical existence and our understanding of thesisism, we have at each individual level a truly justified and moral position where we can apply our thesis-based justifications. We now have our justifications for our movement. Our thesis-based justification illuminates our freedom and liberty. In this way, we can release our freedom and liberty while at the same time we can identify and stop unjustified coercive action.

7. *Our free will depends on the characteristic of our framed-reference.* When we measure our ideas against the human mind, it places us in a vast ocean where we float without any reference. If we push against another boat (another idea), we have two difference forces that results in movement not where we wanted to go. If we push against land, we move to where we want to go. If we have a free-flow framed-reference, we can achieve free will for ourselves. If we have an adhesive framed-reference, we are at the mercy of any residual or parasitic actions. When we measure our ideas against the chaos of the human mind, we can *feel* as if we are in a state of free will. Nevertheless, the same unaccountable and chaotic result *feels* as if we are free because we have attached ourselves to a floating manufactured idea. When we measure against the physical world, we then are free to make definitive actions with definitive movements to our will.

8. *When we have a free will and a measurement system of thought to accountability, we can then claim self-responsibility.* Our self-reliance and individual self-responsibility means we must engage in free will and align ourselves to the truth of existence. Only then can we know what the responsible conduct is. When we as a social group do not meet this minimum, we remain bound to our responsibility because physical existence holds our equations of accountability. Our adults and educators have the obligation to move our understanding of existence to the truth of existence. We as a species have the capacity. Nevertheless, we are not born responsible. We have to understand our reality and learn how we can achieve responsibility. There has to be a path from when we are born to when we become an adult that leads us to our independence. Our independence must maintain our thesis-morality equations. Our independence then means we have individual obligations in terms of our behavior to all other individuals and as one individual of all

individuals to any individual. Self-responsibility is equal to all as our equations in physical existence are the same for all.

9. *Despite that self-responsibility is an equal obligation to all, our self-responsibility in terms of understanding and having conscious awareness of it is dependent on our differences.* It does so because our ability to understand and achieve it falls under physical human differentiation.[12] This physical human differentiation includes both the physical structure of our human mental capacity and environmental learning. The ability to learn, achieve and express self-responsibility can vary between people like the ability to dance or do mathematics. No individual can be self-responsible by any *a priori* knowledge of it. Therefore, it is an ideal that we must strive to achieve. It becomes part of the idea of creating oneself. This means that those of us that achieve conscious understanding of self-responsibility have an obligation to assist in the development of self-responsibility in others.

10. *Self-responsibility for Jean-Paul Sartre came from his idea that all human beings have freedom found in non-freedom.* It goes something like this; we are not free to be not free. We have no choice but to be in a state of freedom. Here are some words of Sartre that show this position. "I am condemned to be free. This means that no limits to my freedom can be found except freedom itself or, if you prefer, that we are not free to cease being free." (4, p567) I think his idea of freedom involved our *evaluate-to-balance* to our physical existence. We are not free not to engage in *evaluate-to-balance*. Because it arises out of awareness and not consciousness, we can ignore it consciously. In the end, whether Sartre and I agree may be more in my misunderstanding of him or in his presentation. In *Being and Nothingness* he wrote, "It is strange that philosophers have been able to argue endlessly about determinism and free will ... without ever attempting first to make explicit the structures contained in the very idea of action. The concept of ... to act is to modify the shape of the world; it is to arrange means in view of an end; it is to produce an organized instrumental complex such that by a series of concatenations and connections the modification ... finally produces an anticipated result ... We should observe first that an action is on principle *intentional*." (4, p559) Notice he was attempting to focus on action. Our actions are physical events. Nevertheless, his *structures* were *intentional*. This *intentional* placed his evaluations right back into our human mind. He ended up doing the same as the philosophers that he complained about in the same paragraph.

11. *Sartre placed action with intention.* If action was intentional, what was behind his idea of intentional? Sartre claimed we were free because we

---

12 Our physical existence as human beings has two expressions. We have equality and inequality between us. We can express this through mathematical equations. The chapters on *Equal thesis-morality* and *Unequal thesis-morality* outline the distinction.

had no choice to be not free. If action is on principle intentional, then his *intentional* holds within it the idea of freedom. The choice was intentional, deliberate and not made as a cause and reaction. His position that we were free because we had no choice to be not free contorted the ideas of free, freedom, action and intention. We have to straighten out his twisted mess. To start, we can say we have to act because we are not free not to act. Even not acting is a result of action. It seemed that Sartre suddenly animated *freedom* not only in a narrowband form without its acknowledgement, but changed the typical master idea of freedom. Freedom in the broadband form means that we initiate action without any impinging forces. We have no unknown and unseen force in play. The broadband view of freedom could even include that we operate independent to the physical world. In the narrowband form from Sartre, freedom became a state to a forced to choose action; thus, we have a forced choice within its position in the physical world. Therefore, our no impinging forces became impinging forces to some action. He placed force behind the idea of freedom, which was an idea that contained the idea of no impinging force. He forced us to choose action because we were not free not to act. We were not free not to act owing to the movement of the physical, which we call time. Now we have eliminated the idea of freedom completely from the view by Sartre that we are not free to be not free. He measured his "not free" with impinging forces. His position that we were not free to be not free was simply; we are with impinging forces to be with impinging forces. We now see that he unnecessarily obscured his position.

12. *Sartre was not acknowledging physical existence to his ideas of responsibility and freedom.* We can see this when he wrote, "The essential consequence of our earlier remarks is that man being condemned to be free carries the weight of the whole world on his shoulders; he is responsible for the world and for himself as a way of being. We are taking the word 'responsibility' in its ordinary sense as 'consciousness (of) being the incontestable author of an event or of an object.'" (4, p707) This "condemned to be free" has its physical connection to our evaluate-to-balance. We have a hardwired aspect for this evaluation of our surroundings and to any subsequent idea animation that may be thesis or manufactured. Until we acknowledge this connection to physical existence, his presentation would not be clear. Once we accounted for this relational aspect of his argument, it becomes clear what he is saying. He continued with, "What happens to me happens through me, and I can neither affect myself with it nor revolt against it nor resign myself to it. Moreover everything which happens to me is *mine*." (4, 708) Here we see his version of our evaluate-to-balance. When we understand his position that we are responsible comes from the input of our physical existence through

our evaluate-to-balance, he directed his view of responsibility not from non-impinging forces, but from the impinging forces of physical existence.

13. *The idea that we are not free to be not free can be better understood by stating we are required by nature to evaluate to a balance, to which we must make our action.* Our evaluate-to-balance moves us because it is the movement of physical existence, which we measure as time. When we move with our evaluate-to-balance, we move to make our action. The *how* we evaluate-to-balance becomes important. We must maintain an open free will. When we do, we move away from a denied free will. When we have free will, we have a free-flow framed-reference that exists. We also then align with reality. When we maintain a denied free will, we have an adhesive framed-reference that exists. Now we have a break from reality. We, by our own physical nature, must engage in evaluate-to-balance and move to action. Our mental life moves as if we were on a snowy hillside sliding down. If our evaluate-to-balance is not to act, then this becomes the action. Nature forces us to evaluate-to-balance, which is not our choice. This means nature forces us to develop a thought system. If we want to break the chains the coercive animal has on our freedom and liberty, we must keep our ideas measured against physical existence.

14. *We cannot confuse freedom with free will.* Kant stated "But freedom is a mere Idea [Ideal Conception], the objective reality of which can in no wise be shown according to laws of nature, and consequently not in any possible experience; and for this reason it can never be comprehended or understood...." (16, 70) Although our idea of freedom does not exist in a form like our orange, it does come about from our observation of the physical world and its sometimes random and free-floating aspects that we can observe. We can animate the random movement of objects and remove all ideas of hard form. These ideas go back to our perceptual capacity for spatial and movement recognition. Freedom that we animate is an idea of no impinging forces. This requires the idea of forces, which we see affect change as they force against something. We then eliminate the sliver idea of impinging forces while keeping the effect of something. Nevertheless, our free will idea does involve no impinging forces from our own mental forces to incoming sensory existence or in our mental animation in thought existence. Our idea of freedom under the idea of no impinging forces is too broadband to bring clarity. It ignores our physical existence. Freedom in physical existence and relational to our thesis-morality splits freedom into two types of impinging forces against freedom. One impinging force comes from manufactured coercion by the misplacement of the sliver idea of reality, whereas thesis coercion can justify impinging forces and restrict freedom. Our law that restricts our freedom to murder is a thesis-justified coercion placed onto ourselves.

15. *We long have had the idea that we cannot comprehend ideas such as freedom.* Interestingly, Kant followed his statement in the above paragraph with "and for this reason it [freedom][13] can never be comprehended or understood, because we cannot support it by any sort of example or analogy." (16, p70) I found this interesting because my first reaction was, if we cannot comprehend it, why then do we have an idea of it. However, this was his precise position, absurd as it was. Nevertheless, he did not seek the physical bases for the idea of freedom. We obtain the idea of freedom by comprehension of our spatial environment and our movement in our spatial environment with the removal of the idea of hard form. He did not understand that ideas do arise from a parallel group of ideas that attach together to make the full idea. We can then strip away, one by one, or in bunches, or all attached sliver ideas, leaving only one idea, like *five* without any relational aspects of mathematics. We conceive the idea of freedom from perceiving the experience of our world. We experience the release of a bird, our child leaving to study at a University and obtain a sliver idea of a release of an impinging force. We experience the appearance of random movement of animals, the feel of wind and obtain the sliver idea of no noticeable impinging forces. These experiences carry all the parallel aspects of the experiences to ideas, and later we strip away the attached sliver ideas and gain the idea of freedom. Freedom equals no impinging forces. Kant saw an interaction of the laws of reason independent of natural construction. He saw the idea of freedom as a singular idea that he never attached to the experience behind other ideas. Through his animation, freedom was broken away from physical reality and made mysterious.

16. *We need clarity in our intellectual discussions.* When we have people that write large books, the question that comes to my mind is why? Does the discussion require it? Are we dealing with mental animation that is leading us to truth, understanding and to a better society? If it is simply an individual saying lots of things because they received attention, or they like to be thought of as some genius, or it perpetuates some academic position, what I claim we often end with is a large heat-sink that diverts future thought by ramming human thought into the ground. The tragedy is that we send our young thinkers down into the basement to perpetuate old ideas that arrived from the motivations of self-absorption and self-gratification. Some people have recognized this. Sir Thomas Pope Blount in 1691 wrote, "That which we so much admire under the name of LEARNING, is only the knowing the fancies of particular men." (19, Essay II, p33)

17. *Our idea of freedom needs to be relational to physical existence.* Our idea of freedom requires actions that occur in the physical world. By the result of physical existence interaction with us to our evaluate-to-balance, we come

13 The word *freedom* in brackets was added for clarity.

to our actions. When we have conflict between individuals and groups of individuals to their evaluate-to-balance, we have clashes of freedom. Therefore, we tend to address freedom only when it clashes. We may know this clash at the time, or we may know it later. This means that just because we do not have a clash immediately around us, it does not mean we are free to engage in action. When we have clashes occur, or become known, we have to resolve them by human thought. Because we have to use human thought, when we use a system of thought without accountability, we end with coercion. A system of thought with accountability would measure against our physical realities to our evaluate-to-balance, which contains thesis evaluations, and provide the thesis-based justifications for the correct course of action. We know that to have freedom and liberty, we must have a free-flow framed-reference to allow free will to input physical existence without distortion. We can then determine our thesis-based actions to prevent coercion and to release our freedom and liberty.

Morality Connected to Our Physical Existence
Section 1: Thesis-Morality

1. *We can make all ideas accountable.* We have seven elements to maintain accountability to all ideas. We can categorize the relationship between the physical world and our thought existence by our four relational characteristics of thought existence shown in Diagram 1a and 1b. When we use language to bring any idea to its narrow form, we can then apply this system of thought to bring accountability to all ideas. By doing this, we stay measured against the physical world. Our physical world determines the truth position of any idea. We can identify coercive manipulation from people when they engage in an adhesive framed-reference motivated by emotion or beliefs of personally held false-reality desires. More importantly, we can then achieve a commonality to our thesis-based system of thought that is independent to human manipulation. We also have a system of thought that has a self-correcting system of thought enclosed. It can self-correct because it measures against the physical world, which is common to all people.

2. *We can measure our ideas of morality against our physical world.* Since our ideas of morality are ideas as well, we can apply the same accountability system to moral ideas. Because morality involves our code of conduct, which is actions in physical existence, we determine our proper code of conduct by looking to our physical world to receive our inputs to moral ideas. Our code of conduct between us is always in relation to humankind. Therefore,

we must view the physical realities of human existence. From this, we can determine our code of conduct between one another.

3. *When we measure our moral ideas against the physical world, we have thesis-morality.* When we measure our code of conduct against the physical world, we determine our thesis action. When we measure our moral ideas against the physical world and draw a code of conduct from it, we have thesis-morality. It is thesis-morality because we connected it to the physical world. Our physical world contains mathematical equations to our moral and justice conduct. Therefore, thesis-morality maintains balance to moral equations derived from our physical existence.

4. *We can break thesis-morality for humankind into two different expressions.* Our thesis-morality for humankind has one source, our humanness, but it has two different characteristics. One of our characteristic is termed equal thesis-morality and the other is termed unequal thesis-morality. Each of our characteristic has an equation and a moral flow of conduct associated with it. It is in the physical aspects of our human existence that our characteristics and expressions base themselves.

Section 2: Equal Thesis-Morality

5. *By the existence of the word humankind, we have recognition that within this group we have equality.* We can cite Volney. "Whatever be the active power, the moving cause that directs the universe, this power having given to all men the same organs, the same sensations, and the same wants, has thereby sufficiently declared that it has also given the same rights to the use of its benefits; and that in the order of nature all men are equal." (6, p136) Volney provided the definition of humankind that included body and mind to an abstract idea of humankind. We can take it further and show that the essence of humankind resides not in the organs, but in the common consciousness we have between humankind.

6. *We have a physical equality that exists between all human beings.* If we strip away all differences between people, we leave ourselves with our equality. Our equality is the minimal physical essence to which we can classify ourselves as human beings. We can even remove our physical bodies, as we can be human without it in every way except one. We have to have physically our human brain to maintain our human status. Our physical brain, in the common structure required for human classification, when activated with awareness and consciousness holds our commonality between every other human being. Our equality creates a relational equation. That equation is $E = E$; that is, our equal equals our equal. We term this physical aspect between all human beings as equal thesis-morality.

7. *Our physical equality includes our brain that leads us to a human consciousness.* In the E = E equation, we have our common brain that we term human. Our common human brain results in our consciousness. Our consciousness arrives from all experiences we have had with our experiential experience. In our experiential existence, we have an equality that is termed human experience. Because we have equality in the experience of experiential existence, this equality overrides any individual differences. We have always *sensed* this fundamental equation.

8. *Our physical equality that exists between all human beings has a directional flow of action.* Our equal thesis-morality flows from the individual person to all other individuals. Each individual has to recognize the equality that exists between all human beings to maintain our thesis equations that reside in physical existence. When each of us reaches this recognition, we express this equality between us and to all other human beings. Even before we develop into adulthood, this equality exists. This equality exists in the physical world; therefore, it does not change if any individual, child or adult, does not recognize it.

9. *We as a community have a responsibility to bring this moral aspect to the awareness of all people.* Because we have equal thesis-morality, we have the required expression of it to all people. It is our responsibility as all individuals to bring an understanding to all individuals of this physical reality. We can speak in terms of ideal. Nevertheless, many different physical influences affect the development and the level of understanding between human beings. It is not that we start with any perfection, but seek to move ourselves toward it.

10. *We have conflict between the ideal verses the practical.* Any human society to act morally must attempt their best effort to bring this reality to our consciousness. We need the largest amount of us to have the understanding of equal thesis-morality to move us toward the correct moral code of conduct. Ideas measured against our physical reality of equality can bring to our consciousness the proper code of conduct.[14] We can also know how to differentiate between causes and motivations of people when we violate equal thesis-morality.

11. *Our equal thesis-morality is that aspect of our physical existence that affects each of us the same.* When someone murders another, we have an action without thesis-based justification. A thesis-based justification is a justification with a connection to the physical world. Without a thesis-based justification,

---

14 This statement is only in relation to our equal aspects as human beings. In the next Chapter, *Unequal thesis-morality*, we look at our inequality. Ideas measured against our physical reality of inequality can bring to our consciousness a proper code of conduct as well. We have a relational expression dependent upon which physical characteristic of human is being expressed.

we have someone acting contrary to our physical existence. They are acting as if their human equality is greater than the equality of the other person. The physical-world equation to murderous action becomes $E > E$, which does not match our $E = E$. Since we have this mismatch to the equation of equal thesis-morality, we have an idea expressed in action that does not exist in the physical existence. This idea to action by the murderer can only exist in human thought existence. When we have two injured people of equal physical states exists and one person is allowed a medical treatment that saves or improves their life while the other is not allowed the same medical treatment that resulted in their death or diminished capacity, we have the occurrence of $E > E$. Life is the same requirement for all of us. When we have human-made systems that differentiate between the status and financial positions of people and create differentiation in our equal-to-us areas, we have an immoral human system. When we have two people where a large disparity to educational opportunities exists and it attenuates the ability of one to develop and express their individual difference, then we have $E > E$. When we have a social system, where there is poverty and extreme wealth, equal thesis-morality is easily offended. People must have the equal opportunity to express their true potential for any society to be a moral society.

Section 3: Unequal Thesis-Morality

12. *By the nature of physical existence, we have within our human existence an inequality.* We have recognized our inequality throughout our history. Volney wrote, "This inequality, the result of accident, was taken for the law of nature. Almost all the ancient philosophers and politicians have laid it down as a principle, that men are born unequal, that nature has created some to be free, and others to be slaves. Expressions of this kind are to be found in Aristotle, and even in Plato, called the divine, doubtless in the same sense as the mythological reveries which he promulgated." (6, p336) Our inequality surrounds us in our physical world. We have the history that Volney referred to as well as the history that followed him. When we are infants and young children, we investigate our world and discover all the variations that surround us. This aspect of our physical existence makes our differences easy to perceive.

13. *We have a physical inequality that exists between all human beings.* When we strip away all that is the same between all human beings, we leave ourselves with our differences. This inequality is the resulted physical variations that exist between people. These physical variations translate into different behaviors and characteristics between people. Some of our different characteristics are height, body stature, as well as differences between abilities

to dance, do math, and fix broken mechanical devices or to create new and novel ideas. When we display our differences, we have a level of variations between each individual. This inequality contains a mean, which in turn creates a relational equation. The resulting equation is $\bar{E} = U \pm D$, the mean equal equals the unequal plus or minus the difference. We term this physical aspect between all human beings as unequal thesis-morality.

14. *Our physical inequality that exists between all human beings has a directional flow of action.* Our unequal thesis-morality flows from all individuals to the individual person. Any difference that any individual holds, we can only measure it against all individuals to the individual. Society makes the determination because each member holds a data point of inequality to the individual. As a child grows to adulthood, any inequality is developed and better expressed. This inequality exists in the physical world; therefore, it does not change if any individual or groups of individuals do not recognize it. For a visual representation of the two different flows between the two expressions of thesis-morality, refer to Diagram 4a.

15. *We have a responsibility as a society to bring this moral aspect to the awareness of all people.* Because our unequal thesis-morality is in relation to all individuals, we have the responsibility to bring it to our attention the correct adjustments to this physical reality. Nevertheless, we have many physical influences that affect our development and our understanding. This expression of unequal thesis-morality that comes from our physical existence is an ideal. We need to attempt to move ourselves as close as we can to our ideal.

16. *We can have conflict between the ideal verses the practical.* Any society to act morally must attempt their best effort to bring this reality to the consciousness of our society so that the largest amount of people can know to act according to the code of conduct that arises out of unequal thesis-morality. Like our equal thesis-morality and its equation, we must bring to our consciousness our unequal thesis-morality and its equation. Then we can engage in action with the proper code of conduct. We can then differentiate between causes and motivations of people when we violate unequal thesis-morality.

17. *Our unequal thesis-morality involves those aspects of our physical existence that affect all of us differently.* When we have someone offer a relative a job over another person and they did not measure against their differences, they have disregarded the differences between them. Immoral conduct can occur depending on the existing physical-world equations. When our unequal is greater to the person not given the job and the unequal is less for the relative, then we have ignored our unequal thesis-morality and have engaged in immoral action. Our unequal position of the relative (U_r) becomes greater

than the unequal position of the other person (U_p). Our U_r is presented as $U_r > U_p$, but the physical reality is $U_r < U_p$. To proceed would mean to engage in immoral action. When we have a person of one race given a job over another in employment because of their race, then the measurement is race A is greater than race B. This violates equal thesis-morality as it ignores the physical realities of the physical equality between all people. The only time race A can be greater than race B, or any other violation, is when there is a thesis-based justification. An actor playing a role that requires a certain race may have a thesis-based justification. If centuries of discrimination of a particular race have created imbedded immoral equations, our governing institutions can respond through thesis-based justifications.[15]

18. *Thesis-based justifications are the result of examination of physical existence.* When we have a society failure that suppressed one race over another for a long period of history, we can point to inequities that we have created in our physical environment that led us to unequal opportunity to equal-to-us situations. We have other equal-to-us situations where society can create unequal opportunity to as well. Education is certainly one. Societies can adjust to correct society failure, but only under thesis-based justifications that are rooted to our physical existence. When our thesis-based justifications no long fit our physical realities, our physically based (thesis) justifications no longer exist. We must remove our actions. We have to keep our moral equations in balance. Sometimes we can replace one moral failure with another, as when we deny education and opportunity to a race and over time, this failure transforms from race to an economic class.

19. *Our unequal thesis-morality is more difficult to evaluate.* Because we measure our differences and not our sameness, unequal thesis-morality requires the evaluation of each and every action and differences over all people. This makes our application of unequal thesis-morality difficult. Despite that it is more difficult, it does not remove this physical reality. We must measure against it as a community of all individuals, and as frequently and accurately as possible.

Section 4: Equal Thesis-Morality Overrides Unequal Thesis-Morality

20. *Our equal thesis-morality overrides unequal thesis-morality.* Thesis-morality has its two expressions. In our lives, we have our complexity of

---

15 An example of a thesis-based justification to unbalance our E = E was given against the claim by Milton Friedman that government interference with affirmative action was coercion to economic freedom. This example is in *Book Three*, under the chapter titled, "*Thesis-Based Coercion: Our Release of Freedom and Liberty,*" in paragraph 6.

social interactions. When we have a conflict occur between equal and unequal thesis-morality, we have to determine which one we follow. Since our equality is the same for everyone, we have a code of conduct that is in relation to all people. Since our inequality is not the same for everyone, we have a code of conduct that is in relation to one person, or a subset of same-difference persons. Based on this physical reality, equal thesis-morality overrides any conflict with unequal thesis-morality.

21. *We have an example of not understanding the dual nature to morality seen in the philosophy of Friedrich Nietzsche.* He wrote, "that what is right for the one may certainly *not* be right for the other, that to demand *one* morality for all is precisely to encroach upon the higher sort of human beings—in short, that there is a *hierarchy* between human and human, and therefore between morality and morality as well." (20, p120) Nietzsche saw only one side of thesis-morality—our unequal thesis-morality. He did not acknowledge our equal thesis-morality. By viewing only our differences, he chose individualism over equality rather than choosing both. When we chose one side, and ignore the other, we then enter into extremist thought. It becomes an extremist view because we move half of our moral equations to the wrong equation. With Nietzsche, we no longer have E = E. When Nietzsche chose unequal thesis-morality only, he chose extreme individualism. He is then doomed to apply individualism to our equality and to create manufactured ideas that can only reside in the human mind, as no counterpart exists in physical existence. This is what Nietzsche did. He went on to create individual types of human beings, and then he created different moralities for his viewed hierarchy of lower and higher types of human beings. He opened up the door for any self-appointed higher types to view themselves higher in every aspect of physical existence, including into equal thesis-morality.

22. *The inability of Nietzsche to view both aspects of thesis-morality and his move to focus on only one side was evident in his writing.* He wrote, "*Morality in Europe today is herd animal morality*—and thus, as we understand things, it is only one kind of human morality next to which, before which, and after which many others, and especially *higher* moralities, are or should be possible." (20, p228) Nietzsche recognized but did not fully understand that one view of morality did not work. Here we have a condescending view of a mass morality, which we can see as a misunderstanding of equal thesis-morality. This misunderstanding belonged to both him and those involved with mass morality. This mass morality was not a correct expression of equal thesis-morality but was a corrupted expression of it as well. Nevertheless, all he had to do was to examine it. If he had sought to understand the source to this misguided mass morality, clarity could have come to his mind. Nevertheless, he had used an incomplete understanding of unequal thesis-morality and

misplaced it in the elevation of certain types of individuals over others in *all areas of physical existence.*

23. *Instead of his weighting the perception of the two possibilities of thesis-morality to how they then interacted, he reacted with what I think was emotion.* He clouded his station and position of equal thesis-morality by elevating egocentrically a perverted view of unequal thesis-morality. He saw injustice coming from people that applied equal thesis-morality to situations where they should have applied unequal thesis-morality. This has truth in history. Nevertheless, rather than taking the time to understand the mistakes in the mechanics of this, he took a bitter and emotional attitude. This may have come from an adhesive framed-reference of seeing and knowing the committed religious injustices around him. He filled his framed-reference with emotion and it skewed his view of physical existence. He did not have a free-flow framed-reference and therefore had a denied free will. In this, we can see that his own character betrayed him. To back my statement, he wrote in *Ecce Homo*, an autobiography of sorts, "I am by nature warlike. To attack is among my instincts."(21, p16)

24. *Our emotion creates an adhesive framed-reference and denies our free will to see the reality of our physical existence.* Nietzsche allowed his emotion and his character flaw to destroy any possibility for achieving clarity. He wrote, "When a *décadence*-species of man has risen to the rank of the highest species of man, this can happen only at the expense of its antithetical species, the species of man strong and certain of life." (21, p100) Here we have the ranking of human beings irrespective to our equality. He was responding emotionally to injustice. The word species implies characteristics common to all of humankind, as we are one species. Nevertheless, he chose to split humankind into various species. His fragmentation of the word species also split our equality and made his idea a manufactured idea that can only exist in his thought existence. He then was able to sub-human our equal aspects. His words demonstrated a self-elevation with contempt for human beings in every way. When we do this, we eclipse our equal-to-us aspects. He had absolutely no understanding that he was shoving both human equality and human inequality down the same hole. Perhaps he could not accept the idea that he had equality to all humans as well as an inequality. Perhaps he saw himself and loved himself so much that he separated himself from his own species. The harsh individualistic man or woman seizes this dangerous road just as the harsh communal man or woman seizes their dangerous road too.

25. *Our emotions not only add to an adhesive framed-reference, which denies our free will to see the reality of our physical existence, but it can add manufactured-based justification and motivation to people that seek power and self-interests.* Nietzsche wrote in his *Genealogy of Morals*, "The sick are the

greatest danger for the healthy: it is not from the strongest that harm comes to the strong, but from the weakest. ... What do they really want? At any rate to *represent* righteousness, love, wisdom, superiority, that is the ambition of these 'lowest ones,' these sick ones!" (14, p87-88) How can this system of thought bring justice and peace when we measure against this type of thought? Once we break away from one side of thesis-morality, whether it is equal or unequal thesis-morality, we immediately set up situations for immoral actions to occur. His contempt that came from perceived moral injustices simply shifted injustices from one side to the other side of thesis-morality. Our thesis-morality can only provide the proper moral code of conduct when we acknowledged and reacted to both sides of thesis-morality. His "higher men" became the self-appointed and provided manufactured-based justifications to racists, holders of dogma and for anyone desiring economic power or government domination.

26. *Nietzsche never saw our physical world and the one source, two expressions of morality.* In failing to see this reality, he viewed morality as relative. When we have relative morality, we attract people with desire to manipulate and those with self-interest independent to others around them. We have given people tools to engage in unjustified coercion. He wrote, "it is the lack of nature, it is the utterly ghastly fact that *anti-nature* itself has received the highest honors as morality, and has hung over mankind as law, as categorical imperative!" (21, p102) Our categorical imperative from Kant did not measure against the differences that Nietzsche saw between people. Nor did it measure against the vague *sense* from Kant of *necessity, duty and universality.* We may indeed have a universality that led us to a duty to pursue a specific code of conduct. We may because the categorical imperative from Kant did not spring forth magically from our human minds, but arrived through our free-flow framed-reference to open our free will to receive physical existence in its purest form, to which we then evaluated-to-balance. When have done so, we have seen that we as human beings have a physical existence, and the nature and structure of this physical existence results in our one source and two expressions of thesis-morality—equal thesis-morality and unequal thesis-morality.

27. *When we have this type of amputated thinking by Nietzsche, people acquire the manufactured idea of individual human superiority over all areas of existence.* When we allow people to amputate equal thesis-morality or unequal thesis-morality from our understanding, we allow opportunities for people to create manufactured-based justifications to their own desired self-interest coercion. Removal of one or the other perverts thesis-morality. When people create false realities to their lop-sided moral evaluations, they create many additional false realities when they attach other sliver and master ideas to these false realities. People that desire domination and power grasp ideas such as

self-interest pursuit of happiness as an *ultimate end* and a god giving them the deed to the planet and special privilege to pursue their narrow self-interests without accountability. When we have a clash of freedom occur between people, these historical manufactured ideas gave many manufactured-based justifications to coercion against others. The unaccountability of reason and rational thought allowed the creation of many different false realities and provided people tools to commit coercion against others without protection. This then resulted in a long history of loss in freedom and liberty.

Understanding Universal and Limited Moral Possibilities

1. *We have the highest level of communications in the history of humankind.* We have an explosion of media that resulted in an abundance of journalists, talk show hosts and bloggers. With our massive amount of media sources, instead of more evaluation of ideas taking place, the media has fractured themselves into various positional programs, and even into full corporate media stations with predetermined ideology. We do not evaluate predetermined ideology with relational thought. It is an adhesive framed-reference designed to bend ideas to fit a false reality. We have liberal and conservative stations load their programming with likely winners and losers. The irony of our increased media availability is that less thought occurs because we do not seriously challenge the positions between each other. We can go to a media source with our predetermined positions and hear what we want to hear. Essentially, we have come to market to the adhesive framed-references of people.

2. *When we do not make evaluations against our ideas further than the simple equation of sameness or not sameness, we lose our ability to think critically.* Our having an explosion of media is not bad in itself. How we come to use it determines its success or failure to our survival as a species. Because each of us can tune in a program that reinforces our own ideas, it helps solidify and harden any framed-reference. It creates durability or adhesiveness to our personally held false-reality desires. Unfortunately, it can contribute to an inability to open our free-flow framed-reference and to engage in our free will. Without our free-flow framed-reference to open our free will, we cannot align with the truth and to the realities to which we live in.

3. *When we chose to listen to ideas that we know will agree with our own, we can open ourselves to manipulation.* We often hear broadband and generalized statements. They make them because they can capture the largest audience. Think about it. If I were to say I am for *Traditional Values*, I would be throwing out a broadband statement that has many different master ideas. Many people watching or listening would think to themselves, "Yes! I am for traditional values too!" However, what I may be animating in my mind about traditional

values may be different from many others. In fact, traditional values for one may mean life, liberty and the pursuit of happiness, thus if a gay couple wanted to marry, they are free to do so. For another it may mean Christian values, thus gay couples may be allowed or may not be allowed to marry. It would depend on the different master ideas of each subgroup under the same heading of traditional values. Nevertheless, imagine these groups bobbing their heads in agreement when the announcer spouts his or hers broadband statement of *traditional values*.

4. *Our moral ideas have two characteristics that we must identify.* We can have the presentation of a broadband statement while it contains a collection of narrowband ideas. We know from the example above that to talk about broadband ideas such as *traditional values*, each person must define their narrowband ideas so that they can then begin to talk relationally to the same master idea. Nevertheless, when we speak of moral ideas in the broadband, we can confuse two different characteristics that moral ideas can contain. These two characteristics result in two types of moral ideas. When we narrowband our moral ideas, we expose and determine which type of moral idea we have. When we do not have an understanding of these two characteristics, ideology through corporate entertainment (or any other source) can take advantage of this incognizant and hidden physical-world reality to perpetrate false ideas. This is especially true when we reduce our action of thought to the simple equation, *does it equal to what I think*. We find our two types of moral ideas in how they relate to our physical world. Similar to our equal thesis-morality and unequal thesis-morality, our moral ideas can be universal or limited in nature. A universal moral idea is finite in the type of physical action but infinite to application. Our evaluation of the application of this type of idea moves from the idea to the physical world without limitations. Our limited moral idea is infinite in the type of physical action but finite to application. The evaluation of the application of this type of idea moves the idea to the physical world with limitations.

5. *We have moral ideas that are universal in nature.* We can make moral statements that are singular in nature. In this singularity, we have the needed connection to physical existence within its definition. We have our physically based (thesis) justification to the idea within the idea. This makes the idea finite. This thesis-based justification flows between our human physical existences to all individuals. We have a visual representation of universal moral ideas shown in Diagram 9. An example would be not to murder. It is a universal moral idea because the thesis-based justification is within the idea. Not to murder is different from not to kill. Murder is to kill without a physically based (thesis) justification. We have a thesis-based justification when we have an equation from the physical realities of existence violated.

The physical reality of this universal idea resides in the physical equality in every individual and the maintenance of the E = E equation. Every situation that brings up this moral idea, the physical connection flows from the idea to physical existence. It is in the flow that we make the application. Therefore, we have a universal type of moral flow. We have one idea with one type of evaluation.

6. *We have moral ideas that are limited in nature.* Certain moral claims are limited in nature. The needed connection with physical existence is not within the definition of the idea; rather, its (thesis) justification in physical existence resides individually out in the physical world. This makes the idea infinite in possible different thesis-based justifications, but there are limited possibilities residing in physical existence to the idea. We have a visual representation of limited moral ideas shown in Diagram 9. An example of a limited moral idea would be to help someone in need. While this moral idea is unlimited in different possible need applications, we have a finite amount of possibilities that actually exist within possible applications that actually connect to our physical world. It is limited because we have a broadband idea, and we have to evaluate each situation to determine its application.

7. *Our limited type of moral idea can have presented moral situations that are not actually moral ideas.* Every situation of *need* is unique. Because of this characteristic, we have the potential for unlimited situations, but the physical world has a limited number of them that are actually moral-based needs. Our thesis-based justification resides not in the moral statement, but relationally to each independent situation. The limited moral idea then applies only to specific and certain need situations. Our idea of need is broadband and contains master ideas that are not moral issues. Every situation that brings up this idea of helping someone in need is dependent on whether a thesis-based justification resides within it that makes it a moral-based need. Importantly, since our thesis-based justification resides not in the idea, but instead in the physical world, the flow of this idea is from specific finite situations back to the infinite idea. This is opposite to the moral flow of the universal type of moral ideas, which is from the idea to our physical existence. Here, we have the flow from physical existence back to the idea.

8. *When we do not understanding this, we can find people attempting to switch limited moral ideas into universal moral ideas to perpetuate false ideas.* We can use the idea that we should be unselfish. This is a limited moral idea. The idea to be unselfish is not a blanket statement to all situations. It requires the evaluation of each possible situation to our physical world to determine if the idea of being unselfish is a moral-based idea. This is how we know if our specific situation should or should not apply as a moral imperative. We must determine if there is a thesis-based justification to move our actions

to unselfishness or not. If, however, we apply the idea of being unselfish as a universal moral idea, we result in absurdity. To act in a constant state of unselfishness does not align with the physical realities around us. To be unselfish without thesis-based justification in a constant manner can only end in hurting oneself by resulting in negative consequences in physical existence. We may deplete our resources so that we do not have food or shelter. We may end with not being able to assist others in their lives as we had diminished our resources, and we made ourselves incapable of assisting when we have real moral-based need for assistance. The physical-world truth to the idea of unselfishness is that it has a limited moral structure. The flow is from the situation in the physical world back to the idea. Our thesis-based justification resides not in the idea of unselfishness, but in our evaluation of each situation. When we find that thesis-based justification, we have found a limited moral situation to which the idea applies.

9. *People can switch between universal and limited moral ideas to bring manufactured-based justification to their position.* The manipulation is that without this real-world recognition to how ideas work within our physical existence, people can apply reality to ideas that it is bad to be unselfish. People can claim that to be altruistic and helping others will only lead us to coercion against an individual. They offer the bizarre idea that an individual cannot engage in their self-interest simply because they have to be unselfish across all situations. They can achieve this because they apply the idea of unselfishness as a universal moral idea. In doing this, we lose sight of our moral obligations and people justify their immoral actions with manufactured ideas that only reside in their minds. It only resides in their minds because they applied an idea that does not reflect our physical reality. If the idea does not connect to our physical world, we have broken away from our physical existence. It then becomes a false-reality idea that leads us away from our moral obligations, our truth and away from achieving long-term quality of success as a species. The idea of unselfishness with a switch from a limited moral flow to a universal moral flow is only one example. Nevertheless, this is what many of our talking heads do with ideas. This allows us to create corporate-circus news, which feeds people what they want to hear rather than to create a real dialog that would move us to a reality-based position. Our understanding the difference between universal and limited moral structure is especially important when we deal with Milton Friedman and F. A. Hayek. As we will see, it resides in their justification to their position, as well as their view of no coercion to their extended order of capitalism.[16]

---

16 The misuse of universal moral and limited moral ideas is not restricted to capitalism. Other human-made systems, such as socialism, can attempt justification of their position by the misapplication of this feature of moral ideas as related to

The Thesis-Morality Filter

1. *Under the accountability method of thesisism, we have a series of actions that we flow through a filter to determine moral position.* We have described our four existences, our relational requirements to our physical world, our physical human structure that leads us to two thesis-morality expressions and the proper flow to each. In Diagram 5, we see the serial events that lead us to our proper code of conduct.

2. *Sensory existence is our first event as it provides inputs from our physical world.* From pre-birth to adulthood, we experience the inputs from our sensory existence that move to our thought and reactive existence. In thought existence, we can obtain and hold the idea of any experience. We also can obtain and hold the idea of any experience from our reactive existence. This is because we experienced it like anything else in the physical world, except that it was the result of physical actions from our reactive wiring.[17]

3. *We have four categories that we defined in our thought existence.* Whether we maintain accountability or not, physical existence determines where our ideas fall into these categories. They fall into these categories because these categories measure against our physical world, independent to any human confusion. Our responsibility, individually to each individual, is to minimize this confusion as much as possible. We can see in Diagram 5 that sensory existence moves the input from physical existence into our thought and reactive existences. To know our reality and our correct code of conduct, we have to maintain our connections to our physical world. By examining our ideas and their relationship or lack of relationship to our physical world, we can begin to maintain the relationship to our reality of life.

4. *If we do not bring accountability to our ideas, we can animate reality falsely attached to any idea.* When we offer ideas as reality and we do not require them to measure against our physical world, we break our alignment to reality. Our four categories of ideas as they relate to our physical world do not match what we animate in our minds. Therefore, when we offer manufactured reality as truth, we create a manufactured filter that bends and maintains non-reality. We create opportunities for anyone to use false realities to grasp and maintain power over others immorally. We have created the essence of coercion. When we operate under coercion measured against false realities, any proper moral actions we engage in are accidental. Since we

---

physical existence. The same argument of applying unselfishness universally when used by the socialist, religious, secularist, or by any other groups, creates the same false-reality argument.

17 When we reference our thesis-morality filter, we do so as that of a normal adult.

can make any mental animation without any accountability, numerous false realities do arise. We can use coercion based in false reality to create a false acceptance that this false reality is truth. Because they are false, they require human coercion by use of domination, intimidation and blind obedience to maintain. These false realities include false ideas of morality. Since we have detached from reality, we can teach and dictate many immoral actions given as moral actions.

5. *If we categorize our ideas by their relationship to our physical existence, we maintain accountability and accuracy.* Once we have our ideas properly aligned to our physical reality, we can begin to filter our ideas and ideas of morality to come to our proper code of conduct. In Diagram 5, we see our first filter after idea categorization. We keep our pure-thesis and conclusive-thesis ideas. We can bring in our high probability theorized-manufactured ideas. From this section of our thought existence, we can let our ideas pass. We have allowed the highest possible accuracy that we have at that moment to pass on to determine our code of conduct.

6. *We then measure our high accuracy ideas to reality against the physical reality of our human existence.* The physical reality of our human existence is our equal-to-us aspects and unequal-to-us aspects. Depending on each idea and how it relates to this physical reality determines the proper code of conduct. We can see in Diagram 5 that this filter is after our thesis idea selection and goes through our human structure made in physical existence. If it is an issue of equal thesis-morality, it follows its flow of conduct from the individual to all individuals. If it is an issue of unequal thesis-morality, it follows its flow of conduct from all individuals to the individual.

7. *It is our responsibility as a community to bring this understanding to the consciousness of all of us.* Whether any of us are aware or not of this reality to moral conduct, the physical reality of its existence does not change. For any adult to violate thesis-morality because of ignorance or alternate systems of thought does not change the physical reality of its existence. How we deal with ignorance, other system of thought and human beings incapable of understanding, we deal measured against this physical-reality-based filter and all their subsequent potential actions in our physical world.

8. *Our thesis-morality filter is the result of (thesis) ideas aligned to our physical reality.* Now we have a system of thought where we can apply reason and rational thought accountably to our social conduct. Note that this thesis-morality filter is individual action across all individuals by all individuals. When we maintain our relational evaluate-to-balance with an open free will to our physical existence, we can create a useful tool that can pull clarity from chaos. Through the collection of individual actions, we can bring intelligence into our *invisible hand* that Adam Smith referenced. We can limit the coercive

actions of people to only thesis-justified situations. In doing this, we release our freedoms and liberties and allow ourselves to progress as a unified species to unified ends.

BOOK TWO
OUR HALF STEP OF RATIONAL THOUGHT

Thesisism and Rational Thought Philosophy

1. *It was through our coercive political history that we developed theology and science, which in turn created a hidden reality that we needed to see.* In our ideas, we created a vacuum between science and theology that led to false and mutually exclusive ideas. We have by convenience and that of political wishes and desires made a line in the sand where each do state where each can and cannot know (or interfere with) the other, and in doing so mortared a wall over the door to truth. We have atrophied our nature of science and forfeited a full system of thought. We kept the study of developing ideas, but ridded ourselves the study of ideas themselves; and in the end, we placed into darkness our ability to understand the seven elements that would bring accountability to all ideas.

2. *Our coercive political history amputated accountability from philosophy.* We know that reason and rational thought have no relational requirement to measure against our reality. Does not this mean our philosophy suffers from politicized science and theology as well? We have those that want to stay in the real world and those that want to transcend. This is possible because in philosophy they continue to have our universe revolving around our earth; that is, in this argument, we have our conscious being revolving around our conscious being. We diminish ourselves by an artifact of our truce with science and theology. Our truce hides thesisism and the idea of accountability of ideas from us. Our truce hides our need to study the nature of ideas in of themselves.

3. *Where does thesisism fit?* Thesisism resides one-step further out from our historical systems of thought. Where our traditional systems of thought

89

will attempt to place thesisism—be it they religion, philosophy or science—is not my concern, for the applied elements of thesisism are not hypothetical, opinion or fancy. Nor does thesisism derive from any particular history. Rather that we know truth exists by definition. That our *sense of it* is because it is there, seen, and that its articulation requires being open and accepting, that our truth of existence comes from what is truly our open free will. Instead of us going to it, it comes to us, because an open free will is a will without impinging forces of self.

4. *Thesisism is a correction that requires historical systems to alter.* I do not find thesisism deriving from any existing historical position, rather it is illuminating a notch of darkness that can in turn explain historical tries and their resulting manufactured models. Thus, I leave it to others to decide if thesisism comes from an empirical system, a newly conceived ontological system, or if it is a religion, a science, a psychology, or a philosophy or for that matter from the simple ranting of a mad man.

5. *Thesisism involves nothing more than thesisism.* It is not my position to make claims to any other system of thought, or to profess absolute understanding of the thoughts of any philosopher, secular or theological. Rather, to make my claims founded on the physical relationship of ideas human beings hold and physical existence. We state the mental animations, assess them against physical existence, determine if they are broadband or narrowband, universal or limited, and determine the appropriate placement and attachment of the sliver idea of reality.

6. *Our historical philosophy of rational thought was unaccountable.* In my assessment, philosophy, in its broadest sense, is extremely painful. Under its wing, to understand the simplest, such as the existence of walking, we have to talk about the existence of space and motion, but they usually referenced their ideas to a fully developed and experienced adult. Their human mental animations of an empty adult begin to determine arguments like, did walking exist before walking or does it only exist after walking or does it only exist during walking. Perhaps walking does not exist at all. Moreover, walking may not exist if there is no existing conscious being to experience walking. Maybe we do need a conscious being to have walking exist, which in turn means walking may not need to exist to have the existence of walking. Often they never acknowledge or even know the jumps between broadband ideas and narrowband ideas. They never acknowledged the difference between universal and limited ideas, moral or not. From this and for most, it becomes confusing. Our darkness from a covered door to truth resulted in no one looking for physically based perceptions that fully mimicked existence. Although truth exists independent of consciousness, it has not reach our consciousness, at least until now, for which we have to ask, if no one saw me walking, did the

existence of my walking exist, and if not, does that mean I do not exist. If my nonsense about walking somehow made sense, then you are a philosopher.

7. *Our unaccountable historical systems of thought led to alternate and yet incompatible systems of thought.* The fact is that philosophy, religion and psychology all have carved out their narrowband niches, and sometimes they bump into one another so much so it is difficult to know which and whom we have dealt with at any given moment. Nevertheless, they all at some point made their claim to morality. Since thesisism is the study of ideas and a method to which we bring accountability, one of the most important ideas human beings have is to understand morality. Because of this history, thesisism becomes part of this mix even if I wish to protest, as thesisism is a new point of view only in that it starts with a shift in the most fundamental position. As we branch out and examine historical thought, we will find fragmented pieces of the puzzle; and when we filter them through thesisism, their shape alters and begins to fall into place.

8. *Our unaccountable and historical systems of thought diminished the good intentions of people.* It would be tempting to claim all else to be nonsense. Although a percentage certainly is—as with our popular metaphysics—the witness I see in the historical lineage are good people that tried to make sense out of the world in which they found themselves. Good people in the sense of sureness and of kindness on my part, as I default that any person that seeks truth of existence, seeks from a sense of want to know good. Good, as we have seen, is the balance of equations. Thus, they tried to find balance in the structure that they saw. Everyone tried to find that model that gave us the impression that we had found a fit to true existence. Nevertheless, our ideas when we filter them through an adhesive framed-reference prior to our evaluate-to-balance, can only lead us to mismatches with our reality. This mismatch leads to conflicting ideas and provides fodder for religious arguments against reason and rational thinking to justify their unaccountable systems of thought as well. Sir Thomas Pope Blount wrote, "little Learning is requisite for a good Mind: Nay, some are of opinion, it rather hindreth it; And that where Learning and Knowledge go in the *Front*, Pride and Ambition always follow in the *Rear*. ... Atheism, Errors, Sects, and all the troubles of the World, have risen from the Men of *Knowledge* and *Learning*. If we search into the *Morals* of the most Learned amongst the *Heathens*, I mean their Philosophers, we shall find but little agreement betwixt their Practices and their Doctrines; And that the one did generally run counter to the other." (19, p35-36) The good intentions of people, whether it is under rational thought or religious thought, have uncertain value when they use unaccountable systems of thought.

9. *Our unaccountable systems of thought can achieve accidental discoveries.* If we indeed had good people that tried to find perfect truth, should not they have come to some assemblage of truth? Although some may argue and make claim of finding perfect truth, I claim we have yet to discover the elements to perfect truth. I further claim that I have found a significant key to these elements, so much so, that from its revelation—moreover, the seven elements of accountability and the physical structure to our humanness that translates to our moral code of conduct—we can begin to make further discoveries.

10. *Our unaccountable systems of thought do not maintain the sliver idea of reality accountable to physical existence.* If we have not applied our seven elements of accountability and we animated and attached the idea of reality despite a break from our physical existence, then we can only have offered realities that are fractured and contradicted. Language, more significant than what most of us may first give, requires us to distinguish with our conscious awareness our broadband and narrowband ideas. When we have understanding of these two aspects of ideas, we can see how shifts between the two can create breaks with our connections to physical existence. This shifting can result in us keeping the idea of the physical connection attached, or to state it differently, the animation of reality can follow the idea despite an occurrence of a break.

11. *When we engage in language manipulation, we can drop our accountability by inadvertently breaking our connections to physical existence.* What we have to maintain with our ideas offered as reality and truth is our connections to physical existence. We can also drop our connections to our physical existence by not acknowledging a movement from broadband to narrowband thought and vice versa. We could engage in a *faithfully unintended* (or in politics and self-interests, intended) shell game. Although our idea of "shell games" attaches the idea of intention, our use of "unintended" here with the adjective "faithfully," makes it understood that we pretended with the sliver idea that we pretended notched out. This often occurs when we have false-reality desires, which create adhesive framed-references. As we have seen in *Book One*, it brings us a denied free will.

12. *When we do not maintain accountability to the sliver idea of reality, it leaves our human mind to move it in any chaotic direction and this chaotic direction becomes contained within the majority.* This is why in our remarkable course of human history and our mental life; that is, our thought existence; we have strayed for so long. This is why our philosophy, psychology and religions all have a commonality of not finding our truth with accuracy.[18]

---

18 This broadband statement contains a limited range of experience. We have many areas of historical thought that this author has not explored in depth. They include, but are not limited to, Eastern Religions, various brands of socialistic and capitalistic

Although we have had good people that tried to find the truth to existence, it appears that those that could put aside their personal desires with false reality may indeed have had to succumb to the majority. We have had a majority that wished not to think of this accountability and did not want their personal desires with false reality challenged. What we have left are good people operating within personal desires with false reality. We have an altered mental reality that then alters physical reality to fit a personally desired false-reality landscape, which contributes to the making of imperfect truth. We have presented our imperfect truths to one another, and we have left ourselves scratching our heads. Paradoxically, in some circles, this conforms to their false-reality desires; and this false reality leaves those that do not want to be challenge—unchallenged.

13. *The purpose of Book Two is not to cater to unaccountable systems of thought, but to demonstrate the value of thesisism.* We will discuss in *Book Three* the subject of how we have engaged in the manipulation of people through ideas. How our unaccountable systems of thought can allow manufactured coercion to appear justified is an important subject. Before we can get to this, we need to show how our reason and rational thought has historically failed us. We need to show how we have picked up manufactured ideas and used them to justify personal self-interests. When our self-interest uses manufactured ideas for justification, we are using unjustified coercion. Our first step cannot be to point out unjustified coercion, but how we come to understand what is justified and unjustified coercion. To do this, we must first have conscious understanding of our true existence. This brings us back to thesisism, for only in thesisism is there a system of accountably to all ideas that removes the human being from being the source to justification. Thesisism requires the outside existence to make the statements of accountability and to provide us the justice equations. We have accomplished this in *Book One*. We must look at our history to see our evolution of human ideas that converges onto us today. We always have had the coercive animal. We continue to have the coercive animal. When we can determine justified and unjustified coercion, we can begin to expose the coercive animal.

14. *Manipulations from the human mind can affect thesisism too.* For the record, our personal desires with false reality can interfere with the application

---

thought and more. Despite rudimentary passes on other thought systems, such as various Eastern Religions, I have not found any system of thought with accountability as presented in thesisism. Some Eastern Religions and Native American Religions appear to have a greater focus on our physical environment. Nevertheless, spirituality was a constant and it allowed for unaccountable thought. I based my presentation of thesisism and this statement on my range of experience. This then biased this presentation of thesisism toward historical Western Philosophy.

of thesisism as well. However, thesisism has a pointer to the physical world, which bypasses human beings. This pointer creates a self-correcting system, and it pushes to expose our adhesive framed-reference and denied free will that any of us can carry.

15. *The qualities of thesisism:* David Hume influenced us to view our moral actions in terms of passion and with a secular form of faith. He wrote, "Since morals, therefore, have an influence on the actions and affections, it follows, that they cannot be derived from reason; and that because reason alone, as we have already proved, can never have any such influence. Morals excite passions, and produce or prevent actions. Reason of itself is utterly impotent in this particular. The rules of morality, therefore, are not conclusions of our reason." (17, p355) Thesisism both agrees and disagrees with this, as he does not connect his ideas back to physical existence. Indeed, reason without any connection to physical existence fails us. What Hume had *sense of* was that reason and rational thought were not accountable systems of thought for social discourse. He did not recognize the difference between science and its cause and effect model and the needed relational measurement of our own ideas to reality. He did not acknowledge that two different existences were involved and the cause and effect model cannot apply to experiential existence. He did not acknowledge our *why-2*.[19] Our morals cannot have influence on our actions, as they are the actions. We do not decide our moral actions and then engage in it; rather we find our moral actions relationally to physical existence, which is to match it to reality, and then engage in it to maintain or correct physical-world equations. In the first, humans are deciding moral actions, whereas in the second it is physical existence that determines our moral actions. Morality is not passion, as reactive responses can only lead us to adhesive framed-references. When we base our morality in passion, we easily end with manipulation and unjustified coercion. It is through our passions that the coercive animal among us has been so successful in keeping us away from our reality and creator.[20]

16. *The qualities of thesisism continued:* What should "produce or prevent" our actions is our evaluate-to-balance with an unrestricted free will. When we bring in our physical existence without influence to any framed-reference, we can identify our moral codes of conduct. What we find in our physical existence, when free will allows evaluation-to-balance to occur, is that we as human beings have equality and inequality. We have our action that our physical existence gives us in terms of balance to physical existence. We then

19 We have an explanation of *"why-2"* provided in the chapter titled, *"Is Our Use of Reason Accountable?"* in paragraph 6.
20 We have an actual historical example provided in the chapter titled, *"Is Our Use of Reason Accountable?"* in paragraphs 11 and 12.

obtain our thesis-based justifications to our moral actions. The idea that the use of reason by any one individual cannot understand the totality of existence, therefore reason fails, is simply movement between the narrowband ideas of reason to a broadband idea of reason. Our use of reason is the mechanism and not the output. Hume confused the end with the mean. The idea of reason does not include comprehension of everything. Therefore, our thesis-based idea of reason becomes a narrowband version of reason. If each individual engaged in thesisism, then we would achieve collectively what Hume could not do with his unaccountable form of reason. Thesisism removes the secular-faith idea that each individual would pursue their self-interest with the greater number of people working toward good, and replaces it with reality-based thought where evaluation of the greater good can occur and we can demonstrate it. Our reality-based measurements, since we base it to our common physical existence, include all individuals. Our common physical existence provides us a uniform accountability to personal self-interest held by any individual, both individually and collectively. Now we have our moral code of conduct operating beyond the comprehension of any individual, yet unified by our common physical existence. We have each individual tied to reality and expressed across all individuals.

17. *We must measure human mental animation against its original source, the physical world.* Our source to understanding existence becomes a product of human beings and their ability to animate ideas. Our ability to animate ideas is a relationship between physical existence and our thought existence. Human history shows that consciousness requires the formation of physical existence into an organ we call the brain. Once this organ is satisfied to its physical requirements, it can begin to engage in the development of thought existence. The level and quality of that existence depends on the evolution of that brain. On this planet, human beings have the most evolved brain. Nevertheless, we should never confuse this with an idea of evolutionary finality, nor that ours is sufficient for long-term survival, and for any current ability to animate and reach a quality of life for all. For what the reality of physical existence is and to what our actions ought to reflect, our actions show disconnects. The question becomes, do we have the capacity, and if we do, how do we obtain the ability.

How Atheism Perpetuates Religion

1. *Atheism is a force of opposition that by its own opposition to religion gives substance to religion.* For atheism to exist, theism must exist. By the creation of atheism, it is an admission on the part of atheists to a lack of discovery to a system of thought for human thought existence. By omission and silence—or

references to arbitrary reason and rational thinking—to a defined atheistic system of thought evaluation, this emptiness during arguments against religion provides an unspoken strength to the same system they oppose. Richard Allestree wrote of atheism, "We call it frenzy to see a man fight with a shadow; but sure it is more so to invoke it." (22, p27) When atheists rail against religion, they not only fight with the elusive non-reality animations of the religious, but they invoke their own shadow that gives the religious animations a false legitimacy. Richard Allestree further wrote, "And indeed it seems a tacit confession, that they have little of their own...." (22, p27) When atheists confront the religious, they offer no positional ideas of replacement beyond reason and rational thinking. Because reason and rational thinking allows unaccountability, to which the religious can legitimately claim use of, this provides the religious a sense of strength to their religious position, as demonstrated in the given statement from Richard Allestree.

2. *Atheism offers no competition to the religious system of thought.* What do atheists offer as competition to religion? Voltaire? Volney? Thomas Paine? Thomas Paine wrote *The Age of Reason.* In it, he delineated the problems with the Christian religion. What did it accomplish? It accomplished to inspire the religious to engage in more saving face animations, that was all. In doing this saving face, they became embolden. They became motivated. We may even argue that *The Age of Reason* ended the enlighten thinking of the Deists. Thomas Paine accomplished more when he provided his alternate system of thought. He changed our world with his writings of *Common Sense, The Crisis, The Public Good* and the *Rights of Man, Part 1 and 2.* These were not arguments against religion; they were the presentation of reality-based, physical-world ideas. They competed with unaccountable systems of thought by associating the physical realities of the times.

3. *Atheism has used reason and rational thought against religion but has seldom applied it to atheism.* Atheism does not provide any cohesive thought system. They are preoccupied to put stray jackets on religious ideas only to find the religious ideas well greased. When they point to people like Sigmund Freud, Friedrich Nietzsche, Jean-Paul Sartre and others, most of the their arguments are again positioned against religion. The religious simply do not care, as they do not reside within the rules atheists want to place. Even when atheists try to create systems of thought to society, the use of reason and rational thought has been unaccountable. We ended with extremes of socialism and communism from Karl Marx, and the extremes of pure capitalism from Ayn Rand. Each ignored the physical-world realities in a complete sense, as they did not have any system of thought with accountability. When they do not have a requirement for their ideas to connect to the physical world, each had swung toward one end of thesis-morality. We have these two expressions

of ideology based on rational thought, to which they have legitimacy, but the legitimacy is only in relation to each other, not as mutually exclusive entities.

4. *The arguments against religion by atheism as a method to eliminate religion denies the reality that religion can animate any false-reality idea it desires.* Religion has in its possession a powerful tool for continuance. They can animate and attach the sliver idea of reality to anything they so desire. Richard Allestree animated in his mind the reconciliation of atheistic thought. He wrote of atheists, "Their most bold Thesis, That there is no God, no judgement, no hell, is often met with an inward tremulous Hypothesis, What if there be? I dare in this remit me to themselves, and challenge (not their consciences, who profess to have none, but) their natural ingenuity to say, whether they have not sometimes such damp and shivering with them." (22, p17-18) We see this common mental animation even today on our televisions regularly. He continued with some manufactured reason and rational thought from his flawed original premise to provide a good argument against atheists. Perhaps I should remind that the problem atheists have here is not the religious providing solid arguments against them. Rather, the religious allow to themselves any mental animations with the idea of reality attached, and then move their ideas with solid reason and rational thought attached to their false-reality arguments. The religious do not argue against the non-believers, they animate to maintain their personally acquired false-reality desires. Allestree continued to write, "If they shall say, that these are but the relics of prepossession and education, which their reason soon dissipates: Let me then ask them farther, whether they would not give a considerable sum to be infallibly ascertained there were no such thing. Now no sensible man would give a farthing to be secured from a thing which his reason tells him is impossible; therefore if they would give any thing (as I dare say they themselves cannot deny that they would) 'tis a tacit demonstration that they are not so sure as they pretend to be." (22, p18) Here was the use of logic and rational thought where he pointed out his perceptions of the frailty of atheistic thought. Again, rational thought does not have the requirement to connect to the physical world, that is, reality.

5. *When atheists make arguments that atheism is a method to eliminate religion, it denies the reality of human animation and human need for thought systems.* We cannot eliminate religion by arguing against it. The fact is that religion provides a system of thought that brings stability to the mental understanding of individual human beings. Do not confuse this with stability to society. Religion, as demonstrated many times during its history, often brings instability, violence and suffering to societies. It brings stability to the minds of individual human beings attempting to understand the world

they find themselves living in. What atheism needs is a system of thought that brings each person a needed stability. That needed system of thought is thesisism. Whether atheists can handle the broadband view of religion under thesisism and accept religious ideas as ranging from pure-manufactured ideas to theorized-manufactured ideas of a low probability we have yet to see. Perhaps they can provide the needed arguments that show all religious ideas are pure-manufactured ideas.

6. *I contend from the presented arguments above, that atheism actually helps perpetuate religion.* There is one more argument I want to provide. The mocking of religion does not work and will never eliminate religion. Allestree wrote, "This is indeed, considering the depravation of the world, a pretty fast tenure for atheism to hold by; yet it has of late twisted its cord, and got that other string to its bow we before mentioned. Its bold monopolizing of wit and reason compels, as the other invited men. This we may indeed call the devils press, by which he hath filled up his troops: men are afraid of being reproached for silly and irrational, in giving themselves up to a blind belief of what they do not see. And this bugbear frights them from their religion; resolving they will *be no fools for Christ's sake.*" (22, p16) Here he spoke of the compelling wit and reason of atheists. He related how it did lead to some leaving religion. Nevertheless, understand that this reference to the wit and reason of atheists was written in the year 1691. In fact, all the quoted material in this chapter on atheism I quoted from the same 1691 source. Here we have evidence that atheists mocked religion for over three hundred years. Where are we today? We are on the brink of an evangelical takeover of this country.

7. *Atheism is only a half step.* Why do atheists fail? They are only a negation. By their own name, their position of reason and rational thought directs them to the monkey that is on their back. They circle endlessly with the theism part of their own name. By accepting the religious-based name, they have help keep alive an unaccountable system of thought. The move from theism to atheism is only one step of two needed. It is a move from *to be with* to the position of *to be without.* The next step is to leave their negation status and move to accountability. We know how to move to reason and rational thought that is reality-based. We accomplish this when we understand thesisism. To understand our current thought systems beyond the religious and into our secular, governmental and economic thought, we need to know where our ideas came from and how they progressed and moved over time to reach us today.

Epicures and Epictetus, the Old Stoic Thought System

1. *We have championed reason and rational thought throughout the history of humankind.* We had Phyathoris engage in reason about the gods. We had Aristotle use rational thought to talk about the pursuit of human happiness measured against the personal desires of individuals. We had Thomas Aquinas use the rational and logical method to move the happiness of humankind into the knowledge of his God. We had John Locke make the pursuit of human happiness the acquisition of property and any other personal desires. We had Fredrick Nietzsche make human beings with certain abilities superior over others in all aspects of existence. Jean-Paul Sartre centered our human consciousness void of any physical existence and interactions. All of these thinkers had used reason and rational thought.

2. *Despite the millenniums, reason and rational thought does not have a solid system of thought to our social structure.* We had many early philosophers that used reason and rational thought. We will look at two. Our first is Epicurus, a Greek philosopher born in 341 BC. He provides us our typical flaws in reason and rational thought that we have carried to date. He wrote, "we must comprehend the meanings that underlie the words, so that, by referring to them, we may be able to reach judgments concerning opinions, matters of inquiry, or problems and not leave everything undecided as we argue endlessly or use words that have no sense." (23, sec 37) This idea from Epicurus sounds in agreement with thesisism. To apply thesisism, we must recognize broadband words and narrowband them so everyone is animating the same idea. For any philosopher to say we must understand our words leaves the question of how can we know to understand our words. Our words are articulations—written, spoken or thought—that pulls up a collection of sliver ideas to make the master idea. If we do not measure our words and the understanding of them against our reality, then the words become the property of the human mind only. This gives us no accountability to the words and for us to know if the understandings of the words are indeed inline with reality. How then can we with any confidence reach sound and correct judgments with words that have no foundation and attachment to reality? The "leave everything undecided as we argue endlessly" is because of human beings animating anything they want in their minds without any measurement system. He referenced at the end the use of words that made "no sense." There it was. The door to thesisism and accountability awaited his opening. Nevertheless, he did not open it. Rather, his *sense* was to use mental animation of ideas by humankind without any system of thought to bring accountability. His use of *sense* referred to an evaluate-to-balance with

false-reality equations from an adhesive framed-reference, and not the input to senses from the physical world to an unrestricted form of free will and to our evaluate-to-balance with reality-based equations.

3. *Epicurus, like other early philosophers, started with human senses but moved toward the human mind.* He wrote some striking lines that came close to thesisism. Here are a few. He wrote, "it is through the senses that we must by necessity form a judgement about the imperceptible by means of reason." (23, sec39) What did he mean here by senses? Epicurus, from a position of a thesisist, was referring to the physical activity of the human mind. This included sensory, reactive and thought existence. It was a true statement if "through the senses" meant that all ideas arrived from the experience of sensory existence, and from that all ideas must maintain accountability to those original percepts. However, if the input of reality from sensory existence is allowed to be judged not to physical existence, but to be judged to the human mind against itself, as the use of reason allows, we are once again back to an unaccountable system of thought.

4. *The use of reason by Epicurus involved unaccountable thought.* Here is a line from Epicurus that demonstrates that his view of reason allowed measurement to be not of the physical world, but of the human mind. He wrote, "Furthermore, we must maintain all of our investigations in accordance with our sensations and especially our ready application whether of mind or of any one of our means of judging, and likewise in accordance with our feelings." (23, sec 38) He had our use of reason as human mental animations applied or judged in relation to our sensations and our feelings. Our feelings are human centered and can close our framed-reference. Sensations may be the input from physical existence, but we process them through reactive and thought existence with application and judgement against them without any requirement to maintain the original relationship to physical existence. When we misplace our sliver idea of reality, we can create preconceptions and alter our incoming reality.

5. *Here is a remarkable statement by Epicurus that demonstrates how early philosophy was nearer to accountable thought than we are today.* He wrote,

> There is always falsehood and error involved in importing into judgement an element additional to sense impressions, either to confirm or deny. For there would be no correspondence between the images that are received as in a picture, or those arising in dreams or as a result of application by the mind or the other faculties, and things that exist and are called real, unless there were such effluences actually brought into contact with our senses. There would be no error, unless there occurred within us some other movement connected with the

perception of images but distinguished from it. It is from this, if it is not confirmed or is contradicted or not contradicted. We must by all means keep this in mind, so that neither the standards of judgement that result from perceptions may be confuted nor error that has thoroughly established itself as truth likewise throw everything into confusion. (23, sec 50-51)

6. *The reason why this is a remarkable statement:* Epicurus understood that falsehood occurred with an additional element introduced to sense impressions. His second sentence stated that our senses could only sense reality. It appears to me that he referred to sensory existence when he wrote, "brought into contact with our senses." Our sensory existence is our player and our interface with the physical world. He then acknowledged that error occurred within us and referred to it as "some other movement." It was here that we had acknowledgement of mental animation. Epicurus had a diffuse and ambiguous understanding that something could happen to our master ideas that were originally pure-thesis ideas. This movement is the movement of silver ideas between many master ideas that we as a mental animal can animate and move. He then pointed out quite correctly that "error that has thoroughly established itself as truth," which is our manufactured ideas as they break from our physical world, then results in confusion to the reality and accountability of ideas. He had a weak understanding that mental animation away from our more direct senses could only lead us to chaos.

7. *Epicurus understood that we needed physical existence for our mental life to exist.* He wrote, "It is not possible to imagine the soul existing and having sensation without the body, and experiencing these movements when there no longer exists that which encloses and surrounds the soul, in which it now exists and has these movements." (23, sec 66) This aligns with the reality that our experiential existence cannot exist without the physical structure to allow its existence. Our experiential existence exists in the action of the physical structure. Once the physical action stops, our experiential existence stops.

8. *Epicurus chose happiness and the avoidance of pain and fear as human goals.* Epicurus stated a set of necessary desires. "There are those that are necessary for happiness, those that are necessary for the body's freedom from disturbance, and those that are necessary for life itself." (23, sec 127-128) He stated that observances of these necessary desires we directed toward the health of our body and the calming of the soul. It was these observances that led to the human "goal of a happy life." (23, sec 128) He concluded with "Everything we do is for the sake of this, namely, to avoid pain and fear." (23, sec 128) Like all philosophers, whether they are secular thinkers or religious thinkers, they always moved toward this idea of pursuit of happiness.

This dovetailed right into our personal desires independent to whether our desires resided in reality or resided in false reality. It opened the door for humankind to begin to animate anything they wanted without any required accountability.

9. *The philosophy of Epicurus terribly lacked universality to humankind applications.* His main thrust was that of avoidance of pain and fear. From this, he developed a *retirement* type of life where students and followers contributed to it sustainability. For them to have a life away from pain and fear, they needed an outside support system around them to achieve this. This meant that others around them had to make the world around them free of pain and fear. In this regard, the philosophy of Epicurus had no ability to sustain society in its entirety. It had no recognition of the equality and inequality of people around them. It was mostly a duck and hide philosophy to life. Nevertheless, this idea that the end for humankind was happiness and avoidance of pain and fear represented the narrow sighted thought to our individual self-interest independent to all other people. Therefore, we had the beginning of individualism without recognition of the equality between us. We see this philosophy today in ideas of individual responsibility to our self-interest as if all people instantaneously start life with completely acquired and developed abilities.

10. *Another philosopher, Epictetus, spoke about our need to measure our mental impressions.* After speaking about intelligence (phronêsis) as something good and lack of intelligence as something bad, he concluded that intelligence studies itself. He wrote, "Therefore, the philosopher's greatest and primary function is to test and discriminate between mental impressions and to accept none of them that has not been tested." (24, p131) Nevertheless, we have to ask the question; mental impressions measured against what? Wisdom? Moral excellence? Integrity? Good judgement? We can continue and continue, but these ideas in their historical use do not have any requirement to stay connected to our physical world. We have Christian and Islamic wisdom. We have the claimed moral excellence of the crusaders and priests that entered South America in the sixteenth and seventeenth century. We have the claimed integrity of European immigration and the good judgments of persecution to those that do not submit to their values.

11. *Epictetus demonstrated the ambiguity of his measurement system of thought by stating his view of the starting point of philosophy.* His starting point involved the measurement of reason and rational thought to be against the human mind. He wrote, "Observe the starting point of philosophy: awareness of human beings' conflict of opinions, investigations of the origin of the conflict, condemnation of opinions, investigations of the correctness of an opinion, and discovery of a certain standard, such as we have discovered in

the case of the scale for weights, or the ruler for things straight and crooked. This is the starting point of philosophy." (24, p102) His starting point of philosophy was human thought. Already Epictetus was dealing with mental animation and not the original source of any particular idea. He implied we needed a scale for weights or a ruler of things within our own mind. He never extended that ruler outside of the human mind and into our physical world. Nevertheless, he did give us a measurement system of thought.

12. *Epictetus had reason and rational thought connected to the human notion of confidence and trust.* He provided the example of his measurement of confidence and trust against the idea of pleasure. He wrote, "Must the good be the sort of thing that merits confidence and trust?" His answer was, "It must." He then asked, "Does something insecure merit confidence?" His answer was, "No." He then asked, "Pleasure is not something secure, is it?" Again his answer was no. He then wrote, "Remove it, then, throw it out of the balance and drive it far away from the domain of good things. ... That is how things are judged and weighed when the standards are established." (24, p102-103) Our question is; does confidence and trust connect to the physical world? Confidence and trust are the result of our evaluation-to-balance. If we evaluate-to-balance connected to our physical world, we can say we have confidence and trust. The people that blasted out into space in the space shuttle had confidence and trust. However, this was due to countless connections with the physical world maintained to bring a high probability level that in reality it will go into space and back. No one would blast out into space if the scientists did not do this but instead claimed they had confidence and trust because they *sensed it* to be in correct working order. Further, if we skew an evaluate-to-balance by an adhesive framed-reference, then our confidence and trust involves a manufactured measurement system against our mental chaos.

13. *Epictetus was confident and trusted that physical existence had a consciousness.* He wrote, "How else could things happen so regularly, by God's command as it were? When he tells plants to bloom, they bloom, when he tells them to bear fruit, they bear it, when he tells them to ripen, they ripen; and again when he tells them to drop their fruit, shed their leaves, contract into themselves, stay quiet and pause, they do these things?" (24, p25) When I read this, I thought to myself, "Does he hear little voices to every action of the physical world around him?" What happens when someone cuts a fruit tree? Does the little voice no longer work? Or did the little voice tell the person to cut the tree? This insistence of humankind to place conscious thought into the actions of the action of physical existence requires our creation and creator to be humanlike. Consciousness may be something human beings

possess. That does not mean our creator has humanlike consciousness. Our creator is our physical world. We are made of it.

14. *Epictetus inflated human rationality to that of manufactured ideas of higher authorities.* We have a long history among our religious and philosophers to associate themselves with their gods. They often place their god or a piece of their god into themselves. Although Epictetus did not realize it, the following is the bases for human suffering. He wrote, "Do you not know how small a part you are in comparison with the universe? That is, as regards the body. But as regards rationality, you are not inferior to the gods nor smaller. For rationality's size is not assessed by its length or height, but by its judgements." (24, p 155) Epictetus described for us what we have been doing for millenniums. If you are religious, confident and trusting, you can elevate yourself to the level of a god. If you are a rational thinker, confident and trusting, you can elevate yourself to the level of false certainty.

15. *Part of our existing view of reason and rational thought is that we sense it.* When we use confidence and trust to our assessment of ideas, we historically have dropped any requirement for it to measure against our physical existence. Our confidence and trust is only good if we connect to the physical world. We have not connected rationality to the physical, but to the non-reality idea of a spiritual rationality and ideas of confidence and trust measuring against this spiritual rationality. Second, since our connection to the physical world is our measurement to reality, we lost accountability to our rational thought when we allowed the movement of the sliver idea of reality to break its required physical connection and then we applied the idea of reality to the chaos of the human mind. Now we can animate anything and begin to dominate human beings with coercion with these self-absorbed and narcissistic psychological views. If you are a philosopher, or a wise man, an economist or a politician and you are confident and trusting to your reason and rational thought, you can elevate yourself to the level of a *god-like* being. This self-absorbed and narcissistic psychological (god-like) state can with false reality elevate any self-appointed individual to the ideal man of Nietzsche. Any self-appointed authority can grasp the view of John Locke that everything on earth is a gift from God to humankind. Any self-appointed grabbers can claim that the pursuit of happiness is to procure and use these gifts from a higher consciousness to fit ones own narcissistic view of what makes their happiness. This rational thought becomes as dogmatic as any religious view. Neither view has maintained their connections to the physical world. Both, religious thought and rational thought engage in unaccountability with the sliver idea of reality attached to any false-reality desires.

16. *The unaccountability of reason and rational thought maintains the sustainability of religious thought.* The main reason—reason as an idea

connected to the physical world—that our religions continue is that reason and rational thought continue to measure against the chaos of the human mind. We have stabilized the chaos of our human mind in *feel* by the religious idea of an ultimate and higher authority that brings justice and purpose to all human beings. Ironically, this acquired stability is in response to the created instability in our mental life when we broke our thought existence from our physical existence. This *feel* is an attempt to balance sensed equations. We need to return to our physical existence for reality-based stability. Nevertheless, the users of reason and rational thought animate their ideas in the same chaos.

17. *Secular thought has a vague foundation.* All secular thought in terms of social structure is fragmented. Even in these fragmentations, some contradictions occur, as our ideas do not have to connect to physical existence. Reason and rational thought has a *feel* for thesisism, but not a *vision* of it. This results in partial connections. Nietzsche is an excellent example of focusing on one side of the physical nature of human beings and while ignoring the other. We find these two sides of physical nature in human beings in their physical existence as equal thesis-morality and unequal thesis-morality. Therefore, since our reason and rational thought are not required to connect to physical existence and does not operate under the accountability of thesisism, their foundations are indeed vague. The uncertainly that this creates in *feel* for most human beings maintains while the religious are able to cover this instability with their manufactured ideas. The absolute requirement from thesisism to maintain our ideas to the physical world allows a stabilization to occur that will appeal to most people. Until this is recognized, religion will continue.

18. *Even in the 21st century, the time of this writing, only religion offers definitive statements to stable social structure.* We continue to have religions that dominate our planet. Religions have contributed to love, peace, and the assistance of humankind during life-threatening needs. They have also contributed to the hellish world of conflict, hate, and authoritative demands on behavior that is inconsistent, chaotic and often vindictive. The irony is that the religious thought system under all individuals is unstable, unpredictable and leads to periodic domination by a few people. Despite the instability that religion brings to all individuals, it brings stability to the individual and a collection of individuals. That is the difference.

19. *The extended order of capitalism also gravitates to religion because of the stability to individuals that religion can bring.* The extended order of capitalism is not in the business of religion. Nevertheless, the extended order of capitalism requires social stabilization for its success. This is why, as we will see in *Book Three*, conservative economists like Milton Friedman and F. A. Hayek make apologies for religion and bring it into their fold. The potential of thesisism to bring not only social stabilization, but also a true and superior stability

makes it likely that the extended order would benefit from the support of thesisism. The only opposing forces to this support would come from those capitalists that would not want to acknowledge their moral obligations for their personal gain.

20. *Our rational thinkers have failed to create a social structure that can sustain itself better than the religious social structure.* The reasons for this are many, with religion itself playing a big role in impregnating reason with impotency. The largest problem we have with reason and rational thought is that it too is an unaccountable system of thought. It has similarities with religious thought in that we allow reason and rational thought to measure their social ideas against the chaos of the human mind. It has repeatedly chosen to grasp an egocentric view that our human psyche is the center of the universe and all else revolves around us. We have advanced an egocentric view that our ultimate goal is the pursuit of happiness, that a god gave the earth to us in both land and animals, and that we can have a successful society when we place faith in our pursuit of narrow self-interests. We have not gotten past our fears, our pains, and our desires of pleasure and our seeking of self-gratification sufficiently to measure our ideas not against ourselves, but the physical world around us. All this historical thought is mindless because our mind only measures against itself and not to any reality. Once we break the chain that we have placed on ourselves and once we make reason and rational thought accountable to our physical existence, we can then truly progress as a species. Each individual has a mind that animates in its actions. Our rational thinkers must understand this need to bring stability to the individual. We achieve our stability when we maintain our relationship with physical existence as our reality. Once this happens, competition with religion occurs. Thesisism is that competition. It competes not just against religion, but also against faith-based capitalism. Thesisism exposes the coercive animal and allows us our freedom and liberty.[21]

John Locke and the Big Give Away

1. *John Locke speculated we could demonstrate morality by some form of measurement.* He wrote, "And hence it follows, that *moral* Knowledge is as *capable of real certainty*, as Mathematicks." (15, IV.iv.7) The idea that we can demonstrate morality was something that Locke made claim to through many years of his life. In his early years, he wrote, "For there are some moral principles which the whole of mankind recognizes and which all men in the world accept unanimously; but this could not happen if the law were

---

21 Thesisism competes against all other thought systems. This sentence was made relational to the contents of this publication.

not a natural one." (25, p282) He further wrote, "This argument is also demonstrated by the fact that the theory of virtues can be comprised within the limits of a science, for it is by this that; 'whatever depends on convention is rightly distinguished from things natural; for things concerning nature, being always the same, can readily be gathered into a science, while those which are the outcome of convention form no part of science, because they often change and are different in different places.'" (25, p282)

2. *John Locke then hesitated on his own position.* John Locke himself removed the last two quotes from his *Essay on the Law of Nature.* W. von Leyden offered, "He deleted it probably because it contains views concerning the general consent of men that run counter to those expressed in his fifth essay." (25, p282) The title of the fifth essay by John Locke was, "*Can the Law of Nature Be Known from the General Consent of Men? No.*" (25, p161) The title alone seems to confer with Leyden's assessment. John Locke started with an absolute statement of unanimous consent in his removed quotes and moved to the ambiguous idea of general consent. Leyden also noted that, "I have preferred to render the Latin consensus by 'general consent' rather than by 'consensus'." (25, p161) We could argue that *General Consent* meant *Consensus*, as John Locke used the Latin word "Consensu." This makes a difference in understanding the dilemma John Locke had. General consent measures from a different source than consensus. The latter source measures from our physical existence, the former from our human mind. John Locke could not reconcile the two and remained in their ambiguity.

3. *Locke began to divide the idea of consent into different types.* In his fifth essay, he distinguished between positive and natural consent, with consent akin to consensus. His positive consent "arises from a contract," (25, p161) which he concluded with "does not prove a natural law, but should rather be called the law of nations." (25, p163) Locke claimed natural consent to be "one to which men are led by a certain natural instinct without the intervention of some compact." (25, p165) Nevertheless, his general consent falls apart. It does so by his insistence, as well as the history of humankind, to keep humankind in the center of measurement. His general consent involved the judgment of individuals without establishment of reality. If we measured our judgement against the backdrop of the human mind, we would not only end with variations of consent to ideas, but outright contradictions. He knew this dilemma, as he wrote, "What immorality would not be allowable and even be inevitable, if the example of the majority gave us the law?" (25, p165)

4. *The dilemma of John Locke with his attempts to reconcile consensus with general consent rested on his measurement of ideas against the human mind.* I suspect John Locke, in his mind, actually wanted to mean *consensus* and not *general consent*, as if he indeed thought morality to be demonstrable, would

not then this mean that all consent measured against his law of nature be consistent. His general consent implied there was permission or agreement in kind by human beings. This also implied there was non-consent. This demonstrates that he made the final measurement of ideas against the human mind. *His law of nature became tied to human beings without having to have it remain connected to nature!*

5. *When he made the human mind over physical existence the final source of measurement, he made the law of nature to have relativism to it.* This relativism comes from the result of our mental animations by the vague measurement system of rational thought to social and moral ideas. General consent then opens humankind to possible coercion and domination by any self-appointed authority or groups. I suspect Locke *sensed* that humans and their general consent to ideas was not the driving authority. Rather, what he strove for arrived from some other authority. To open oneself to that view meant removing the authority position of those in power, be they the elite of wealth, education and the dominate religion. In the same removed paragraph, Locke wrote, "But if these laws were positive and arbitrarily laid down by men without any concept or obligation antecedent to such laws, they would not be everywhere so similar to one another." (25, p282) The word consensus implies agreement within human beings not tied to their own human created system of evaluation. He was seeking *consensus*, yet most of the human behavior around him only showed *general consent*. Effectively, he chose to focus on the wrong side of nature, the nature of the animating human mind.

6. *By not connecting to physical existence, he had to remain in the chaos of the human mind.* In his fifth essay, he acknowledged that consensus to moral actions had been poorly established and portrayed throughout human history. He had an understanding of our "general consensus," yet not a conscious understanding that there were two types of consensus within his own ideas. There was a manufactured-based consensus and a thesis-based consensus. The thesis-based consensus made its evaluation-to-balance against the physical world. The manufactured-based consensus made its evaluation-to-balance against the individual human mind. We can clearly see this when he wrote,

> No one, therefore, has attempted to build up a law of nature upon this most unfortunate agreement among men. It may be said, however, that the law of nature is to be inferred not from men's behaviour but from their innermost ways of thinking—we must search not the lives of men but their souls—for it is there that the precepts of nature are imprinted and the rules of morality lie hidden together with those principles which men's manners cannot corrupt; and that, since these principles are the same in every one of us, they can have no

other author than God and nature. And it is for this reason that the internal law, whose existence is often denied by vices, is acknowledged by men's conscience and the very men who act perversely feel rightly. (25, p165-167)

He then followed with, "then, there does not occur among men a general consent concerning moral rectitude." (25, p167) He placed measurement of our moral ideas against our "innermost ways of thinking" and we must search our "souls." This is opposite to what we need to do. He ignored the silver idea of reality and gave reality to the animating human mind without any accountability. We must make our ways of thinking relational to physical existence and open our free will. Nevertheless, part of the mechanism of thesisism is within the statement by John Locke.

7. *In the passage above by John Locke, we see the mechanism to his truth and morality.* When he wrote, "we must search not the lives of men but their souls," he was attempting to understand our human character of free will. His statement or attempt was actually the following. We cannot search the fancies of particular men or women. Rather, we must connect into our physical existence through our open free will obtained by a free-flow framed-reference. We can now understand his statement that "for it is there that the precepts of nature are imprinted and the rules of morality lie hidden." Under this view, where we evaluate physical existence by the evaluate-to-balance of our open free will (soul), John Locke hit it precisely correct. He knew thesisism in the terms of *sensing* it, but could not find its articulation.

8. *John Locke unwittingly mixed a manufactured idea with his thesis view of nature.* When Locke wrote "no other author than God and nature," he combined the two. You can see that he was trying to connect to the physical world, yet he could not do so without violating the prevailing higher authority idea. His words came close to stating that we do not determine morality, rather the physical world determines morality. Because he could not distinguish manufactured ideas from thesis ideas, he struggled with the appearance of incompatibility between his fifth essay and what he was struggling to get to on his deleted paragraph. This was probably why John Locke removed his passage, not because it was necessarily false, but he did not have a way to back up what he *sensed* to be true.

9. *This brings us to the fundamental flaw in the philosophical theory of the law of nature.* Even though it appears based into nature, when we examine it further, we will see that it really measured against the human mind and not nature. There was a sort of handshake that occurred that allowed humankind to get closer to the truth. Certainly, it was a terrific testimony to John Locke, as he was one of the first to wedge between a long history of dominated human

thought with a new and more reality-based human thought. This move to a more reality-based thinking was not pure, nor necessarily full. Nevertheless, he did live near where the sword of the magistrate lingered. He was also a part of the educated and economic class, and we will see how this contributed to a philosophy of self-justifications.

10. *We have maintained within the philosophy of the law of nature a fundamental flaw, and it has led to a chaotic intrusion into many areas of study and thought.* Locke stayed with the idea of morality being demonstrable, yet he also stayed measured to human minds. We indeed have the capability to measure morality. We can measure morality if we know how to remain connected to the physical world that we are born in and within our lived lives. The accuracy of our judgements, in his time or ours, depends on the population of any given society in how well we know, consciously or via reactive awareness, what source to use to measure our judgment of ideas. He saw that agreement and disagreement of our ideas between people "will produce real Knowledge, as well as in Mathematical Figures." (15, IV.iv.7) My interpretation is that we should change the word "will" to "could" in that we are not born with a full innate understanding or a conscious understanding of how to stay measured against reality. Rather we are born with the capacity to evaluate-to-balance, which is a broadband and generalized capability. We will see that in his understanding of his ideas about ideas, he had all the ingredients to discover thesisism.

11. *His measurement of agreement with disagreement was only as good as the thinking abilities of the people at that time.* He took the agreements and disagreements as the measure toward whether an idea was moral and where it stood in relation to people. However, this measurement placed morality against the human mind. His agreements and disagreements was a crude and noisy calculation. His agreements and disagreements between people suggested to him that we human beings have an evaluative system. Unless we are aware of an evaluative system and to what we ought to measure against, it can be unreliable. If we measure our agreements and disagreements against the broken physical connections of any animation, anything can happen. If we stay measured against our physical world, which is our creation, then a singular and uniformed backdrop of measurement occurs.

12. *John Locke understood a form of measurement was taking place, but could not identify with it.* What John Locke saw in his perception of agreements and disagreements perceived was that there was a sense of measurement taking place. Nevertheless, he did not stay connected to the physical world. Our agreements and disagreements follow the natural evaluative makeup of people to evaluate their physical world. We have a natural move toward balance without our necessarily understanding how or why we do. If he had

kept his connection to the physical world in place, he would have seen that his agreement and disagreement would have correlated to whether one had a free-flow framed-reference to allow one to maintain the physical connections to their ideas or not. To use his word, a *soul* that was open to physical reality as the pure source of measurement.

13. *Locke understood that the process of understanding the physical connection to morality (our morality filter) we do not achieved by tradition, but by individual exploration.* What this means is that we do not study ideas given as morality; rather we study the tools to their discovery and understanding. He wrote, "But since the law of nature cannot be known by tradition, all that remains is that it becomes known to men by the light of nature alone." (25, p133) We cannot create repetitive actions within our society and expect people to come to an understanding of our relationship to the physical world. Each of us has to move and work toward this achievement through acquired tools. When we do not know what this tool is, we are lost. When we recognize the existence of the tool, it brings the light of nature to our perceptions. It is against this light of nature that we evaluate.

14. *Since John Locke operated under unaccountable reason and rational thought, he could not push accountability to ideas back to its source.* Locke wrote, "But since, as has been shown elsewhere, this light of nature is neither tradition nor some inward moral principle written in our minds by nature, there remains nothing by which it can be defined but reason and sense-perception. For only these two faculties appear to teach and educate the minds of men." (25, p147) Thesisism teaches this relationship between reason and sense perception. By maintaining this relationship between our thought existence and physical existence, we have accountability to ideas. This accountability we apply to master ideas. What is important here is that he was correct that our moral principles were not written in our minds; rather they were to be read from our physical world. Our evaluative ability to balance seeks its form. It was there in his words. Yet he did not require that "sense-perception" maintain any relationship to reason.

15. *He could have revolutionized human thought and social systems if he only made one further step and required the relationship between physical existence and our ideas to remain.* Unfortunately, he did not maintain the connection to the physical world and he never was able to present such a model. In his correspondence to Molyneux, he wrote, "Though by the view I had of moral ideas, whilst I was considering that subject, I thought I saw that morality might be demonstratively made out, yet whether I am able so to make it out, is another question." (26, L1538) When he wrote, "I thought I saw...," he was *sensing* it through his evaluate-to-balance within him. Nevertheless,

he did not acknowledge that this internal *sensing* was relational to incoming sensory existence from physical existence.

16. *John Locke knew he had to start with the understanding of ideas before he could create an accountability method for morality.* We must have an understanding of how ideas work and how we bring accountability to them before our ideas can have stability and value. It was in his presentation of ideas, how he perceived them that made him so interesting and valuable. His ideas on ideas were an early attempt to bring accountability to human knowledge. Although he started with an understanding that ideas source from the physical world, he did not maintain that connection. He quickly turned away from the physical world and ran into the abyss of human animation. He did not maintain accountability with the sliver idea of reality relational to the real world. Although he maintained a closer relationship with the physical world with his ideas of government, which helped propel him into the well-respected person he is today, he folded his ideas of morality back into the human mind. Under this backdrop, he could not find his accountability method to morality.

17. *The ideas of government by John Locke had closer connections to physical existence.* We can see this in what he wrote. "The state of nature has a law of nature to govern it, which obliges everyone: and reason, which is that law, teaches all mankind, who will but consult it, that being all equal and independent, no one ought to harm another in his life, health, liberty, or possessions." (27, 2nd Treatise, 6) He was saying that the physical world, when measured against, had our code of conduct. By this universal nature to all of us, we were obligated to it. We used reason to find its laws, which in turn taught us our code of conduct. We could find our code of conduct in physical-world items such as our own physical existence, our health, our freedoms and our possessions. This was touching on thesisism. He was pointing out where we could find our code of conduct, which was nature, and which was physical existence. Unfortunately, he did not see that we needed to remove ourselves from the center of existence and place the physical world as the center of existence.

18. *When he included "possessions," he measured against a different expression of physical existence as well.* He cited items that were equal thesis-morality first, such as life, health and liberty. These items are equal to all of us by the virtue of physical existence. Nevertheless, possessions was not an idea based in equal-to-us but in unequal-to-us. John Locke further referenced life and liberty in his book, *A Letter Concerning Toleration.* He wrote, "Civil interest I call life, liberty, health, an indolency of body; and the possession of outward things, such as money, lands, houses, furniture, and the like." (25, p218) His placing possession of things along with life and liberty has had a profound

influence on our subsequent history to our time. The first four are equal-to-us moral issues. Possessions are unequal-to-us moral issues. We handle and respond to these two types differently.

19. *John Locke then added the pursuit of happiness to the idea of liberty.* He wrote, "As therefore the highest Perfection of intellectual Nature, lies in a careful and constant Pursuit of true and solid happiness; so the Care of our selves, that we mistake not imaginary for real Happiness, is the necessary Foundation of our *Liberty.* The stronger Ties we have to an unalterable Pursuit of Happiness in general, which is our greatest Good, and which, as such, our Desires always follow, the more are we free from any necessary Determination of our *Will* to any particular Action, and from a necessary Compliance with our Desire…." (8, II.xxi.51) He took our liberty, which resides in our equal-to-us flow, and colored it with the reactive response of happiness. He had the measurement of our "Perfection of intellectual Nature" not connected to physical existence, but to our ambiguous reactive existence. Having our "highest Perfection of intellectual Nature" tied to the emotion of happiness is different to the view by thesisists that perfection of our intellectual nature is to maintain our thesis-morality equations. We then can pursue our happiness knowing that we have not violated our thesis-morality equations from physical existence and wrongly engaged in coercion. This is intellectual honesty whereas happiness has no requirement to honesty.

20. *John Locke then tied the idea of possessions and property to the idea of happiness.* He wrote, "for the observance of this law gives rise to peace, harmonious relations, friendship, freedom from punishment, security, possessions of our property, and—to sum it all up in one word—happiness." (25, p215) We now have a set of master ideas that sets us up for unjustified coercion. We have no distinction between our equal-to-us moral obligations under liberty and our unequal-to-us moral obligations under possessions. In fact, we have the two paired. There is nothing to stop anyone to begin to animate our unequal-to-us moral obligations as being the same as our equal-to-us obligations. One aspect of equal thesis-morality is that it overrides unequal thesis-morality when conflict occurs. Here we can easily make them the same. When we add in our master idea of pursuit of happiness without the distinction between our two expressions of morality, we provide a potential for manufactured (false) justifications to make our unequal thesis-morality to be equal and even greater than our equal thesis-morality.

21. *Confusion between pursuit of happiness and liberty occurred.* Our pursuit of happiness is a narrow component to our human existence. When we make our pursuit of happiness our greatest good, we expand our ideas to measure against our self-interest desires in an overreaching way. The idea of liberty is a universal type of idea that resides outside of us as a singular entity. Since

liberty is universal, that is, the same for all of us, it is dependent on physical existence for our justifications to limit liberty. It is also independent to our experiential existence, as justification to limit liberty does not reside in any unaccountable movement of sliver and master ideas to create manufactured-based justifications to coercion. Liberty resides in physical existence whereas happiness resides in our experience of reactive existence. The word "pursuit" mixes our universal idea of liberty, which based in physical existence since pursuit involves actions in our physical world, along with our reactive existence of happiness. Nevertheless, our pursuit of happiness is a limited idea that resides in our experiential existence because the result of the pursuit is an individual type of specific happiness.

22. *The pursuit of happiness is a component of liberty and its limitations remain measured from the physical existence of liberty.* Our actions to happiness are numerous and they vary from individual to individual. Each of our movements in the pursuit of happiness is from variations in the physical structure of the human mind and dependent on all thought and reactive variations that occur with the subsequent movement of sliver and master ideas. This makes happiness and the pursuit of happiness relative to each individual. This means that justifications to limit liberty do not come from measuring against happiness or the pursuit of happiness. Our justifications continue to measure against physical existence to determine if we have or not have justifications to limit our liberty to pursue our happiness. When we measure this idea of happiness as being our greatest good, it moves us away from measuring against physical existence and moves us to measure against our personal self-interests independent to accountability. We begin to animate mistakenly that pursuit of happiness is the same as liberty.

23. *John Locke made our pursuit of happiness idea a narrowband idea by the association of possessions and property.* When John Locke, like so many people, added to their pursuit of happiness as our greatest good the possessions and property of material things, he focused his natural law to the inequality between human beings. He actually began to justify limited unequal considerations under the universal idea of liberty. One possession under the pursuit of happiness was, and continues to be, land. This idea goes to the *status* of landowners of his time. Nevertheless, all human beings need space. Land ownership is unique in that it not only involves our equal-to-us aspect of required space, but our unequal-to-us aspects in our differences in need to space. There is individual need for land as well as all-individuals need for land, such as land for crops for food. Land is both relational to the individual and to all individuals (full community). Further, how one uses land can fall under our unequal abilities as well. Because it has both equal-to-us and unequal-to-us expressions, it requires an understanding of both flows,

individual to all individuals and all individuals to individual. In other words, the liberty of land ownership must be under thesis-based justifications as well as no thesis-based justifications for non-ownership. These justifications derive from both of our thesis-morality equations, $E = E$ and $\bar{E} = U \pm D$.

24. *Our justifications for land ownership must arrive from physical existence.* How can we procure any piece of land that which belongs to physical existence and transfer it to any individual? John Locke had this transferred under two arguments. One was that his higher authority gave human beings land. He stated, "it follows from this that he [God][22] has not created this world for nothing and without purpose. ... Hence it is quite evident that God intends man to do something." (25, p157) John Locke animated in his mind that his higher authority gave earth to humankind. He wrote, "God, who hath given the world to men in common, hath also given them reason to make use of it to the best advantage of life and convenience. The earth, and all that is therein, is given to men for the support and comfort of their being. And though all the fruits it naturally produces, and beasts it feeds, belong to mankind in common." (27, 2nd Treatise, 26)

25. *John Locke had just given away the earth.* Where did John Locke get this big give away idea? Nowhere did he show any give away by his higher authority in relation to his higher authority. In relation to his writing, it was outright random declarations. However, if we replace his higher authority with physical existence, then physical existence becomes a measurement source common to all humankind. Physical existence is not a humanlike consciousness; thus, it cannot give away anything. The statement that physical existence was common to all humankind was true. However, the statement that physical existence belonged to humankind was not. Except to the property of oneself, no human being ever had any ownership granted anywhere to anything by a spiritual and conscious higher authority that was not claimed from a book and self-proclaimed authorities. Thomas Paine wrote, "There could be no such thing as landed property originally. Man did not make the earth, and, though he had a natural right to *occupy it*, he had no right to *locate as his property* in perpetuity any part of it: neither did the Creator of the earth open a Land-Office, from whence the first title-deeds should issue." (28, p9)

26. *John Locke gave away the earth to his own like-minded people without any accountability to the taking.* John Locke pandered to the desires of the wealthy. "Though the earth, and all inferior creatures, be common to all men, yet every man has a property in his own person: this nobody has any right to but himself. The labour of his body, and the work of his hands, we may say, are properly his." (27, 2nd Treatise, 27) This was his second argument

22 [God] added for clarity.

for land transfer. Nevertheless, shortly afterward, he wrote, "God gave the world to men in common; but since he gave it them for their benefit, and the greatest conveniences of life they were capable to draw from it, it cannot be supposed he meant it should always remain common and uncultivated." (27, 2nd Treatise, 34) What happened to the "belong to mankind in common" that he wrote earlier in paragraph 24? My goodness, John Locke just gave away the whole store, and if you were not there for the grab, you were just out of luck. It is one thing to make a pot and claim it. To seize large tracts of land is another. We have a mix of a *give away* that involves a specific moment in time mixed with humankind over all time. Was John Locke saying his God gave the earth to humankind at one moment in time during the late seventeenth century, or was the give away across all human beings across all time?

27. *John Locke provided a source of measurement of how and where his God gave land to specific people.* He wrote, "He gave it [land][23] to the use of the industrious and rational (and labour was to be his title to it), not to the fancy or covetousness of the quarrelsome and contentious." (27, 2nd Treatise, 34) With his system of measurement, we have no accountability attached to industrious and rational. Each individual can self-appoint himself or herself to determine if others, he, or she were industrious. Whether one was industrious or filled with fancy, we determined by rational thought. Nevertheless, each individual can use rational thought without the sliver idea of reality required to connect to physical existence. What we determined industrious thus became limited to those that acquired power and determine themselves industrious and not fanciful. This could, and did, result in power to self-appointed landowners to create manufactured-based justifications to use coercion to maintain their power position. John Locke understood that land was common to all humankind. By not having a physically based system of measurement that thesisism offers, he could not provide thesis-based justifications to human actions. Instead, he provided an unaccountable system of thought that allowed those with power to create self-justifications to their individual and personal desires independent to reality.

28. *We can begin to see the perversions that manufactured ideas create.* He stated that no one can steal the property of another, yet allowed his higher authority to seize property. He wrote, "it is a law of nature that every man should be allowed to keep his own property, or, if you like, that no one may take away and keep for himself what is another's property, yet at God's command the binding force of this law can lapse, for this actually happened, as we read, in the case of the Israelites when they departed from Egypt and journeyed to Palestine." (25, p201) W. von Leyden in the footnote stated this

---

23 [land] added for clarity.

referred to the goods they seized from the Egyptians. In other words, any self-proclaimed authority could seize property from others under the claim that their God permitted them.

29. *This is a major problem with manufactured ideas concerning a higher authority.* Anyone can animate anything. This, as we will see in subsequent chapters, creates a null effect. This is how major human injustices survive, such as slavery in the United States, as ideas about property can be animated in anyway anyone wanted. It allows manufactured-based justifications to violate our equal thesis-morality and to justify falsely the use of coercion. Therefore, those that had the correct moral position had to contend themselves with their own constituencies. If we connected property to our pursuit of happiness and that a god gave us property, then disaster can strike, as it did with slavery. John Locke contributed to this notion with ideas such as this when he wrote, "as when God, to whom all things belong; has transferred parts of His dominion to someone and granted the right to give orders to the first-born, for example, and to monarchs; or by the right of contract, as when someone voluntarily surrendered himself to another and submitted himself to another's will." (25, p185) When we have statements like these, as well as his "and all inferior creatures, be common to all men," it led us to wild animations because we had measured against the human mind. When we do not connect our ideas to the physical world, we can create ideas that move all over the place and end with outright contradictions. To give a couple of concrete and narrowband examples, which serve as demonstrations, please allow me the following.

30. *Moral ideas based off human thought existence leads us to moral relativism.* When we have movement of sliver and master ideas in our thought existence that allows the attachment of the sliver idea of reality not to be relational to physical existence, it leads us to conflicting moral stances. This leads us to moral relativism. Early American slavery is an example of the occurrence of moral cancellation when we measured our ideas against thought existence. The idea of slavery as held in the United States prior to emancipation provides us an example of how higher authority ideas can in effect cancel each other out. We have the following examples from the book by William Goodell titled, *Slavery and Anti-Slavery*, printed in 1852.

31. *Example 1:* Goodell wrote of Mr. Stewart, an elder from Illinois. He reported that Mr. Stewart spoke to his General Assembly in 1835 and said, "In this church, a man may take a free-born child, force it away from its parents, to whom God gave it in charge, saying, 'Bring it up for me,' and sell it as a beast, or hold it in perpetual bondage, and not only escape corporal punishment, but really be esteemed an excellent Christian. Nay, even ministers of the Gospel, and Doctors of Divinity, may engage in this unholy traffic, and yet sustain their high and holy calling." (29, p153)

32. *Example 2:* A few pages later, Goodell referenced a pamphlet from the Pittsburg press attributed to Professor Hodge of Princeton. It read, "At the time of the advent of Jesus Christ, slavery in its worst forms prevailed over the world. The Savior found it around him in Judea, the apostles met with it in Asia, Greece, and Italy. How did they treat it? Not by the denunciation of SLAVEHOLDING as a necessarily SINFUL. The assumption that slaveholding is, in itself, a crime, is not only an error, but it is an error fraught with evil consequences." (29, p155)

33. *John Locke found slavery offensive.* He wrote, "Slavery is so vile and miserable an estate of man, and so directly opposite to the generous temper and courage of our nation, that it is hardly to be conceived that an Englishman, much less a gentleman, should plead for it." (27, 1st Treatise, 1) Nevertheless, we have to ask ourselves to what set of sliver ideas to this master idea did he have in mind? Did slavery for John Locke include all races of humankind, or was it restricted to certain races? John Locke had directed this opening sentence from his first treatise against Sir Robert Filmer and his treatise, Patriarcha. Filmer had argued that "'Men are not born free, and therefore could never have the liberty to choose either governors, or forms of government.'" (27, 1st Treatise, 5) The fact was that John Locke was not including other races such as the Africans. The first treatise by John Locke involved argumentation in relation to biblical scripture and Adam. Therefore, his idea of slavery only included races restricted to his narrowband version of slavery. In an essay by Ian Shapiro titled, *Locke's Democratic Theory*, he referenced in note 38, "[John Locke][24] supported and even profited from the African slave trade and slavery in America—not least because African slaves were not captured in war and women and children were enslaved which was expressly prohibited on the just war theory." (27, p334) Here is an example of how two people could agree to the same set of words, but have different narrowband versions of associated master ideas. I would argue that John Locke had a moral reach that was limited in understanding to our equal aspects. In modern times, and as a broadband statement, our moral reach in understanding to our equal aspects has improved.

34. *Unless we measure our ideas to our physical realties, we will articulate moralities that conflict.* Moral cancellation is a dilemma for the holders of god-ideas. They have nothing to measure against except the sliver and master ideas invoked by words on a book that they in turn have the license to shuffle into any desired set of sliver ideas to master ideas. Thus, anyone can make any unaccountable statement. How would thesisism hold against mental animation? No one can stop presentations of absurd mental animations. Nevertheless, when we have our ideas accountable to the physical world,

24 [John Locke] added for clarity.

which is our creation and creator, we can bring ourselves to a focus that can expose the absurd perpetrators. We must measure the words in books—and it includes this book too—against physical existence. Therefore, no thesisist is ever a self-proclaimed authority. Each person deals with the same ultimate authority, physical existence without a self-proclaimed human authority placed in between. The ideas presented by this author represent one attempt to open to our common physical existence. As more and more thesisists measure against physical existence, the greater we can achieve our accuracy. Even holders of higher authority ideas, to which thesisism is not compatible with, can use thesisism. They can if they use the creation of their manufactured higher authority, the physical world, to measure against for his word. Many organized religions probably would not accept this, as it would place the relationship of accountability between each person and the physical world, or in religious terminology, the individual person with their creator, which would bypass them, the self-proclaimed authorities. The physical reality is that we all have human consciousness. We have equality in this human consciousness. No one human consciousness can take as property another human consciousness, even if one willingly surrendered it.[25] It is not for the individual to surrender it and it does not conform to the physical reality of E = E.

35. *We need to evaluate the influence of the inclusion of pursuit of happiness as a human end for all human beings.* We must understand at the onset that our *pursuit of happiness* idea is not a problem in the sense that we need to eliminate it. Rather, we will examine the difference in its character and demonstrate how pursuit of happiness as an end, when not understood and evaluated to physical existence, can lead us to many undesirable ends. Unaccountable systems of thought can and does easily move our pursuit of happiness to extreme individualism while ignoring all individuals. The pursuit of happiness idea without accountability can lead us to the expression of the coercive animal.

36. *To begin to understand why our pursuit of happiness idea can lead us to coercion, we need to examine John Locke.* He wrote, "Thus, how much so ever Men are in earnest, and constant in Pursuit of Happiness; yet they may have a clear View of Good, great and confessed Good, without being concern'd for it, or moved by it, if they think they can make up their Happiness without it." (8, II.xxi.43) He has our happiness not tied to good, but to the pursuit of happiness independent to good. John Locke acknowledged that pursuit

25 When we invoke the idea that no one can surrender their consciousness to another, we are operating in the realm of normal and healthy minds. For dysfunctional and other issues, we always measure against our physical existence for thesis-based actions.

of happiness could just as easily involve the pursuit of bad actions. Our self-interests to our pursuit of happiness are independent to any required moral action. If we link our pursuit of happiness to self-interest, then our self-interests loses its relationship with doing good. We have in a subtle way already began to set aside our E = E equation and our Ē = U ± D equation. It does so because E = E and Ē = U ± D represents our justice equations to equal and unequal thesis-morality respectively and good is expressed when they are balanced. Therefore, John Locke has begun to move our equal thesis-morality and unequal thesis-morality away from its equations by allowing unbalanced and manufactured expressions of justice. We now have opportunities to use out-of-balance equations to create manufactured-based justifications that in turn we can use for arbitrary coercion.

37. *When we have human beings in a constant state of pursing happiness, we have an unnatural human state.* Is the "constant in Pursuit of Happiness" as presented by John Locke really a characteristic of human beings? Certainly, we want to avoid pain, suffering and misery. We saw this with Epicures and we can go back to the beginning of our existence. Human beings do seek happiness in things. A constant pursuit of happiness implies a desired constant state of happiness. It also implies an obsessive state of mind. Adam Ferguson wrote, "Those men are commonly esteemed the happiest, whose desires are most frequently gratified. But if, in reality, the possession of what they desire, and a continued fruition, were requisite to happiness, mankind for the most part would have reason to complain of their lot. What they call their enjoyments, are generally momentary; and the object of sanguine expectation, when obtained, no longer continues to occupy the mind: A new passion succeeds, and the imagination, as before, is intent on a distant felicity." (30, p67) If a constant pursuit led to a constant state of happiness, would a constant state of happiness really be a reasonable statement of human beings. Would not the chemistry of our brains after a while begin to saturate and render the person out of a state of happiness, or perhaps place that person into a state of insanity! What I am leading to is that human beings must seek balance. We have our swing of everyday life and we can justify our swing into happiness frequently, but a constant state of pursuit is an obsession and a form of behavior that leads to isolation between people.

38. *The ideas of life and liberty are different in nature from the pursuit of happiness idea.* Life and liberty are universal in character. They are each a singular idea. The life of everyone is physically equal to all people and no one can remove it without thesis-based justification. Without any thesis-based justification, it becomes immoral action. Liberty too is physically equal to all people, and we cannot deny it without thesis-based justifications. When we measure the idea of liberty properly against the physical world, our liberty is

freedom to physical action contained within thesis-based justifications. Our life and liberty exists in the physical world.

39. *The pursuit of happiness idea does not reside in physical existence, but in thought existence.* We do not have an idea of happiness as a singular idea or multiple ideas that exists in physical existence. The reason for this is that our happiness does not reside in physical existence, but resides in our experiential existence. It is a state of mind. The pursuit of happiness involves the personal desires of people without any requirement to maintain a relationship with reality. When we measure our action to happiness, we do not measure against physical existence, but thought existence against reactive existence back to thought existence. We then are measuring against the chaos of the human mind. We allow ourselves to animate anything to reality or to personal desires of false-reality. When we animate with false reality, we begin to create manufactured-based justifications to any unaccountable end. If people actually achieved the end of their pursuit of happiness and ended in a constant state of happiness, we would render our ability to run society impossible. Nevertheless, we could not achieve a constant state of happiness without saturation and in the end the destruction of our self.

40. *Although the pursuit of happiness idea as a general statement is fine, the pursuit of happiness as an end leads to manufactured ideas by placing ideas through the filer of personal and false-reality desires.* We can connect our experience of happiness back to the source of physical existence. We may have found love, gathered consumer goods or did drugs. Nevertheless, happiness itself only exists in our minds. Happiness does not exist in physical existence. Our life exists in physical existence. Our liberty to move about in our actions requires the balance of actions to our physical existence in relation to all other individuals in physical existence. To experience our happiness may require our actions in physical existence, it also may be independent to our actions by the involvement of nature, but we acquire the idea of happiness by the experience of a coloring of reaction. Our pursuit of happiness as it brings pleasure to life is fine only as a limited idea. Applied universally, a serial killer receives his happiness in the murder of another human being. When we make it an end, it separates us from physical existence. It moves us to seek an altered state of mind that cannot bring balance thought to our society. We create an adhesive framed-reference to alter incoming reality away from truth to preserve personal self-interests without a required accountability.

41. *The pursuit of happiness idea as an end to human beings opens us up for coercion.* John Locke wrote, "For God, having, by an inseparable Connexion, joined *Virtue* and *Public Happiness* together; and made the Practice thereof, necessary to the Preservation of Society, and visibly *beneficial* to all, with whom the virtuous man has to do...." (8, I.iii.6) What John Locke was saying

was that the code of conduct by virtue based on divine law also brought public happiness. Divine law has no physical-world connection. We had to accept the virtue given as divine law, which they provided with self-appointed authorities. If we followed their virtue, we would be happy. If we did not follow it, we were working against the preservation of society. This is a passive-aggressive form of authority. When we apply thesisism, here is our truth. The physical world provides us the source to our code of conduct to which we follow that leads us to a stable society. John Locke dangled the carrot of our pleasure-seeking principle while he tied it to virtue. His virtue comes from his God. Only his self-appointed authorities know his God. We have to rely on the judgment and wisdom of self-appointed authorities. We are now dealing with a measurement system where we *measure against the mind of any self-appointed authority*. His theory allowed the ruling entities around him to rule in any fashion. It did because he had made the pursuit of happiness an end to human actions relative to divine ideas. We have a serious problem because our pursuit of happiness idea without thesis-based justifications becomes a form of coercion.

42. *The pursuit of happiness idea as a human end leads us not to social health, but to a form of obsession and self-indulgence.* Under a thesisistic view, the physical world has made virtue and public contentment its practice, not happiness, necessary to the continuance of our society. Our virtue is our moral thesis equations. Our public content comes about when our thesis-based moral equations are balanced. We express our virtue from each individual to all individuals that equal thesis-morality requires. We express our virtue by the actions of all individuals to each individual that unequal thesis-morality requires. When we conduct ourselves to the physical world, both in ideas and to our thesis-morality filter, as well as our accountability methods to ideas and morality, we find our individual and our all-individuals balance. It is in this moral balance that we find our public contentment. When we have our virtue and public contentment, we can have our individual pursuits, which include our individual pursuit of happiness. We can use the idea of public contentment because we find it in balance to our physical existence, just as life and liberty involves physical-world balance.

43. *John Locke, in some ways, had touched on thesisism.* He wrote, "A state also of equality, wherein all the power and jurisdiction is reciprocal, no one having more than another." (27, 2nd Treatise, 8) This is our equal thesis-morality. He further wrote, "In transgressing the law of nature, the offender declares himself to live by another rule than that of reason and common equality." (27, 2nd Treatise, 8) His statement places our required balance of justice equations squarely in the physical world. Unfortunately, he did not attach the required physical connections to the specific transgressions.

He measured against reason with reason, which was to say the human being mind against the human being mind. He needed to measure reason with physical existence. If he had measured against the first part of his statement, "transgressing the law of nature," he would then have been measuring human being reason against the physical world. There it was, before him and in his hands. He maintained this mixed mode more so with government ideas while not acknowledging the required physical connections. When it came to morality, he broke away completely.

44. *A summary of the life, liberty and thesis pursuit of happiness:* When we have life and liberty followed by pursuit of happiness, we have our equal thesis-morality and universal thesis ideas of the first two followed by a limited thesis idea that resides in a different existence than physical existence. In our idea of life, we have our aspects of equal thesis-morality stated, in that each of us has an equal requirement to life. In our idea of liberty, we each have an equal right not to be restrained to our desired thesis-based actions of liberty. We then followed it with a statement that each of us has the right to be individualistically hedonistic.[26] Under this view, each person has the right to individualism that places the equal aspects of life and liberty on an equal plane to pursuit of happiness. John Locke had his happiness and his continued state of mind in happiness achieved by the acquisition of property and possessions. We ended with animating our unequal thesis-morality to be reasonable acquisition of property and possessions as having priority based on the false idea that pursuit of happiness is equal to life and liberty. We shifted the $\bar{E} = U \pm D$ equation to $E = E$. This then resulted in $U = E$, which is contrary to physical existence and can only exist in human thought existence. We had animated our unequal aspects in our pursuit of happiness to our equal-to-us ideas of life and liberty. We mixed our equal-to-us with our unequal-to-us. This allowed our actions to be justified by ideas that only could exist in our minds. We then ended with manufactured-based justifications to use coercion. This flaw resulted in immoral actions. These flaws permitted acceptance of slavery for a long time. This flaw remains in our current human thought. What we need is life (universal), liberty (universal) and the pursuit of thesis-based happiness (limited), or life, (universal), liberty (universal) and pursuit of public contentment (universal), which allows us to pursue our pursuit of happiness within our thesis-based justifications.

---

26 This statement concerning the idea of pursuit of happiness is in relation to the current view of the general population. Academic or political arguments that the idea of the pursuit of happiness and as an end were relational to specific narrowband arguments, as defined during the times of John Locke, ancient philosophy or current academia or political posturing, does not address our current outlook nor the flaw of ambiguity built-in the various narrowband arguments.

45. *Freedom is actions that we back with thesis-based justifications and do not alter with manufactured-based justification.* John Locke had his ideas about freedom of the individual. He understood that "The freedom then of man, and liberty of acting according to his own will, is grounded on his having reason." (27, 2nd Treatise, 63) He is correct if our use of reason is with accountability. When we back our actions of liberty with thesis-based justifications and rid ourselves of manufactured-based justification, we have our freedom. Thesis-based freedom encompasses all of existence and justifies our action under liberty. Freedom is, and we pass laws to protect it. John Locke understood that we do not grant freedom. Rather, we maintain our freedom by restricting the restrictions to it. He wrote, "So that, however it may be mistaken, the end of law is not to abolish or restrain, but to preserve and enlarge freedom: for in all the states of created beings capable of laws, 'where there is no law, there is no freedom;' for liberty is to be free from restraint and violence from others...." (27, 2nd Treatise, 57)

46. *The last statement by John Locke had strong influence in how the government of the United State of America was intended to run.* We were to design laws only when to avoid the infringement of freedom on people. Our freedom did not translate to the idea that one could do whatever they wanted. Locke understood when he wrote, "for liberty is to be free from restraint and violence from others; which cannot be where there is not law: but freedom is not, as we are told, 'a liberty for every man to do what he lists....'" (27, 2nd Treatise, 57). When we connect our ideas to our physical world, we not only bring clarity to this understanding, but how to distinguish what every man or woman can and cannot do. When Locke wrote "restraint and violence," he was talking about physically based violations. Even when others demand you to think a certain way, this would involve others altering your being in a physical manner. These demands would involve confinement and force by physical actions. To understand the problem with John Locke and his ideas of freedom, we have to look at how he measured his ideas.

47. *Here we have the beginning of our extended order of capitalists taking their cue to use their "no coercion allowed" against them idea.* When John Locke wrote his, "for liberty is to be free from restraint and violence from others...." (27, 2nd Treatise, 57) he gave a broadband statement that was an idea in negation. He provided no information in how to determine what restraint to liberty was. Rather, he spoke to us in our more primitive and reactive evaluate-to-balance. Certainly, most people would agree we ought not to restrain liberty. The problem in the presentation John Locke gave was how could we separate thesis from manufactured restraint? How do we separate thesis from manufactured coercion. If it was true what John Locke wrote that liberty was not, "a liberty for every man to do what he lists," (27, 2nd Treatise,

57) then there are justified times to use coercion in economics just as we use coercion to the idea that we are not allowed to murder.

48. *John Locke gave manufactured-based justifications to give away the earth to selected people, provided false-reality equations that made the pursuit of happiness the same as life and liberty and gave an open-ended view of freedom.* The big give away by John Locke played into the hands of the wealthy of his time. They took the prevailing Christian ideas that invoked ideas of equality and transformed them into their advantage. He further provided manufactured-based justifications to the actions of the wealthy to engage in their actions under the pursuit of happiness idea without any definitive accountability. He had mixed the narrowband and individualistic idea of pursuit of happiness with the all-individuals idea of liberty and life. This provided a predisposed focus on individual actions that in turn carried the same weight and justification to life and liberty. Finally, his view of freedom was diffuse and did not address the problem of when freedom is justified and when perceived or claimed freedom is not freedom. We then have the idea of freedom under the bases of personal desires of individuals to their personal pursuit of happiness independent to physical existence to which no one is allowed coercion against them and god sanctioned all their actions. We now have the beginning of the modern extended order. Since all these collected master ideas worked well for the aristocrats of the time, true rational thought based on nature became a threat. This is where David Hume came into play to protect the ruling class.

David Hume, Rational Thought Sent to the Gallows

1. *David Hume, born in 1711, continues to have his influence today, although few of us realize this fact.* His influence came from his philosophy that brought uncertainty to existence. We have acquired ideas that religion and science not only fails, but also does not exist. We have ideas that physical existence does not exist, that our existence consist of thought existence only. We have arguments that if all we can know is what our mind paints for us, we then can never know reality. It is with this use of reason and rational thought that we have ideas where no one else exists, only you. Some argue not even you, though they may try to save themselves.

2. *These ideas have roots that derive from Hume origins.* Hume had responded to the problem that philosophy historically had, that it could not explain everything. All Hume did was to swing to the opposite end, that perhaps we could not explain anything. He took the limitation of human understanding to a humble form. Nevertheless, if we cannot know the world around us, and we only know what our mind makes, this isolates us from

physical existence. *It amputates the relational action between physical existence and our minds.* Now we have only our own mind to measure against. We animate ideas to unknown ends clouded in darkness. This is where we begin to see the influence of Hume today. I contend that the rise of understanding from those like Thomas Paine and other Deists we had begun to extinguish by the end of the eighteenth century by apologetic Christians. For those with power that desired power over moral actions, Hume provided justifications for a rational argument that rational thought does not apply to economic and social behaviors. We have an irony that Hume used rational thought to dispel rational thought. When we do not have any rational arguments to economic and moral behaviors, how then can we justify any actions we engage in? The darkness of David Hume and a small phrase by Adam Smith took hold within these apologies and brought us a new dark age that continues with us.

3. *During the eighteenth century of Hume, science progressed and landowners and aristocrats grew in numbers.* Specialization in skilled work became even more prominent. New revolutions were taking place in France and in the new country that became the United States. Adam Smith, a political economist during the time of Hume, and a friend of his, published his famous *Wealth of Nations* the same year that Hume died in 1776. Others, such as M. de Vattel, called on the nations an obligation to engage in moral behavior and to measure this obligation against the natural law that people spoke of during that time. (31, p1-2) Nevertheless, the influence of Hume was well established. Nine years before the "invisible hand" publication by Adam Smith, Adam Ferguson wrote, "Every step and every movement of the multitude, even in what are termed enlightened ages, are made with equal blindness to the future; and nations stumble upon establishments, which are indeed the result of human action, but not the execution of any human design." (30, p205) We will see that this statement by Ferguson is astonishingly similar to modern economists, such as Milton Friedman and F. A. Hayek.

4. *Adam Smith provided political and economic justification to the stumbling forward idea to the rise and continuance of an unaccountable form of capitalism with his famous "invisible hand" statement.* Adam Smith dipped into the philosophy of Hume with his "invisible hand" statement that we, under religion and the idea of cause and effect from science, could not understand or comprehend all human actions. We could not comprehend with the *cause and effect* idea from science what was morally correct and what was morally corrupt. Adam Smith and his contemporaries followed with historical philosophy that none of this mattered because we all worked to our mutual benefit and self-interests. In doing this, we chose more often than not to do good over bad. Adam Smith wrote that it was as if we are "led by an invisible hand to promote an end." (1, Book IV, Chapter II, p335) This tiny statement

by Adam Smith, along with pointing to the rejection of reason and rational thought by Hume, and fitting in with the apologetic religious conversation of faith during its time, we were led by the extended order of capitalism to justify their own behavior. They created a faith-based economic system, to which, I think, Hume never intended, and to which we have suffered since and suffer with today, over two hundred years later.

5. *The idea that we cannot comprehend and make models and predictions of human actions may or may not be true, but we do not need to know everything to move with accountability.* The complaint, be it from Hume to the modern extended order of capitalists, assumes an *all or nothing* model. They failed to see that society and social behavior are only the collected actions of individuals. If we have a model that is for each individual, and each individual applies it, we can bring intelligence and moral conduct to the "invisible hand" by Adam Smith. This is what we acquire with thesisism. Thesisism holds this value. Instead of each individual animating in the chaos of their mind, attaching the sliver idea of reality to anything desired, we find our commonality to which we measure our ideas. This commonality is our reality, and our reality is the same for each of us. All arguments that we do not perceive reality directly, that what we see, know, feel and think are creations of our minds does not matter. We all have our common reality, even if painted by our minds, and it results in our common reality to thought existence because of our common physical existence. Under all normal functioning individuals and from our common physical existence that we all find ourselves in, we have common experiences. It is under these common experiences through our interactions with physical existence that we take our cue and begin to conduct ourselves accordingly. Our physical existence is our creator. We as a society must learn to live with our creator under its terms.

6. *Hume, like Locke, started with a definition of what ideas were.* As we have seen with the reason and rational thought from our philosophers, Hume too did not stay connected to physical existence with his ideas. He, like so many others, became Sir Thomas Pope Blount's, "Learning does but serve to fill us of Artificial Errors. That which we so much admire under the name of LEARNING, is only the knowing the fancies of particular Men. (19, Essay II, p33) Likewise, it was with Hume too. After reading many works by philosophers, theologians and economists, what I perceive from each is an output that reflects the thought process of each individual. Perhaps I too could be accused. Yet when I compare thought systems, I am the first to use our physical existence as a source of measurement for *all* ideas. With time, I am sure others will do a better job than I had done. I do not present myself as a great thinker, simply one individual that requires ideas to measure its

relationship, or lack of a relationship, with physical existence. Nevertheless, Hume gave weak definitions of what consisted of ideas.

7. *We can see Hume move his ideas of ideas within our Diagram 2.* He started his *Treatise of Human Nature* immediately with, "All the perceptions of the human mind resolve themselves into two distinct kinds, which I shall call Impressions and Ideas. The difference betwixt these consists in the degrees of force and liveliness, with which they strike upon the mind, and make their way into our thought or consciousness." (9, p5) He referred to his impressions entering with "force and violence" while ideas were "faint images." Already he ignored physical existence in his first statement. His force and violence were in reference to our sensory existence and reactive existence. We find evidence of this when he continued, "We may name *impressions*; and under this name I comprehend all of our sensations, passions and emotions, as they make their first appearance in the soul." (9, p5) His faint images were in reference to our thought existence. He wrote, "By *ideas* I mean the faint images of these in thinking and reasoning; such as, for instance, are all the perceptions excited by the present discourse, excepting only, those which arise from sight and touch, and excepting the immediate pleasure or uneasiness it may occasion." (9, p5) This idea of separating sensory existence with thought existence by evaluating the force and violence verses faint images seems a poor way of starting ones position. He continued with "The first circumstance, that strikes my eye, is the great resemblance betwixt our impressions and ideas in every other particular, except their degree of force and vivacity." (9, p6) It amazes me to read this as he wrote, "that strikes my eye," a common and original source to experience. It revealed one of our original input or sensory sources to our ideas from our sensory existence. However, as used here, the strike of the eye was not this original sensory source but his animating mind!

8. *The force and violence of his impressions was due to its close relationship with physical existence.* Sensory existence is our player to physical existence. It involves a direct interaction. Our sensory existence brings in the actions of physical existence and results in awareness to us. Our reactive existence has its ties to sensory existence as well. Therefore, we have awareness occur to us in the same or near same level of experience that our senses provide us.

9. *The faint images of his ideas were due to their removed relationship from physical existence.* Our ideas reside in our thought existence. All ideas we have were inputted by experience through our sensory or reactive existence. We have faint images because we no longer have the direct perception, or the direct reactive occurrence. Our ideas are always the replay of inputted experience.

10. *Hume then split impressions and ideas into two more distinctions.* He created the idea of simple and complex ideas. His simple impression and ideas

were the sliver ideas to ideas. He never really provided us concrete examples and always wrote of it in the abstract. The best he gave was the following vague example. He wrote, "Simple perceptions or impressions and ideas are such as admit of no distinctions nor separation. The complex are the contrary to these, and may be distinguished into parts. Tho' a particular colour, taste, and smell are qualities all united together in this apple, 'tis easy to perceive they are not the same, but are at least distinguishable from each other." (9, p6) One sliver idea he ignored was the sliver idea of reality. His apple had attached to it the external world experience, and in that experience, we had the common experience of reality. His complex impressions and ideas were the pooling together sliver ideas to make a master idea.

11. *Hume ignored the relationship of physical existence to his ideas of ideas.* By his ignoring the physical-world input and losing their relational aspects to this collection of sliver ideas, he brought in an unaccountable system of thought. Within his first few pages, he already recognized the problem without understanding it. He wrote, "I observe, that many of our complex ideas never had impressions, that correspond to them, and that many of our complex impressions never are exactly copied ideas." (9, p6) When we have ignored the relational aspects of experience to physical existence and we have animated within our human mind the movement of sliver ideas, of course we have ideas that no longer match experience. He gave the example of imagining himself in Jerusalem with pavements in gold and walls with rubies. Why did not he acknowledge that he had rearranged his simple ideas (sliver ideas) into a manufactured idea of Jerusalem that broke the connection to the physical world? Then he related that he saw Paris, but could not form a perfectly copied idea of it in his mind. Why did not he acknowledge the physical limitation of the human mind? Why was he equating the direct experience of something, even as simple as his apple, to that of being an exact copy in the mind? The two are in difference existences. The apple is in physical existence. When we experience the apple, we have the impression created by the physics of physical existence, as with the light bouncing off the apple to the eye and so on. We have the physical events that then traveled our physically created brain to its construction, to which it created the idea. The idea may have good or poor accuracy, even in something as simple as an apple, let alone a complete city!

12. *Hume had the understanding of pure-thesis ideas.* He wrote, "I first make myself certain, by a new review, of what I have already asserted, that every simple impression is attended with a correspondent idea, and every simple idea with a correspondent impression." (9, p7) The experience of his apple came with many impressions that created the sliver ideas, which when pooled together made the pure-thesis idea of an apple. He had the

means to understand the relationship of physical existence with thought existence. He wrote, "This priority of the impressions is an equal proof, that our impressions are the causes of our ideas, not our ideas of our impressions." (9, p8) He had the flow of sensory and reactive existence going in the right direction, to thought existence. Nevertheless, he amputated the connections to physical existence. He wrote, "Ideas produce the images of themselves in new ideas; but as the first ideas are supposed to be derived from impressions, it still remains true, that all our simple ideas proceed either mediately or immediately, from their correspondent impressions." (9, p9) His statement was a good example in how we animate our ideas in relation to our human mind and not to the physical world. The same old problem occurred in that he had us producing new ideas without any relational requirements to ideas that remained connected to physical existence and to those that broke the connections to physical existence. Hume amputated, as with all other philosophers, the relational aspect of physical existence to ideas. If all ideas have sliver ideas to physical existence, does not that mean we have a relational connection to this physical existence, and should not we maintain that relationship. In Diagram 2, Hume worked within the figure in every way except physical existence. Remove physical existence from Diagram 2 and you have Hume and the fancy of everyone in his or hers own minds.

13. *Hume operated close to thesisism, but failed for the same reasons all others failed, the amputation of physical existence.* He acknowledged that, "Since it appears, that our simple impressions are prior to their correspondent ideas, and that the exceptions are very rare, method seems to require we should examine our impressions, before we consider our ideas." (9, p9) Here he was knocking at the door of thesisism. However, what did Hume mean by "before we consider our ideas." Was he saying that this consideration was in relation to truth? Was not to consider impression before our ideas exactly thesisism? Nevertheless, even here we continue locked into the egocentric thought of human beings. The method was not simply the impressions to the ideas, but the relationship these ideas had back to our physical existence. He moved from thought existence in Diagram 2 to sensory existence, but not all the way back to physical existence. Without this additional understanding, we could not see that our moral ideas derived from our physical existence and in our physical structure of being human beings. We could say the idea of angels was the impressions of human beings mixed together with impressions of wings on birds. If we do not measure to our physical existence, we could incorrectly attach the sliver idea of reality to this idea. If our ideas on how to treat people involved the incorrect movement of the sliver idea of reality, it would not matter if we could identify the impressions to each sliver idea. Each master idea, not sliver ideas, by the realities of experience has to fit that experience.

When we make our moral decisions between people, not only the impressions and the simple ideas of Hume must to go back to our physical structure as humans, but his complex ideas must maintain some form of accountability to the sliver idea of reality. When we measure against this physical reality, we can determine if we are dealing with a moral issue that is equal thesis or unequal thesis. The mention of method by Hume does not bring us back to our impressions of ourselves from our viewpoint from physical existence to see what our moral obligations are.

14. *We have further evidence of the fancy of individual philosophers when Hume broke impressions into two further divisions.* Hume wrote, "Impressions may be divided into two kinds, those of SENSATION and those of REFLEXION." (9, p9-10) His sensation seemed to be our reactive existence. It was something that "arises in the soul originally, from unknown causes." (9, p10) Reflexion seemed to be our thought existence. He wrote, "An impression first strikes upon the sense, and makes us perceive heat or cold, thirst or hunger, pleasure or pain of some kind or other. Of this impression there is a copy captured by the mind, which remains after the impression ceases, and this we call an idea." (9, p10) He had sensory existence in play. Heat and cold arrives from our sense of touch. Thirst and hunger arrives from our internal sensing ability in the brain. Pleasure and pain arrives from various senses, be it visual, sound, touch and more. Hume placed ideas into the copy of the mind. This we can interpret to be thought existence. He understood that these ideas could move back to reactive existence to trigger reactive responses. He wrote, "This idea of pleasure and pain, when it returns upon the soul, produces the new impressions of desire and aversion, hope and fear, which may properly be called impressions of reflexion, because derived from it." (9, p10) We now begin to see that he was developing a model of the human mind, but consistently ignored physical existence and the relationship that any idea may or may not have had to it. Just like our lungs breath in air, our mind brings in physical existence.

15. *He made the distinction between thesis and manufactured ideas while ignoring the needed connection to physical existence.* He wrote about the difference between memory and imagination by measurement against the idea of vivacity. He applied vivacity to memories and when the idea lost its vivacity, it moved to imagination. His move from memories of experience to imagination by use of vivacity was crude. We commonly think of memories as derived by our experience. However, memories do not have to connect to physical existence. For example, we can have memories from induced altered states of consciousness. However, memories typically are from our experiences that arrive from our senses. During the time of Hume, no one considered altered states. Imagination for Hume was essentially our thought existence.

Our imagination can involve the movement of sliver ideas. We do not allow this movement for our memory. Hume recognized this when he wrote,

> There is another difference betwixt these two kinds of ideas, which is no less evident, namely that tho' neither the ideas of the memory nor imagination, neither the lively nor faint ideas can make their appearance in the mind, unless their correspondent impressions have gone before to prepare the way for them, yet the imagination is not restrained to the same order and form with the original impressions; while the memory is in a manner tied down in that respect, without any power of variation. (9, p11)

He was distinguishing between pure-thesis ideas and ideas that have undergone mental animation; that is, the movement of sliver ideas. He could classify memories with the same strength as pure-thesis ideas and perhaps even conclusive-thesis ideas when he wrote, "The chief exercise of the memory is not to preserve the simple ideas, but their order and position." (9, p11) Understand that his simple idea was the individual sliver idea, whereas memory was the master idea that related back to our physical existence in a complete manner.

16. *What he never made clear and what he left open to manipulation was the sliver idea of reality.* If his "order and position" meant to be relational to physical existence, then he would have accounted for the sliver idea of reality and he would have been correct. If his "order and position" meant to be relational to thought existence, then he would not have had the sliver idea of reality accounted for in any reordering of sliver and master ideas. Nevertheless, we could definitively say Hume meant the latter, as Hume had never made the sliver idea of reality required to follow ideas to truth, and in his imagination, the accountability of the sliver idea of reality was never specifically stated. In doing this, all ideas—pure-thesis and conclusive-thesis, and pure-manufactured and theorized-manufactured—could fall under his imagination. We can see this when he wrote, "The same evidence follows us in our second principle, *of the liberty of the imagination to transpose and change its ideas.*" (9, p11) This means he only had memory equal to pure-thesis ideas. Anyone that placed the sliver idea of reality into any idea could claim that reality as truth independent to memory. He had no relational measurement to when we reorder our sliver and master ideas in our thought existence.

17. *Hume came close to thesisism.* In his attempt to dissect human thought, he wrote,

> The fables we meet with in poems and romances put this entirely out of the question. Nature there is totally confounded, and nothing mentioned but winged horses, fiery dragons, and monstrous giants.

Nor will this liberty of the fancy appear strange, when we consider, that all our ideas are copied from our impressions, and that there are not any two impressions which are perfectly inseparable. Not to mention, that this is an evident consequence of the division of ideas into simple and complex. Where-ever the imagination perceives a difference among ideas, it can easily produce a separation. (9, p11)

All Hume needed to do was to ask the following question. How could we then keep accountability of ideas to the "order and position" of nature? His thinking was close when he wrote, "As all simple ideas may be separated by the imagination, and may be united again in what form it pleases, nothing would be more unaccountable than the operations of that faculty, where it not guided by some universal principles, which render it, in some measure, uniform with itself in all times and places. Were ideas entirely loose and unconnected, chance alone would join them; and 'tis impossible the same simple ideas should fall regularly into complex ones...." (9, p11-12) Unfortunately, Hume never questioned what the "universal principles" were. Instead, he moved to the chaos of the human mind.

18. *Our universal principle resides outside of ourselves.* Our philosophers and theologians understood our minds reacted to some "universal principles." Nevertheless, no one ever understood that the *universal principle* we *sensed* was our relationship with physical existence. The physical structure of our mind gives us the impression that the *universal principle* is internal, as it results from physical existence operating against our evaluate-to-balance. Nevertheless, the source always was and is outside of us.

19. *Hume moved away from thesisism and into cause and effect.* He wrote, "The qualities, from which this association arises, and by which the mind is after this manner conveyed from one idea to another are three, *viz.* RESEMBLACNE, CONTIGUITY in time or place and CAUSE and EFFECT." (9, p12) He then wrote, "I believe it will not be very necessary to prove" and "Tis likewise evident" when referring to resemblance and contiguity. He quickly moved to cause and effect. It was, however, in the resemblance and contiguity that the answers resided. Perhaps the idea of cause and effect from science, which had intellectual popularity during his time, shifted his attention to cause and effect when trying to deal with the idea of ideas. It was here that he fatally fell into the chaos of the human mind. It was so because resemblance and contiguity were relational to physical existence. Cause and effect was the animation between ideas. When he started without the requirement that his simple ideas and set of simple ideas to the complex idea maintain a status with the sliver idea of reality, he embraced the same "unaccountable" "operations of that faculty" he just claimed we needed in

paragraph 17. His idea of "universal principles" was the same source to his own conception of simple ideas, which was physical existence. Perhaps he had, as well as humankind in general, an egocentric belief in the grandness of humankind and our thinking machine that made the ideas of resemblance and memory, contiguity and reality insignificant to the greatness of our mental animation abilities. Nevertheless, without this simple connection, physical existence was denied, ignored and made insignificant.

20. *When he moved to the idea of cause and effect, he broke away any capability to bring accountability to ideas.* By moving his thought to cause and effect, he brought in science to explain human understanding. Science wiggles the physical world and observes its effects. When it comes to ideas, what is there to wiggle? There is nothing to wiggle. There is a measurement of scientific ideas to the physical world. When in science a wiggle results in something, we understand its existence better in terms of cause and effect. However, our ideas in science we make made relational to physical existence to physical existence. For science, cause and effect is a way to evaluate their ideas about the physical world. How well the ideas connect to physical existence determines the end evaluation and categorization. We do not need any wiggle for our social ideas. Instead, social ideas are a relational quest to our physical world and our thought existence. Part of that physical world is other human beings and our behaviors between us. We observe, and not wiggle, that we have a common physical existence call human consciousness. We observe, and not wiggle, that we have differences between human beings. It is then no surprise that Hume found fault with cause and effect reason for social actions. We have a square peg for a round hole.

21. *Hume never distinguish ideas of reality with manufactured realities, thus he rejected reason and rational thought.* He wrote, "I would renew my question, *why from this experience we form any conclusion beyond those past instance, of which we have had experience.*" (9, p73) When we try to find cause and effect in human behavior, we are dealing with a different reality than with science. In science the cause and effect is in relation to physical existence to physical existence. We have cause and effect with the interaction of physical existence and the input into our minds that result in the possibility to bring up ideas in experiential existence. This nevertheless remains relationally physical existence to physical existence. For human behavior, the attempt at cause and effect is in human *experiential existence* and the arrangement of each sliver idea to master ideas. If the attachment of the sliver idea of reality is not required to measure back to the physical world, we have lost our common measurement point. Since we can make any random mental animation with the attachment of reality, we cannot begin to measure against our minds when our measurement points, our attachment of the sliver idea of reality, can be different for every

individual. The physical world operates within its laws of physics. Human beings on the other hand can animate anything within the acquired sliver ideas from physical existence into any form we desire. At some fundamental level, there may be cause and effect in the action of experiential existence derived by the physical action of physical existence. Nevertheless, without any accountably to human thought, we cannot even begin to find cause and effect to ideas. The only possibility is if a uniformed thought existence was somehow to occur and then we change ideas in certain populations to see the different outcomes. Nevertheless, this is not feasible and certainly not practical. Cause and effect in physical existence is not equal to cause and effect in experiential existence. In paragraph six of the chapter, *"Is Our Use of Reason Accountable?"* we have a *why* to explain the cause and effect. This *why* for science is always relational to a stable and uniform physical existence. When we apply the cause and effect idea to human thought, we have an additional *why*, which we refer to as *why-2*. This *why-2* explains the unstable and non-uniform thought existence between human beings.

22. *Hume was correct that reason broke down under the cause and effect idea applied to human actions.* Reason is only accountable when measured against physical existence. We have allowed our mental animations not to be accountable to physical existence. We have allowed our mental animations to be free to think anything we have wanted and we have allowed ourselves to place the idea of reality anywhere we wanted. Since this is a fact during the time of this writing, it is only reasonable, if I may say, that Hume wrote the following. He wrote, "Thus not only our reason fails us in the discovery of the ultimate connexion of causes and effects, but even after experience has informed us of their constant conjunction, 'tis impossible for us to satisfy ourselves by our reason, why we should extend that experience beyond those particular instance, which have fallen under our observation." (9, p73) Our failure with reason resides in the unaccountable system of thought we have allowed. Consider what Hume wrote here. "Reason can never shew us the connexion of one object with another, tho' aided by all past instances. When the mind, therefore, passes from the idea or impression of one object to the idea or belief of another, associate together the ideas of these objects, and unite them in the imagination." (9, p73) We can see that the reason for the breakdown of reason was that "when the mind passes from the idea of one object to another," we had no accountability. We have allowed our sliver ideas to move without any requirement on our part to connect to our physical world. This same problem showed itself when Hume wrote, "Reason can never satisfy us that the existence of any one object does ever imply that of another; so that when we pass from the impression of one to the idea or belief of another, we are not determined by reason, but by custom or principle of

association." (9, p77) Since our custom had for its source manufactured ideas or the "principle of association," this principle allowed the sliver idea of reality to be placed without any measurement back to physical existence. Certainly then our "reason can *never satisfy us,*" as we are filled with false-reality and adhesive framed-references.

23. *Hume revealed his lack of understanding that our use of rational thought must maintain accountability to the movement of the sliver idea of reality.* He wrote, "If one person sits down to read a book as a romance, and another as a true history, they plainly perceive the same ideas, and in the same order; nor does the incredulity of the one, and the belief of the other hinder them from putting the very same sense upon the author. His words produce the same ideas in both; tho' his testimony has not the same influence on them." (9, p77) What he neglected to understand here was that we have a different framed-reference created for each person. As they read the book, the attachment of sliver ideas to the incoming ideas from the book would change their perceptions to different directions. What he implied here, and what the extended order of capitalists jumped onto, was that the same experience between people could lead to different outcomes. However, our two readers to the same book will never come with the same life experiences and framed-references. He was incorrect that they "plainly perceive the same ideas." Perceptions reside in our experiential existence. The words on the pages are only words on pages. Many, like Hume here, used this to conclude the inability of reason to assist humankind in social affairs.

24. *Hume confounded himself with his confusion between physical-world actions and developed experiential existences.* What Hume misunderstood was that this was not physical existence measuring against physical existence. It was physical existence triggering experiential existence through different individual framed-references. Without the accountability of the sliver idea of reality, we could not begin to measure, as our measurement base is unknown and different for each person. We actually can use the reading a novel example under different percepts to demonstrate how breaking the connections to our physical world leads to different mental animations. The attached sliver idea of implied reality, one a romance book, the other a book of true history, contributes to two different framed-references. When we add in that each person lived a life of unaccountable thought, we widened the different responses even further. The physical reality was that the book was a romance novel, a history, or something else. To align the book with truth and reality, we have to narrowband to what it actually was to create the common influenced framed-reference needed for the understanding. If the master idea of what the book was about was different for each person, the subsequent animations would be different and each would have different experiential existence occurrence.

In his own example, one framed-reference had non-reality attached as a romance and the other framed-reference had reality attached as history. The two situations were not the same. Therefore, of course the outcomes would be different, even without any additional influence from an adhesive framed-reference. His own premise of different outcomes to the same book was flawed. Hume had demonstrated the problem of unaccountable reason and rational thought without having a clear understanding or presentation to why it was not usable.

25. *Hume seemed to fall for the idea that our mental world had no relationship with physical existence.* In his conclusions, he wrote,

And how must we be disappointed, when we learn, that this connexion, tie, or energy lies merely in ourselves, and is nothing but that determination of the mind, which is acquired by custom, and causes us to make a transition from an object to its usual attendant, and from the impression of one to the lively idea of another? Such a discovery not only cuts off all hope of ever attaining satisfaction, but even prevents our very wishes; since it appears, that when we say we desire to know the ultimate and operating principle, as something, which resides in the external object, we either contradict ourselves, or talk without meaning. (9, p203-204)

He was lamenting that what we could ever know was only our experiential existence. Our experiential existence could not know our physical existence, as it was only an impression of physical existence. Hume trivialized and amputated our physical interactions between mind and physical existence. Because our mind colors in the physical world around us does not lead to his conclusion that we must be disappointed and that it is nothing but. Our experiential existence is the real *result* of physical interactions.

26. *Hume confused human conscious experience with a manufactured idea that physical existence had consciousness of itself.* Physical existence has no conscious experience and thus there are no direct impressions of physical existence in existence. Nevertheless, our experiential existence is the interactions of physical existence and we have a common relationship with our experience and physical existence. To put it another way, Hume laments that we are not imaginary divine beings. Under this absurd measurement, he concluded we were stupid, disappointing and talked without meaning. When we accept that reason and rational thought are unaccountable systems of thought, his conclusion of our breakdown of rational thought was correct. He was referring to the absurdities that came from our historical use of reason and rational thought, since it too measured against the human mind when trying to understand humankind. He wrote, "Nothing is more dangerous

to reason than the flights of the imaginations, and nothing has been the occasion of more mistakes among philosophers." (9, p204) Hume found that reason and rational thought were unaccountable systems of thought. What he did not know was how to bring accountability to it. Instead of reaching out to physical existence, he shut it out. In doing that, he opened the door to those that desired coercion to cite Hume as justification to their unjustifiable ends.

27. *Hume opened the door for people to set aside reason and rational thought and to move forward ideas based on faith.* The ruling class now had a method of providing justifications to ideas given to them by John Locke. The extended order of capitalism found a way to justify itself and their personal pursuits without required accountability. Hume wrote, "Shall we, then, establish it for a general maxim, that no refined or elaborate reasoning is ever to be received?" (9, p205) If we could not know from our reasoning, what then could we do? He wrote further,

> We have, therefore, no choice left but betwixt a false reason and none at all. For my part, I know not what ought to be done in the present case. I can only observe what is commonly done; which is, that this difficulty is seldom or never thought of; and even where it has once been present to the mind, is quickly forgot, and leaves but a small impression behind it. (9, p205)

Hume created a narrowband idea that excluded examination into other forms of reason. Well, let us accept the challenge that Hume presented. Let us think about his claim that we only had a choice between *a false reason and none at all.*

28. *Is our choice between false reason and none at all, all we have?* What stuck me first was the adjective *false* to the word reason. If Hume found reason to be false, then what made it false? He faulted reason to the imagination and the cause and effect of ideas that which could move to ends different from what reality showed us in the end. This was so because we had an unaccountable form of reason. The cause and effect by Hume resided in the movement of ideas within the human mind, but they had no relationship to the original inputs from physical existence. He never considered the idea that we have reality attached to clusters of sliver ideas to the master idea and that we must maintain them relationally to their origins. When we bring accountability to reason, we no longer have a false form of reason. We have reason with accountability per individual with a common measurement point, our physical existence. Wrongly convicted, Hume sent reason and rational thought to the gallows.

29. *If we bring accountability to reason and rational thought through thesisism, this changes all the subsequent thought that came from David Hume and transferred to the extended order of capitalism.* It changes the "invisible hand" idea of Adam Smith from a system of thought where we rely on a mysteriously hand to a system of thought to where we can guide the hand accountably individual by individual. We will see in *Book Three* that this removes the position of Hayek and Friedman that we cannot govern ourselves because reason and rational thought fails. It changes their claim that we have to accept their faith-based capitalism and their self-created rules of the game. It also places more credence into the position by Thomas Paine that every individual has equality and that every individual has say in his or her existence in relation to others. When we consider this, we end back to our equal and unequal thesis-morality.

30. *It changes the ideas of morality by Hume as well.* Since Hume viewed reason under the cause and effect idea applied to the animations in human thought, and the cause and effect idea of science was a misuse of experimentation with physical existence extended to human thought existence, we had the use of a form of reason that did not exist in reality. Thought existence and physical existence are two different existences where cause and effect cannot cross. The use of cause and effect in thought existence broke the connection to physical existence and it became a manufactured idea. Therefore, Hume was correct when he wrote, "Since morals, therefore, have an influence on the actions and affections, it follows, that they cannot be derived from reason; and that because reason alone, as we have already proved, can never have any such influence." (9, p355) He quickly followed with "The rules of morality, therefore, are not conclusions of our reason." (9, p355) When we allow the use of reason to have ideas that start with broken connections to physical existence, his statement indeed becomes correct.

31. *We can see the significant difference between thesisism and historical reason and rational thought when we examine a statement made by Hume himself.* He wrote, "As long as it is allowed, that reason has no influence on our passions and actions, 'tis in vain to pretend, that morality is discovered only by a deduction of reason. An active principle can never be founded on an inactive; and if reason be inactive in itself, it must remain so in all its shapes and appearances, whether it exerts itself in natural or moral subjects, whether it considers the powers of external bodies, or the actions of rational beings." (9, p355) When we look at the sky, we respond to its existence. How our sky looks, we may reason to what actions we may engage in, be it rain or shine. However, the sky is not something you reason, as it simply is, but how it differs or not differs, move the actions of people based on experience. That would be a thesis use of reason. Morality, when made relational not to

the idea, but to physical existence, becomes the sky. Our minds and bodies are the same as the existence of the sky, as they have physical existence. How our minds and bodies differ or not differ, moves the actions of people based on experience. It is not that reason is the active principle; it is that physical existence is the active principle.

32. *Despite Hume claiming we could not understand morality with the use of reason, he continued to make claims to a maxim that contradicted his claim.* He wrote in his chapter, *Of Justice and Injustice,* "In short, it may be established as an undoubted maxim, *that no action can be virtuous, or morally good, unless there be in human nature some motive to produce it, distinct from the sense of its morality.*" (9, p369) If this is so, then could not we measure morality against a form of reason with accountability? His word "motive" is part of the historical definition of reason and rational thought. If we could connect this to the physical world, we could then bring it to a form of accountability. Further, in the same sentence, he used the word "sense" in relation to morality. Again, we had Hume using words that were part of the historical definition of reason and rational thought. You could replace those words with the word reason and it would remain the same. "*unless there be in human nature some* reason *to produce it, distinct from the* reason *of its morality.*" This seems to me a contradiction to what Hume claimed about reason. Yes, he was referring to justice and injustice. Nevertheless, in thesisism, as in physical reality, morality is the balance of the justice equations. When our E = E and Ē = U ± D justice equations are met, morality is met. When they are out of balance, morality is out of balance; meaning immoral actions are taking place. Therefore, Hume again bumped into thesisism when dealing with the idea of justice and injustice. He had ideas of artificial justice and natural justice. His natural justice mimicked thesis-based justice by suggesting a connection to the physical world while his artificial justice mimicked manufactured-based justice by suggesting a missing connection to the physical world.

33. *Unfortunately, the inability of Hume to discover reason with accountability, which led to the only option of false reason or none at all, gave way to provide the extended order of capitalism free access to unaccountable actions.*[27] It allowed people to justify under manufactured ideas, actions that led to coercion of others. The nature and the extent of their manufactured ideas and coercion we have yet to define more fully. I have already hinted at a few

---

27 Hume provided the extended order of capitalism free access to unaccountable actions. This is not an absolute statement that members of capitalism always use immoral actions. Rather, it provided opportunities for people to animate in their mind, manufactured-based justifications to engage in immoral actions. Whether individuals engage in immoral actions, knowingly or unknowingly, depends on each individual situation.

ideas, such as our pursuit of happiness, God granting earth to humankind and a universal application of no coercion allowed to stop freedom and liberty as a few. Individually these ideas vary in truth, but how they have been pulled together to create and use coercion becomes problematic. Until we bring accountability to reason and rational thought in our thought existence, manufactured coercion will continue. The accountability system of thesisism occurs when each individual begins to understand it and uses it to bring control to coercion by thesis-based justifications. Once this occurs, it will release our natural freedoms and liberties.

Ethan Allen, Rational Fantasies

1. *Ethan Allen is a good example of how close humankind had come to a system of thought with accountability.* When we hear the name Ethan Allen, most of us think of him as one of the Green Mountain boys during the revolutionary war. What most of us do not know was that he was a Deist. His thought system is an excellent example of how our broadband definition of reason could lead us in right direction and how any fundamental manufactured idea attached to its beginning skewed the reality it sought. The reluctance to view physical existence as not only creation, but our creator as well, has allowed thinkers of our times to animate their positions in relation to their personal existence. John Locke, David Hume, Adam Smith and more developed their ideas in relation to their personal needs and not relational to physical existence. They justified themselves to their found position, not to the truth of our physical world. We can see this flaw well demonstrated with Ethan Allen because he reasoned away from his found position and came close in eliminating self-justification.

2. *He knew that when he applied reason in relation to the law of nature, it led to improvement of reason.* He wrote, "The desire of knowledge has engaged the attention of the wise and curious among mankind in all ages, which has been productive of extending the arts and sciences far and wide in the several quarters of the globe, and excited the contemplative to explore nature's laws in a gradual series of improvements, 'till philosophy, astronomy, geography and history, with many other branches of science, have arrived to a great degree of perfection." (32, p23-24)

3. *Ethan Allen recognized that most people did not engage in a form of reason with accountability.* He wrote, "It is nevertheless to be regretted, that the bulk of mankind, even in those nations which are most celebrated for learning and wisdom, are still carried down the torrent of superstition...." (32, p24) He saw that for most of the human population around him, they carried ideas that did not line up with his *nature's laws.*

141

4. *Nevertheless, he continued to maintain the manufactured idea about a higher consciousness.* He wrote, "to endeavor to reclaim mankind from their ignorance and delusion, by enlightening their minds in those great and sublime truths concerning God and his providence." (32, p24) We can see his attempt to align the unaccountable system of thought of those around him with the reality of nature he saw. We can see his attempt to focus on the physical world when he wrote,

> Though, '*None by searching can find out God or the Almighty to perfection*,' yet I am persuaded, that if mankind would dare to exercise their reason as freely on those divine topics, as they do in the common concerns of life, they would, in a great measure rid themselves of their blindness and superstition, gain more exalted ideas of God and their obligations to him and one another, and be proportionally delighted and blessed with the views of his moral government, make better members of society, and acquire many powerful incentives to the practice of morality, which is the last and greatest perfection that human nature is capable of. (32, 24-25)

5. *Ethan Allen viewed his God in terms of dependency on existence and self-existence.* Ethan Allen pointed out that our physical world had "THE Law of Nature having subjected mankind to a state of absolute dependence on something out of ... gave them the first conception of a superior principle existing...." (32, p25) The first idea connects to our physical world. We are dependent on our physical existence. This dependency is not in relation to whether we can manipulate it or not, as in science, but that our existence is dependent on the existence of the physical world. It is something we come "out of." It is something that all things come "out of." Ethan Allen then applied rational thought to this idea to create the superior principle idea.

6. *He could not break the snare of manufactured ideas concerning a higher-authority consciousness.* He continued with, "But this sense of dependency, which results from experience and reasoning on the facts, which every day cannot fail to produce, has uniformly established the knowledge of our dependence to every of the species who are rational, which necessarily involves or contains in it the idea of a ruling power, or that there is a GOD, which ideas are synonymous." (32, p25-26) What Ethan Allen failed to understand was that when he changed from his observation that we are dependent on nature and the ruling power it had on us and moved it to the ruling power having a consciousness, he broke from physical existence. He broke it because nothing in physical existence demonstrates consciousness. The order we bring with our mind is not the same as the order in physical existence. He had, as like so many people, animated the idea of human order to a non-human

system. He moved the sliver idea of human, a being with consciousness, to the non-human existence of physical existence. He had the *bases* of the god-idea as a ruling power on the dependency we had on our physical world. As we will see in short, he pushed back the idea of a conscious God and placed our immediate concerns to the reality around us. Nevertheless, his *bases* to the notion of a ruling power on our dependency, remarkably aligns with the position of thesisists that our physical existence is our source of measurement because the ruling power is physical existence.

7. *His alignment came in with the relational aspects of idea position.* The religious made our physical world the product of a conscious authority and called it creation. They had animated a creator to this creation. Because they had moved the sliver idea of a human consciousness to this manufactured creator, it set up the manufactured idea that communications between this manufactured creator and us was humanlike. That is, it talked and wrote like human beings. In thesisism, creation is the action of physical existence. Our creator is physical existence. This places our creator one-step closer. It also becomes apparent that our creator is not a humanlike consciousness. How our creator communicates to us is by the non-conscious action of physical existence to create our minds. Our minds are the product of physical existence that we use to understand the reality we live in. Therefore, our communication with our creator is a combination of our (accountable) rational abilities, which we must rest on the principles of thesisism, measured against the existence of our creator and the results that our (accountable) rational thought engages in. This is why our moral code of conduct is the examination of the human physical structure, which reveals our equal and unequal physical aspects. For Ethan Allen the idea of a higher consciousness remained, but he pushed it back and made our physical existence greater in importance to our rational thought abilities. Although it remains incorrect, it was in the correct direction.

8. *Ethan Allen moved his idea of God to the background.* He viewed his ideas about his God in terms of cause and effect, to which cause and effect is what science concerns itself with in physical existence. He recognized that the problem with cause and effect was that it had no beginning or end. He wrote, "Although we extend our ideas retrospectively ever so far upon the succession, yet no one cause in the extended order of succession, which depends upon another prior to itself, can be the independent cause of all things: nor is it possible to trace the order of the succession of causes back to that self-existent cause, inasmuch as it is eternal and infinite...." (32, p28) His self-existent cause was his God. He tied his god-idea to the actions of the physical existence around him. He wrote, "so that we may with certainty conclude that the system of nature, which we call by the name of natural causes, is as

much dependent on a self-existent cause...." (32, p29) It was actually a nice argument. He did not claim any consciousness to this self-existence because, simply by his reasoning, there had to be a self-existent, otherwise we continue in an endless succession of backtracked causes. With this idea of a self-existent cause, it moved any intervening, humanlike god away to a greater distance, and to a whisper. He attempted to remove the chatter of the human mind and remove the human being between people and truth by writing, "Thus it is from the works of nature that we explore its great author...." (32, p35) What then does Ethan Allen bring up to the front for humankind to observe and measure against?

9. *The God of Ethan Allen became an animation of physical existence with an original mover far in the distance.* His original creator became less important that the creation. If we replaced his idea of God with physical existence, what would happen? We have some evidence that we can. He wrote, "A sensibility of mere dependence includes the idea of something, on which we depend (call it by what name we will) which has a real existence, in as much as a dependency on nonentity is inadmissible, for that the absence or non-existence of all being could not have caused an existence to be. But should we attempt to trace the succession of the causes of our dependence, they would exceed our comprehension...." (32, p27-28) What "on which we depend" is, is our physical world, and our physical world "has a real existence." Physical existence is, from a human life timeline, unchangeable. It is also our source to our moral code of conduct. Listen to his words with God as physical existence. "But as God (physical existence) is unchangeably and infinitely just and good, as well as infinitely wise and powerful, he (physical existence) can therefore never vary from the rectitude of his moral character...." (32, p37) Ethan Allen had the just and the good obtained by rational thought with accountability (thesisism), as it measured against the physical world. Physical existence is our source to truth. Therefore, non-conscious expression of human attributes was infinitely wise and powerful. Physical existence is absolute, thus the moral code of conduct we derive from it never could vary.

10. *Ethan Allen came close to the fundamental principle of thesisism that accountability of ideas requires the maintenance of the relational aspects of sensory input to thought existence. Part 1:* One of the positions of thesisism is that we have sensory input that we can convert to ideas. Sensory existence includes not only ideas from our vision, hearing and other senses, but from our internal actions of our body and reactive existence as well. He wrote, "Human nature is compounded of sensation and reflection." (32, p142) Ethan Allen used the word sensation to acknowledge this flow of physical action. He used the word reflection to acknowledge the resulting idea in thought existence. He recognized that experience of our senses moved to our ideas. He wrote,

"WHATEVER external object presents itself to the senses, gives the mind an apprehension of it." (32, p144) He moved this apprehension of it to the idea of "simple ideas." (32, p144) I suspect his idea of simple ideas derived from having read John Locke and David Hume, but Ethan Allen did not state this. Nevertheless, he never maintained the relationship between the sources of the simple ideas to accountability of ideas. He wrote, "It is on simple ideas, which the mind thus mediately obtains through the instrumentality of its senses, that all our proficiency in knowledge and sciences is predicated." (32, p145) He then followed with, "WHATEVER improvement the mind makes in its reflection, invention and reasoning, upon simple ideas, are the proficiencies of intelligence; for sensation is one entire and simple exertion, which does not admit of improvement; but it is the mind which improves upon those original images. The ideas thus deducible from those which we denominate simple, are vastly more numerous than those original images themselves...." (32, p 150-151) Ethan Allen had recognition that the mind created many ideas derived from experience. Nevertheless, he said nothing about the relationship of the original experience to the mental animation that had occurred to create those numerous ideas.

11. *Ethan Allen came close to thesisism. Part 2:* He had attempted to describe thesisism without his own understanding of it. He attempted to connect rational thought to the physical world, but his inability to reject ideas about a higher conscious prevented him in making that next needed step. Here is an example. He wrote, "When from a deduction of reasoning on the works of nature, or from any particular part thereof, we draw an inference of God's goodness to man, by reasoning on the ultimate tendency of the natural world to subserve the moral, we deduce a moral inference from elementary and material things, which is that which we denominate to be the progressive act of raciocination." (32, p151) He tried to connect ideas to the physical world, as he *senses* in his rational thinking that accountability applied to this type of thought. When we replace his idea of "we draw an inference of God" with "we draw an inference from physical existence," which he actually replaced his God with the "natural world" later in the same sentence, we begin to see that he had a *sense* of where to go for accountability to ideas. He stated that moral ideas were obtain from the "inference from elementary and material things," which he said could be logically followed. This is a move toward thesisism.

12. *The problem was that in his reflection, our thought existence, he never required the measurement of reflection to maintain from his simple ideas the position of the sliver idea of reality.* He viewed sensation and his simple ideas as not being able to contribute anything. He wrote, "We may nevertheless for certain, determine that sensation is not reflection." (32, p155) It was true that sensory existence and thought existence were not the same. He further made

this distinction by writing, "It is as natural for the mind to reflect, reason or philosophize upon the works of nature, as it is for sensation to represent to the mind the first and simple perception of them." (32, p155) However, like John Locke, he never carried it to the next needed step. He did not see that to maintain the reality position of any idea, one had to maintain it to our physical existence. Rather, he left the mind to reflect unaccountably against itself, which included reason and rational thought. When we have unaccountable reason and rational thought, even the idea of faith could become a rational idea. If you do not believe me, here is how Ethan Allen did it.

13. *Ethan Allen connected the idea of faith with reason and rational thought.* He viewed faith as the final move of rational thought. He wrote, "Faith is the last result of the understanding, or the same which we call the conclusion, it is the consequence of a greater or less deduction of reasoning, from certain premises previously laid down; it is the same as believing or judging of any matter of fact...." (32, p331) He also wrote, "And inasmuch as faith necessarily results from reasoning, forcing itself upon our minds by evidence of truth...." (32, p332) Through his use of reason, faith was the *logical* conclusion leading to its acceptance as fact. He continued with "for the faith of the mind, and the sight of the eye are both of them necessary consequences, the one results from the reasoning of the mind, and the other from the perception of the eye." (32, 333) Ethan Allen seized the obvious function of the eye to perceive physical existence that in turn illuminates the human brain, and moved it to an eye with the function of faith. The real eye provides us with pure-thesis ideas and the brain creates them with reality attached. When we have ideas that are not pure-thesis ideas that our mental animations give us, we move into conclusive-thesis or theorized-manufactured and pure-manufactured ideas. They hold a relationship to the sliver or set of sliver ideas of reality. We then form levels of probability. The idea of faith uses an idea that is a pure-manufactured or a theorized-manufactured idea with low probabilities and places the sliver idea of reality in a way that the idea moves to certainty. The idea of faith incorrectly moves these ideas into the pure-thesis idea category. When we misplace the sliver idea of reality, we end with a false reality, as it only exists in the human mind. The slight of hand by Ethan Allen was pairing the eye that plays physical existence and its reality to our minds as being the same as our mind that then receives these experiences, shuffles them around and does not attempt to manage the sliver idea of reality with accountability. Nevertheless, Ethan Allen uses rational thought under the *sensing it* definition.

14. *Perhaps the secular users of reason and rational thought would cry foul.* However, they could not cry foul without crying foul on themselves. In a recent argument with an atheist, he decried that religious thought was devoid of rational thought. In asking for a definition of his view of rational thought,

he never provided one and left in silence. I must add here, that before my asking for his definition of reason and rational thought, I had provided all the definitions I knew and explained why each one was an unaccountable method of inquiry.[28]

15. *An unpleasant fact exists.* The argument made by Ethan Allen, under the rules set forth in the definition of rational thought, was indeed valid. It may not align with truth and reality, but it was rational thought. It may be rational thought, but it also was an unaccountable form of rational thought. It was an unaccountable form of rational thought because rational thought was not restricted to the requirements of thesisism. Thesisism would require the premise that preceded his conclusion—that faith was the result of rational thought—to connect to the physical world. The idea that preceded it was the idea of a higher authority with consciousness existing in reality. Under rational thought, it allowed him to start with a manufactured idea, as he *sensed* and *deemed* it rational to his idea of a higher authority in his perception of an orderly physical world. He *sensed* his conclusion that an original conscious being had authored our physical existence was reasonable. Reason and rational thought allowed these ideas their place with reality attached. We provided the religious and any other false-reality makers a place of legitimacy.

16. *The secular-rational thinkers, since they too allow the unaccountable definition of sensing it to be true, are part of the false-reality makers too.* It is as if their acceptance and understanding of hard science, which contains the absolute requirement to remain connected to the physical world, some how magically translated to the chaos of their mind as being the same. Hard science definitely connects to the physical world. Secular-rational thought to social and moral ideas measures against the arbitrary and ambiguous sensing ability of the human mind. It may move closer to an accountable system of thought, but it is not yet one. To add to this argument, allow me to quote Ethan Allen when he wrote, "so that our faith in all cases is as liable to err, as our reason is to misjudge of the truth…." (32, p332) Well said Ethan.

17. *Rational thought allows religious thought to exist.* When we had an unaccountable form of rational thought allowed with acceptance, it played into the hands of the religious. It allowed them to start with any flawed premise and rationally think their way from that position. Ethan Allen understood this, although not from the viewpoint of a thesisist. He wrote, "The short of the matter is this, that without reason we could not have faith, and without the eye or eyes we could not see, but once admitting that we are rational, faith follows of course, naturally resulting from the dictates of reason." (32, p333) By allowing the unaccountability of reason and rational thought to

---

28 See sections on *"Is Our Reason Accountable"* and *"Is Our Rational Thought Accountable"* in *Book One*.

exist, which meant we allowed the measurement of ideas against the human mind and not the physical world, we brought unaccountable ideas into the fold. That included religious thought that started with ideas inappropriately given as reality.

18. *The unaccountability of rational thought is unveiled.* The rational thinkers with conclusions of relativism *sense* this unaccountability when their conflicting ideas occur. Ethan Allen wrote, "It is observable, that in all cases wherein reason makes an erroneous conclusion, faith is likewise erroneous...." (32, p333) Ethan Allen is effectively apologizing for the mistakes of faith in relation to mistakes resulting from the broadband definition of reason. The reason why faith has errors is due to the existence of the broadband idea of reason. He is correct for the wrong accountable reason. Mistakes in reason are another way of saying that when we use manufactured ideas and inappropriately apply an incorrect truth position, error occurs. When we do not make accountable the ideas resulting from reason and rational thought, people under reason and rational thought allow themselves to animate anything that they find acceptable to their senses. The use of senses here is not the maintenance of the relationship from sensory existence to our ideas, but to the diffuse and ambiguous backdrop of their mind. It is specifically our evaluate-to-balance filtered through our adhesive framed-reference in thought existence rather than through our unrestricted form of free will to our physical existence.

19. *Why do rational thinkers think they are accountable using their sense based in the human mind as the source of measurement?* Ethan Allen dealt with the problem of errors by rational thought in a way that articulated why secular-rational thinkers thought rational thought was fine. He wrote, "We must therefore adopt the principle of sincerity, since it is always supposed to aim at perfection, and to come as near it as the infirmities of our nature will admit, (for otherwise it could not be sincerity) which is the highest pretension to goodness, that we can lawfully aspire to." (32, p334) As long as you were *sincere* in your *sensing* reality against your human mind, you were doing *goodness*. This idea of sincerity is a common component to the validation of reason and rational thought. Isaac Watts gave nine rules to reasoning, none of which had any requirement to be connected to physical existence. Nevertheless, his rule number nine was, *"In your whole Course of Reasoning keep your Mind sincerely intent in the Pursuit of Truth; and follow solid Argument wheresoever it leads you. Let not a Party Spirit, or any Passion or Prejudice* whatsoever, stop or avert the Current of your Reasoning in the Quest of true Knowledge." (10, p337) The idea of measuring against your *sincerity* self-validates the use of unaccountable-rational thought. Rational thinkers were responding to their internal understanding that they were being sincere, and

that in being sincere, they were being good. Hidden in the idea of good, was that of correctness. Nevertheless, with this, they prevented the application of required accountability to their ideas. If they were sincere and good, you did not need to be correct, as that was sufficient for rational thought.

20. *Ethan Allen understood that morality came from his idea of nature, with nature being the physical world.* We can bring understanding to his ideas if we apply the correction of thesisism. He wrote, "for morality does not derive its nature from books, but from the fitness of things...." (32, p466) If a book on morality was shared ideas that connected to our physical world, we could then learn about morality from books because its nature would maintain and the book contains the expressions of the original physical connections. We could then verify it by experience. As Ethan Allen implied, even books must maintain the "fitness of things," which from a point of view of a thesisist is the physical connections to any idea.

21. *Ethan Allen challenged that mainstream religion was not following the fundamental idea of religion, and that was moral obligation.* He wrote,

> Most people place religion in arbitrary ceremonies, or mere positive institution, abstractly considered from the moral rectitude of things, and in which religion does not and cannot consist, and thus delude themselves with an empty notion of religion, which, in reality is made up of tradition and superstition, and in which moral obligation is not concerned; not considering that a conformity to moral rectitude, which is morality in the abstract, is the sum of all religion, that ever was or can be in the universe; as there can be no religion in that in which there is no moral obligation; except we make religion to be void of reason, and if so, all argument about it is at an end. (32, p468-469)

First, we are not in the argument of what is required for religion to be religion. The word religion is a broadband word. What we need to narrowband here was his "moral rectitude of things" did not reside in tradition and superstition, but resided in his natural religion that required the use of reason to his perceived nature, that is, his physical world. Here again, we can see how he connected the use of reason with religion, which led to his idea that faith came from reason.

22. *When we replace his view of God by natural religion with physical existence, we can see his attempts to connect to thesisism. Example 1:*[29] He wrote,

---

29 Note: In the following paragraphs, italicized words in parenthesis were added to show similarities with the Deism of Ethan Allen and thesisism. When the words in

[F]or that it is founded in eternal right; and whatever writings, books or oral speculations, best illustrate or teach this moral science, should have the preference. The knowledge of this as well as all other sciences, is acquired from (*accountable*) reason and (*sensory existence*) experience, and (as it is progressively obtained) may with propriety be called, the revelation of God (*physical existence*), which he (*the action of physical existence*) has revealed to us in the constitution of our (*accountable*) rational (evaluate-to-balance) natures; and as it is congenial with (*accountable*) reason and (*reality*) truth cannot (like other revelations) partake of (*manufactured ideas*) imposture. This is natural religion. (32, p466-467)

23. *Example 2:* "the priests have it in their power to amuse us, with a great variety of visionary apprehensions (*animations of manufactured ideas*) of things in the world to come, which, while in this life (*physical existence with experiential existence*), we cannot contradict (*allowing the sliver idea of reality to attach to a manufactured idea*) from experience." (32, p469)

24. *Example 3:* "and being at a loose (*no accountability requirements*) from the government of reason, please themselves with any (*pure-manufactured ideas*) fanaticisms they like best...." (32, p470)

25. *Example 4:* "And as they exclude (*accountable*) reason and (*thesis*) justice from their (*pure-manufactured ideas*) imaginary notions of religion, they also exclude it from (*accountability*) the providence or moral government of God (*our physical world*)." (32, p471)

26. *Example 5:* "The superstitious (*people engaging in manufactured ideas behaviorally*) thus let up a spiritual (*experiential existence*) discerning, independent of (*without accountability*), and in opposition (*physically and mentally given hostility*) to (*accountable*) reason, and their mere (*pure-manufactured ideas*) imaginations pass with each other, and with themselves, for (*true-reality*) infallible truths." (32, p471)

27. *Example 6:*

(*Accountable*) Reason therefore must be the standard (*of measurement against the physical world*), by which we determine the respective (*truth position of the sliver idea of reality*) claims of revelation (*mental animations*); for otherwise we may as well subscribe (*attach the sliver idea of reality*) to the divinity (*physical existence*) of the one as of the other (*ideas not measured against our physical world, rather measured against our human mind*), or to the whole of them, or to none at all. So likewise on this thesis (*the idea of a system of accountability*

---

parenthesis are not italicized, they are as originally written. The insert of (*accountable*) in front of the word reason means thesisism.

founded on thesisism), if (*accountable*) reason rejects the whole of those (*presented mental animations*) revelations, we ought to return to the religion of nature (*physical existence*) and (*the accountability system of thesisism*) reason. (32, p475)

28. *Example 7:* "As certain as we determine contrary to (*accountable*) reason, we make a wrong conclusion (*mismatch our sliver idea of reality position*); therefore, our wisdom (*reality*) is, to conform to the nature (*physical existence*) and (*accountable*) reason of things, as well in religious (*moral code of conduct*) matters, as in other sciences." (32, p476) Note that Ethan Allen does not give a free pass to religion to be exempt from any requirements to examination.

29. *Example 8:*

All our knowledge of things is derived from God (*physical existence*), in and by the order of nature (*the action of physical existence*), out of which we cannot perceive (*the unknown origin of physical existence*), reflect or understand any thing whatsoever (*inadequate physical connections to create conclusive-thesis or theorized-manufactured ideas of reasonable probability*); our external senses are natural (*sensory existence derives from the physical*) and so are our souls (*experiential existence*); by the instrumentality of the (*sensory existence*) former we perceive the objects of sense (*experiential existence*), and with the latter we (*engage in animation of ideas in thought existence*) reflect on them. (32, p476)

30. *Example 9:*

We may and often do, connect or arrange our ideas together, in a wrong or improper manner, for the want of skill or judgment, or through mistake or the want of application, or through the influence of prejudice; but in all such cases, the error does not originate from the ideas themselves, but from the composer; for a system, or an arrangement of ideas justly composed; always contains the truth; but an unjust composition never fails to contain error and falsehood. Therefore an unjust connection of ideas is not derived from nature, but from the imperfect composition of man. Misconnection of ideas is the same as misjudging, and has no positive existence, being merely a creature of the imagination; but nature and truth are real and uniform; and the rational mind by reasoning, discerns the uniformity, and is thereby enabled to make a just composition of ideas, which will stand the test of truth. But the fantastical illuminations of the credulous and superstitious part of mankind, proceed from weakness, and as far as they take place in the world, subvert the religion of REASON and TRUTH. (32, p476-477)

31. *I left Example 9 for your attempt to see thesisism so close to the surface, yet not quite there.* "For the want of skill or judgement" is the want of thesisism. The "influence of prejudice" is our bending ideas through an adhesive framed-reference to ones personally acquired false-reality desires. Our unaccountable ideas come from human beings "composing" without any accountability method. His "arrangement of ideas justly composed; always contains the truth" is our requirement to connect to the physical world through thesisism. An "unjust composition" does not operate under thesisism's accountability method, as it did not "arrive from nature." This means it does not reside in physical existence, but in our thought existence only. False-reality ideas are incorrectly categorized ideas to the sliver idea of reality. When misconnection occurs, they become "merely a creature of the imagination," which is manufactured ideas that only exist in our thought existence. "Nature and truth are real and uniform" because they are the reflection of the physical world, which is the same for everyone. By measuring against the physical world we can "discern(s) the uniformity" of it and can pass the "test of truth."

32. *Why Ethan Allen, like John Locke, did not move to thesisism was their adherence to the idea of a higher-conscious authority.* Ethan Allen started with preconceived ideas about a higher consciousness. It was at the end of the book by Ethan Allen that he began to start writing in terms of *ideas* and *thesis*. John Locke started his book with an examination of ideas and worked his way to the preconceived ideas about a higher consciousness. Because Ethan Allen spent the majority of his book using reason and rational thought to vindicate his manufactured idea about a higher consciousness having reality, it required his mental animations to measure against the human mind. Concerning ideas of morality, Ethan Allen started wrong and ended closer to the correct position. The opposite of John Locke occurred. He started close to the correct position and led himself to away from correct position. Neither of the two men made the extra needed step when thesisism showed itself. They were too possessed in the idea of a higher consciousness creating the world around them.

33. *When we compare the philosophy of Ethan Allen with John Locke or other philosophers, we reveal to ourselves an important understanding concerning historical philosophy.* John Locke was immersed in the ruling class of his time. Ethan Allen did not write in relation to the ruling class around him. This is why we know about John Locke today and have numerous modern publications of his writings. Finding a copy of the book by Ethan Allen is a challenge. What this means is that our prevailing philosophy comes from a skewed source. When we look at John Locke, David Hume, Adam Smith, Adam Ferguson,

Edmond Burke and all the way to modern times of Milton Friedman and F. A. Hayek, we see that we had written our philosophy to fulfill the desires of the surrounding ruling powers.[30] We then have political-philosophical thought that contributes to an adhesive framed-reference. It was not that our popular and well-known philosophers were necessarily and knowingly engaging in coercion. It was that we did not have a system of thought with accountability. This allowed people to use philosophical arguments that fit their personal self-interests to engage in coercion, knowingly or not knowingly, to their self-interests ends. Without a measurement system to bring accountability, no correction of false-reality ideas can occur within the *sense* and *sincerity* of people, inside or outside the ruling power. `

34. *Ethan Allen had written a statement to the importance of connecting to the physical world, his nature, that to which I most thoroughly agree.* "Through life we struggle with physical evils, which eventually are certain to destroy our earthly composition; and well would it be for us did evils end here; but alas! moral evil has been more or less predominant in our agency, and though natural evil is unavoidable, yet moral evil may be prevented or remedied by the exercise of virtue. Morality is therefore of more importance to us than any or all other attainments...." (32, p472-473) Once we bring accountability to moral ideas, as we can do with thesisism, we have our thesis-based justification for where coercion is appropriate and not appropriate. With our physically based system of thought, we now have a visual sighting of the invisible hand of Adam Smith.

The Beginning to Our End of Happiness

1. *We have two types of pursuit of happiness ideas.* I have presented historical ideas that led to the idea that happiness was the ultimate end humans sought. I have presented how religious ideas and how reason and rational thought have contributed to false ideas we continue to hold today. I have presented how to perceive our physical existence and the circular interaction we have with our mental existence. I am going write this chapter through a historical time line to follow these ideas, and in the end, explain our ultimate human end. To understand this, we need to move toward ending our end of happiness as a universally applied idea, and to understand our natural pursuit of happiness as a limited idea. Otherwise, we end up with the obsessive and destructive aspects inherent to a human end without thesis-based justifications.

---

30 We have a history of philosophers, especially in the nineteenth century, where a counter-philosophy to ruling power had occurred. Nietzsche and Marx are a few examples.

2. *The US Declaration of Independence and the Pursuit of Happiness:* The *Declaration of Independence* of the United States of America has written into it, "Life, Liberty and the Pursuit of Happiness" as an end to our nation and to ourselves. These words are wise in intent. However, what did they mean by pursuit of happiness?

3. *Life and Liberty connects to physical existence.* First, we have a consensus on what *Life* means, as it is our physical existence. This connection to physical existence gives us the right and ownership to our own life as the result of the action of physical existence. Liberty is our movement in this physical existence. Our nature and structure provided by physical existence grants us our liberty. This nature and structure we have resides in our equal-to-us and our unequal-to-us aspects in our human design. These two ideas, life and liberty, are universal ideas when properly connected to our physical existence. Our freedoms reside in our liberty measured against our thesis-morality equations.

4. *We obtain our Life and Liberty from our law of nature.* When we were children, we had guardians. As we moved from child to adult, parental and societal responsibility transferred to the individual. Our physical self then belonged to ourselves without needed nurturing restraints. We have the liberty afforded to us by our physical existence and its movement that can only be restricted by the structure of nature, from which we obtain our laws of nature.

5. *Human law is not to restrict natural law.* The purpose of any government is not to pass laws to restrict freedom and liberty, but to pass laws to prevent the restriction to freedom and liberty not curtailed by the structure of nature. John Locke wrote, "the end of law is not to abolish or restrain, but to preserve and enlarge freedom." (27, 2nd Treatise, 57) This type of natural law thought was instrumental to the formation of the Constitution of the United States of America.

6. *Natural law became political and included ideas about happiness of humankind.* Historically, we have seen that natural law ideas included ideas about happiness. Natural law also worked its way into political thought during the time of the formation of the US government. During the eighteenth century, M. de Vattel wrote,

> We call that the *necessary law of nations that consists* in the application of the law of nature to nations. It is *necessary*, because nations are absolutely obliged to observe it. This law contains the precepts, prescribed by the law of nature to states, to whom that law is not less obligatory, than to individuals; because states are composed of men,

their resolutions are taken by men, and the law of nature is obligatory to all men, under whatever relation they act. (31, prelim.7)

Natural law ideas tied to ideas of human happiness were prevalent during the founding of the United States of America. Political writers like William Godwin wrote in the eighteenth century, "The true object of moral and political disquisition is pleasure or happiness." (33, a4)

7. *We have had ideas of happiness and the pursuit of it for as long as we have had recorded human history.* However, what does the *pursuit of happiness* mean? Why have we discussed it for such a long time? What did our founders have in mind when they wrote it? Was it a solid thesis idea? If we move backward in time, we find that John Locke connected happiness with liberty. The subtitle of one paragraph by John Locke was "The Necessity of pursuing true Happiness, the Foundation of Liberty." (8, II.xxi.51) Within the paragraph, he pooled together our "unalterable Pursuit of Happiness ... which is our greatest Good ... a necessary Compliance with our Desire." (8, II.xxi.51) We had human happiness tied to our liberty and freedom and to our desires. Our question becomes, was this correct?

8. *Our ideas of happiness have a distinct root.* To understand why John Locke thought this way we have to realize that he too was a learned man and he too had acquired many of these ideas. Although John Locke truly had original and wonderful ideas, like all of us, we acquire our knowledge through experiences that we have throughout our lives. They include the interaction we have between people. It also includes our reading the opinions and statements of others. The ideas of happiness that John Locke held came from previous history and his contemporary discussions on what was the ultimate end of human pursuit.

9. *Purpose of this chapter is to compare our historical ideas of happiness against thesisism.* It is the intent of this chapter to look at selected written history and argumentation about the ultimate end of human beings to shed some light on how our ideas developed to become what they are today. We will look at ideas over time under the accountability method of thesisism to see if they stand or not. This presentation contains historical extractions to show how some ideas that started two thousand and more years ago were indeed flawed and how they continue to affect us today. Since most of the referenced philosophers have passed on, they cannot defend their position against any of my claims. It is under a respect that I should provide them their best defense. We can best accomplish this by providing their words directly and fully.

10. *It was Aristotle's position that all actions were ends to good.* Aristotle, in his writing of *The Nicomachean Ethics*, started immediately with, "Every art and every investigation, and similarly every action and pursuit, is considered

to aim at some good. Hence the good has been rightly defined as 'that at which all things aim.'" (34, BI.1094aI) This start of Aristotle, as we will see, essentially rendered the rest of his writings useless. This was due to his having the human being as the center of existence. His animations moved from within us to the outer world and not from the outer world to within us. This stood everything on its head. The use of the word "good" here is broadband. If we define "good" as the balance of thesis (physically based) equations, then Aristotle missed terribly. As given, Aristotle makes all individual human action a movement to a balance of good. Nevertheless, Aristotle did not define "good" in such a way to bring any stable nor reality-based equations. We have no method to assure accuracy. Allow me to continue presenting my rationale and eventual consequential follow.

11. *Aristotle wrote of happiness as a human end.* Aristotle continued with, "Well, happiness more than anything else is thought to be just such an end, because we always chose it for itself, and never for any other reason." (34, BI.1097b.I) We can see our self-centered position further since we thought in terms of ourselves. We can see it in "because we always chose it." We did not begin with the correct relationship with our physical existence. Instead, we went directly to an unaccountable form of personal desires, which in turn led us to create an adhesive framed-reference.

12. *The idea of happiness as an end by Aristotle did not meet the requirements of thesisism.* Aristotle had our measurement of ideas not measured against our physical world, but to our own animating mind. Our animating mind, as we know, can animate anything within our acquired pool of sliver ideas. If we can animate self-made collection of sliver ideas and include the attachment of the idea of reality to them, how then can we know anything? At that point, we are all living in a mentally created world, which becomes a manufactured reality into itself, but not the reality of our physical world. We will see that once we convinced ourselves that happiness was our ultimate end, an idea broken away from physical reality, we could not stop any subsequent perversion of ideas that moved from this position of false reality. These perversions could lead us anywhere.

13. *Aristotle presented the idea that happiness was the perfect virtue.* Aristotle wrote,

> If happiness is an activity in accordance with virtue, it is reasonable to assume that it is in accordance with the highest virtue, and this will be the virtue of the best part of us. Whether this is the intellect or something else that we regard as naturally ruling and guiding us, and possessing insight into things noble and divine—either as being actually divine itself or as being more divine than any other part of

us—it is the activity of this part, in accordance with the virtue proper to it, that will be perfect happiness. (34,BX.1177a.15)

14. *Happiness as a perfect virtue did not meet the requirements of thesisism.* Aristotle had happiness tied to an idea of virtue. Since he had the human being as the center of existence, connections to physical existence were mostly broken from any idea. In doing this, he allowed our mental animation to attach the idea reality and truth to any moral justification that came along, as long as we found it noble and divine. Note that he wrote, "it is reasonable to assume...." Traditional reason and rational thought only had to *sense* it. Aristotle viewed our traditional idea of sensing it to only assuming it. Nevertheless, this meant there was no accountability method to determine the position of any idea by Aristotle about nobility and divinity, or the ideas of anyone else.

15. *No other philosophers met the requirements of thesisism.* This was certainly not restricted to Aristotle. If you look at the Platonists, Stoics, Epicureans and others, the same mistake had occurred. Each searched for the end to which human beings strive for in existence. Each held a perspective of human beings that looked within and animated their ideas against whatever random ideas arrived. They all placed us center of existence.

16. *Although the Stoics touched on thesisist type of thought, they never crossed over into it.* Cicero wrote a line of interest. "There are philosophers who began with the senses but then saw a grander and more divine vision, whereupon they abandoned the senses." (35, IV.42) Was Cicero implying that perhaps we needed to stay within our own senses? However, he was not thinking in terms of ideas and its relationship to our physical world. Cicero wrote just before this, "Virtue cannot be brought into play at all unless everything that it chooses and rejects is related to a single all-embracing good."(35, IV.40) This a wonderful idea as our physical world has this single all-embracing source. Our physical existence provides us our source to determine our evaluate-to-balance. Our "all-embracing good" is the balance of our thesis-morality equations. Nevertheless, he was not measuring against the backdrop of the physical world. He followed with "We are seeking a virtue that does not abandon our nature but protects it." (35, IV.41) Under the right narrowband idea, it could be a conclusive-thesis idea. Nevertheless, "our nature" as he used was relational to our mental nature while he never acknowledged the rest of physical existence. The measurement system of philosophers was always against our internal nature, and not of our external nature, to which we are part.

17. *Our beginning in philosophy was flawed and foolish.* Under the help of Philautia of self-love, Folly wrote of human beings, "yet they're under my

obligation to me on several important counts, notably for their happiness in their self-love, which enables them to dwell in a sort of third heaven, looking down from aloft, almost with pity, on all the rest of mankind as so many cattle crawling on the face of the earth." (36, p86) Regrettably, we have been viewing our internal existence totally in relation to ourselves. We have removed ourselves completely from our creator, physical existence. We have made ourselves godlike. In doing this, we have been viewing ourselves not in relation to the physical world, but in relation to our own human animations. We measure *our* ideas against *our* thought existence. Once again, we can quote Sir Thomas Pope Blount. He wrote, "Learning does but serve to fill us of Artificial Errors. That which we so much admire under the name of LEARNING, is only the knowing the fancies of particular Men, Deliri veteris Meditantes formia vana, in effect but like Gossiping Women telling one another their Dreams." (19, Essay II, p33) Thought existence is not physical existence. Without accountability, we can with our thought existence take the sliver idea of reality and attach it to any master idea we want. An unaccountable idea does not measure against the physical world. We have made this egocentric mistake since the beginning of known human knowledge. Pythagoras, an early philosopher from about 530 BC, taught the immortality of the soul and having sins resulting in a downgrade in your future life.

18. *Science too operates with egocentrism as it relates with curiosity and personal desire, and not with a relational interaction.* First, relational interaction refers to our evaluate-to-balance to our thesis-morality equations. Our science works despite the egocentrism between the physical world and us, as we place the physical world in relation to ourselves only. This egocentric position of the scientist and the physical world does allow them to discoveries. Pythagoras, who taught of the immortality of the soul and spoke of our achieving upgrades or downgrades in future lives, also discovered the ratios under musical concords. (34, Appendix 2) Our science seldom relates the position of humankind to the physical; thus, science often becomes consumption and manipulation without understanding the required balance we need in relation to it. This inadequacy resides within the scientific community, but in defense, this inadequacy is not relational only within the scientific world, but to all of society. Although our science mostly acts independent to social and political issues, our science can never truly divorce themselves from social and political issues. Science has been cowering to these institutions, just as they have been with moral institutions, because we have misappropriated power by allowing coercion to narrow self-interest by those with power.

19. *We have had attempts to connect to the physical and to lose our egocentric view.* There were times when this centralism appeared to people, as when Cicero

wrote, "Since all appropriate actions originate from the natural principles, so too must wisdom itself. ... Similarly it is the starting-points of nature which first introduce us to wisdom, but it is no surprise that we then come to cherish wisdom herself far more than we do those objects by which we came to her." (35, III.23) It too often feels good to wallow in ideas of grandeur rather than accepting a diminutive tool that diminishes your position in existence as having commonality with those that we often find undesirable. John Locke, in his book, *An Essay Concerning Human Understanding*, started his investigation with the nature of ideas. Nevertheless, he remained incomplete due to a division that directed him into two different directions. This division was divine law and natural law. One began to put humankind in our place whereas the other maintained our self-aggrandizement.

20. *When we have historical ideas that were broken from our physical existence, we can only move ourselves to more false-reality ideas. Thomas Aquinas, step one:* When we start with an idea not connected to the physical world, animations of any kind can occur. Thomas Aquinas seized the idea from Aristotle that *everything acts for an end aimed at a good* and moved his acquired sliver and master ideas around it. In his *Summa Contra Gentiles, Book Three*, Thomas Aquinas started with "Therefore, the agent that acts with nature as its principle is just as much directed to a definite end, in its action, as is the agent that acts through intellect as its principle. Therefore, every agent acts for an end." (37, III.ch2.6) We can see him accept the idea by Aristotle that all human intellectual acts were for an end.

21. *How our broken connections to physical existence led to further false-reality ideas. Thomas Aquinas, step two:* Thomas Aquinas too attached goodness to the agent acting to an end. He wrote, "the intellect is only motivating by virtue of the rational meaning of the good, which is the object of the will. Therefore, even the natural agent is neither moved, nor does it move, the sake of an end, except in so far as the end is a good; for the end is determined for the natural agent by some appetite." (37, III.ch3.7) We can see him accept the idea by Aristotle that all human intellectual acts to an end were for a good. Like Aristotle, Thomas Aquinas presented the idea of good without definition and measurement.

22. *How our broken connections to physical existence led to further false-reality ideas. Thomas Aquinas, step three:* Like other philosophers, Thomas Aquinas then added in happiness. He wrote, "Since happiness is the proper good of an intellectual nature, happiness must pertain to an intellectual nature by reason of what is proper to that nature. ... Therefore, happiness, or felicity, consists substantially and principally in an act of the intellect rather than in an act of the will." (37, III.ch26.8) Thomas Aquinas is pairing happiness as our "proper good" to the nature of reasoning. Now he has set up the following

series of ideas that *all acts to an end were for a good,* tied it to happiness and associated reason with nature. When he associated reason with nature, it gave a sense or a feel of truth to what he was saying, as nature here implied reality. Nevertheless, the "proper good of an intellectual nature" and "intellectual nature by reason" have no statement of accountability beyond the traditional definition of reason and rational thought. It allows us to connect reality to any movement of sliver and master ideas as long as we deemed it "proper good" determined by an unaccountable thought system from the "intellectual nature of reason." Finally, he claimed happiness derived from intellect rather than our will. Our will arrives from our evaluate-to-balance. By having happiness tied to our intellect, he can circumvent our natural evaluate-to-balance and create ideas of what happiness is and embed them into the thought existence of others. This created a coercive tool that works to create an adhesive framed-reference. None of his use of reason and rational thought measured against physical existence. Instead, his use of reason and rational thought was to achieve a personally desired end, and that was to create "divinely given laws" to coerce the "interior acts" of individuals. We expose his personally desired end and his adhesive framed-reference in paragraphs 35 and 36.

23. *How our broken connections to physical existence led to further false-reality ideas. Thomas Aquinas, step four:* Thomas Aquinas then continued with his rational presentation to state what human happiness was not. It was not surprising then, since he was not measuring against the physical world, that he finally concluded that human happiness was the contemplation of his manufactured idea about a higher consciousness. He made his rational and reasoned argument over several paragraphs on human felicity. I have combined selected elements for quickness and clarity. He wrote,

> We are left with the conclusion that the ultimate felicity of man lies in the contemplation of truth.... (37, III, ch37.1)

> ...

> In addition, through this operation man is united by way of likeness with beings superior to him, since this alone of human operations is found also in God and in separate substances. (37, III, ch37.4)

> ...

> However, it is not possible for man's ultimate felicity to consist in the contemplation which depends on the understanding of principles, for that is very imperfect, being most universal, including the potential cognition of things. Also, it is the beginning, not the end, of human enquiry, coming to us from nature and not because of our search

for truth. Nor, indeed, does it lie in the area of the sciences which deal with lower things, because felicity should lie in the working of the intellect in relation to the noblest objects of understanding. So, the conclusion remains that man's ultimate felicity consists in the contemplation of wisdom, based on the considering of divine matters. (37, III ch37.8)

...

[M]an's ultimate felicity consists only in the contemplation of God. (37, III, ch37.9)

We have an example of what happens when we do not connect to physical existence and allow our ideas to be animated detached from our creation. Without accountability to ideas, anyone like Thomas Aquinas could animate further unaccountable ideas not connected to physical existence and bring them to any end they desired.

24. *Thomas Aquinas removed happiness from our experiential existence that we receive by the action of physical existence and gave it to a false reality.* He removed happiness from our experience when he wrote,

Again, the ultimate end of man brings to a termination man's natural appetite, in the sense that, once the end is acquired, nothing else will be sought. For, if he is still moved onward to something else, he does not yet have the end in which he may rest. Now, this termination cannot occur in this life. For, the more a person understands, the more the desire to understand increased in him, and this is natural to man. ... Therefore, it is not possible for man's ultimate felicity to be in this life. (37, III, ch48.2)

His last line here appears to contradict his "man's ultimate felicity consists only in the contemplation of God" statement in the previous paragraph. During his rational arguments on human felicity, he had our ultimate felicity connected to our contemplation during our lifetime, and a few chapters later, he had our ultimate felicity connected outside our lifetime. However, his argument as given stands only because he was attempting to indenture human actions. Reason and rational thought has no requirement to measure against truth, even when we use it under the claim of truth!

25. *The movement in his argument was one based in coercion.* He took a normal and desired human attribute, the ability to experience happiness, and used the action of contemplation that takes place in physical existence to pair it with his God. His god-idea only measures against the thought existence of the holders of the idea. Now we have achieving happiness measured against a

thought system of particular individuals. Thomas Aquinas set up the method of construction to create adhesive framed-references to bend our evaluate-to-balance to maintain their misplaced sliver idea of reality. Now we accessed happiness not relational to physical existence, but to particular system of thought developed by unaccountable rearrangements of sliver and master ideas by capricious people. Rather than finding our thesis-based justifications to happiness during our lifetime, he indentured humankind mentally to follow whatever arbitrary and self-proclaimed form of contemplation dictated to them to reach the false-reality idea of ultimate happiness after death. What is important in relation to the rational thought by Thomas Aquinas was that he had changed the fundamental meaning of happiness with the adjective of ultimate. He was attempting to transform happiness from a limited idea to a universal idea.

26. *Human happiness is not infinite, but finite.* His argument was intellectually dishonest. Like many of his ideas, they were declarations. They were declarations because he had the luxury of unaccountability. In having this, he could start with any unaccountable idea presented as reality, and then move with reason and rational thought under legitimate use of logical movement, sensing it, in good sense, deemed lucid and any other justification desired to attach reality to non-reality ideas. Nevertheless, we can go to physical existence to see how sliver and master ideas are corrupted. In order to transform a limited idea into a universal idea, he had to remove it from our physical and finite existence and place it into an infinite existence. His infinite existence could not be our thought existence, as it too was finite. Thomas Aquinas had rearranged his internal sliver ideas to a new master idea of an ultimate and static end of humankind, despite the reality that humankind is finite, as physical existence under its actions made us finite, and transferred his new master idea along with the sliver idea of reality to a non-existent, yet infinite conscious entity.

27. *Thomas Aquinas took our happiness away from our physical world.* Our happiness results in the interactions of our experiential existence and physical existence. He removed our happiness from our physical existence and experiential existence by the misplaced attachment of the sliver idea of reality. He could achieve this by the nature of faith to create a false-reality room of divine status. He, as others, could then attach the sliver idea of reality to non-reality ideas. These non-reality ideas include existences of a higher consciousness and other beings beyond our physical and experiential existences. To maintain non-reality ideas, we have to force incoming reality from physical existence, as well as other incoming human ideas, to fit the desired non-reality ideas. We achieve this by the rearrangement of sliver and

master ideas relational to the misplaced sliver idea of reality. This develops into our adhesive framed-reference.

28. *Thomas Aquinas has our moral code of conduct determined by an existence of a higher authority with consciousness that is beyond physical existence.* In order to evaluate-to-balance to our moral code of conduct under an idea of a higher being with authority that exists beyond our physical and experiential existence, that particular thought system has to become an adhesive framed-reference to bend incoming reality to adjust to false-reality positions. The moral code of conduct arrived by the evaluate-to-balance under such unaccountable systems of thought is simply the evaluate-to-balance of individuals against ideas from human beings presented as divine by the misplaced sliver idea of reality. We have humankind not educating themselves to our reality, but to thought systems created by various individuals. This system of thought delivers us into the hands of the self-appointed authorities of any mental design. These self-appointed authorities claimed knowledge and special position with manufactured ideas about a higher consciousness.

29. *The tragedy of the thought system from Thomas Aquinas is that it created systems of thought for people to engage in manufactured justifications to arbitrary coercion.* If his ultimate end of happiness idea were to have reality, we could only achieve our ultimate end of happiness when we died. Except for contemplating their higher-consciousness idea, this would render everything we do in our lives to be secondary or dreadful. This also would subject us only to their system of thought. Under these types of systems, people could be convinced to be miserable and accept it, as they would have the ultimate end at their death. I see this as a form of violence against humankind. It is a form of evil, as with the Nietzsche view of evil, with the actions of human beings' given as a God. Thomas Aquinas, and his likes, moved us away from our creation, and in doing that, took away our relationship to it and handed our lives over to any self-appointed authority for any personal form of false-reality thought animation.

30. *Aristotle and Aquinas operated with no system of accountability to their ideas.* Under the argument by Thomas Aquinas, his manufactured idea about a higher consciousness was the end all, as he wrote, "From the points that have been set forth we have adequately established that God is the end of all things." (37, III, ch64.1) Again, we had another declaration. He did not; nor did Aristotle; provide proof that good was the end of human being action. Nor did he or Aristotle prove that happiness was what human beings endeavored to obtain in relation to the ultimate end of human being actions. They were declarations of ideas made without connection to physical existence. When they made their choice of happiness as an end, they did not make it relationally to physical existence, but rather to the chaos of our own

minds. Remember that Aristotle connected happiness to virtue. Virtue is our morality. Our morality is evaluation of our existence to a code of conduct. He may have attempted to connect to physical existence, but Aristotle, as well as others, never made any requirement that our sliver idea of reality remain appropriately assigned. It became defaulted to the broadband idea of *sensing it* that rational thought allows. That in turn opened the door for religion to commandeer happiness and to use it for their manipulation.

31. *When our system of thought moves toward thesisism, people move it away.* If these fundamental statements had false starts, then declaring that happiness was the pursuit of a manufactured idea about a higher consciousness does not hold. With all subsequent animations made by human beings, we find that the *ultimate end* of human beings, when not tied to the physical world, became the objects of any human being desire. With John Locke, we find the connection of happiness to property.[31] This was possible by the division of divine law and natural law that clearly existed during his time. This division occurred centuries before John Locke. Natural law made the holders of manufactured ideas about a higher consciousness nervous, as it did during the time of Thomas Aquinas. This was why religion moved to fold into their wing any and all ideas of natural law, for if people began to view the physical world for their source of understanding subjects historically relegated to divine things, they may have discovered thesisism.

32. *Aquinas animated his idea of eternal law with broken connections to physical existence.* Thomas Aquinas created a web to grasp and bend natural law ideas into his system of thought. He shuffled around different animations of natural law to fit the established and untouchable ideas that he had assimilated. Thomas Aquinas was a good example of an adhesive framed-reference. Allow me to pull together a string of his thoughts to make the point. All were from his, *The Summa of Theology, Question 91.* He wrote, "Then the very idea of the governance of things existing in God as the prince of the universe has the character of law. And because the divine reason conceives nothing temporally but has an eternal concept, as is said in Proverbs 8.23, such a law ought to be called eternal." (38, Q91.art1) If he had tied it to physical existence, and not to the manufactured idea about a higher consciousness, his statement would have been good. Physical existence, by our standard of time, is eternal. It is true that we know our universe has a limited amount of time, but again, in relation to our existence, it has an eternal quality to it. Allow me to rewrite his sentence. "Then the very idea of the governance of things existing in physical existence as the prince of the universe has the character of law. And because

---

31 To read John Locke make the connection of happiness to property, see chapter titled, *John Locke and the Big Give Away*, paragraph 20.

reason with accountability conceives nothing temporally but has an eternal concept, such a law ought to be called eternal."

33. *Aquinas animated his idea of natural law with broken connections to physical existence.* Thomas Aquinas took eternal law, which from a viewpoint of a thesisist is our physical world, and from it defined natural law. He wrote, "the rational creature is subject to divine providence in a more excellent manner. ... Hence in him the eternal reason is participated in in such a way that he has a natural inclination to the fitting act and end. Such a participation in eternal law in the rational creatures is called natural law." (38, Q91.art2) Under thesisism, the physical world is eternal. Our participation in it is natural law. Our "natural inclination" is our evaluate-to-balance. However, evaluate-to-balance can occur through a free-flow framed-reference or an adhesive framed-reference. Without the requirement to connect our ideas to physical existence, "natural inclination" becomes the same as *sensing it.*

34. *Aquinas animated his idea of human law with broken connections to physical existence.* When we apply reason and rational though without our sliver idea of reality placed properly, our divine law, natural law and human law can lead to coercion. We can apply reason and rational thought based in false reality to move logically off physical existence to grander false-reality ideas. Thomas Aquinas wrote, "It should be said that practical reason is concerned with things to be done, which are singular and contingent, and not necessary things as speculative reason is. Therefore human laws cannot have the infallibility that the conclusion of the demonstrative science have. Nor is it necessary that every measure be in every way infallible and certain, but only to the degree possible in its domain." (38, Q91.art3) Human law became the human animation derived from practical reason. Practical reason has no required connection to physical existence. We can make our human laws relational to thought existence. Here we had something important. Reason implied an intellectual understanding that one can more confidently rely in the conclusion of the reasoning action. For example, the launch of the space shuttle depends on the reasoning abilities of many people for a successful launch. However, when we tied reason to science, we measured these actions, that is, the calculations and all the experimentation, against the physical world. In doing this, our confidences that we had obtained the correct conclusions were greatly increased. Nevertheless, when it came to ideas of human laws and morality, we never made the same move that science did. It is not the cause and effect of science that never moved; rather, we never moved our relationship with thought existence to include physical existence. In these subjects, we historically did not measure human reason against the physical world, but rather against the animating human mind. We had a division occur, and that division was divine law and natural law.

Thomas Aquinas used the physical limitations of human structure to create an argument for divine law utilizing the unaccountable structure of his practical reason and rational thought.

35. *Aquinas animated ideas of eternal law with broken connections to physical existence to create divine law ideas.* Thomas Aquinas wrote, "It should be said that the eternal law is participated in according to the proportion of human nature's capacity by natural law. But man needs to be directed in a higher way to the supernatural ultimate end. Therefore, a law divinely given was added, by which the eternal law is participated in a higher mode." (38, Q91.art4) He broke natural law away from physical existence when he created his "man needs ... a law divinely given" idea. He based his divine law idea on the idea that it was "necessary for the direction of human life ... to be directed ... to the supernatural ultimate end," which we will see in paragraph 36 is "eternal happiness."

36. *He justified his "law divinely given" under four given reasons.*

First, because a man is directed by law in his proper acts as ordered to the ultimate end. ... But because man is ordered to the end of eternal happiness, which exceeds the proportion of human natural capacity ... he should be directed to his end by a divinely given law.

...

Second, on account of the uncertainty of human judgement ... from which different and conflicting laws arise. ... it was necessary that he be directed in his proper acts by a law divinely given, which he would know could not err.

...

Third ... Man's judgement cannot bear on internal movements, which are hidden ... Therefore human law cannot sufficiently restrain and order interior acts, but it was necessary that a divine law supervene for this purpose.

...

Fourth ... human law cannot punish or prohibit all the evils that are done ... In order that no evil should escape prohibition and punishment, it was necessary for a divine law to supervene by which all sins are forbidden. (38, Q91.art4)

37. *We have in Thomas Aquinas a mixing of existences to create a manufactured justification for divine law with a false sense of truth.* Our experience of physical

reality provides us a sliver idea of truth. Thomas Aquinas moved humankind from our limited capacity given to us by physical existence to an unlimited capacity for eternal happiness. One half of his argument is in physical existence and the other half of his argument is only in the thought existence of the holder of the idea, as it has no connection to physical existence. He then outlined the limitations of thought existence with his statement on contradictions in human judgment and the physical limitation of experiencing the internal thoughts of other people. He ended by citing another physical limitation of ours that we could not know everything. What we have is a manufactured idea of a "law divinely given" that is justified by references to physical existence to bring in a false sense of truth. The slight of hand is that these reasons based in physical existence he based on his "ordered" idea. Physical existence moves, therefore we move, as with Jean-Paul Sartre and his *we are not free to be not free* type of idea. Therefore, the unconscious movement of physical existence orders or directs us to whatever succession it engages in. Nevertheless, he has us not "ordered" to physical existence, but "ordered" to "eternal happiness."[32] This requires consciousness or awareness that is greater than ours, to which his "divinely given law" appears. This moves our creator from physical existence into our thought existences with a false-reality room of divine connection. Our divine laws then arrive from the position of power and influence by the random placement of birth and circumstance of any individual that harbors self-justified ideas to divinely given manufactured ideas from thought existence. Thomas Aquinas had stopped the progression of humankind and actually kept us away from our creation and creator, because our creation and creator is our physical world.

38. *Our natural law ideas moved toward thesisism.* If we look to our physical world, natural law does have physically based laws to which the ideas of natural law were tending its course to become. Our natural law ideas drifted us toward the physical world. Divine law ideas led us back to the chaos of the human mind, preventing progression of the human condition. Cicero wrote in relation to the Stoics while quoting Cato, "With no systematic doctrine, they follow nature herself, and achieved a great deal that is praiseworthy. In my opinion they were better instructed by nature than they could have been by philosophy, had they adopted any other philosophy than which holds morality to be the only good, immorality the only evil." (35, III.11)

39. *If we historically operated our ideas with broken connections to physical existence, what is our question?* If all of our written history involved mental animation broken from physical existence and their ultimate end idea came from their false starts, then we have reached a point to question. Do we have an ultimate end, and if so, what is the real ultimate end of human being

32 See the first of four reasons given in paragraph 36.

activity? Does this ultimate end involve constant happiness or only potential happiness or does it involve something else?

40. *We can begin to understand our failure by looking at some coercive actions.* Let me start by providing something William Godwin wrote.

> Implicit faith, blind submission to authority, timid fear, a distrust of our powers, an inattention to our own importance and the good purposes we are able to effect, these are the chief obstacles to human improvement. Democracy restores to man a consciousness of his value, teaches him, by the removal of authority and oppression, to listen only to the suggestions of reason, gives him confidence to treat all other men with frankness and simplicity, and induces him to regard them no longer, as enemies against whom to be upon his guard, but a brethren whom it becomes him to assist. (39, XIV, p119-120)

41. *We can evaluate coercive action in relation to our historical and current societal systems.* What William Godwin provided us was that when human beings were free from coercion induced by other people, and a governmental system existed that empowered all its members, then human improvement could occur. Nevertheless, his statement also included, "to listen to the suggestions of reason." This meant that despite that we provided freedom and liberty to all, unless we as a people could "listen to the suggestions of reason," and to do that meant to be able to reason as well, democracy does not truly exist. What happens to a democratic government that does not properly support the education of its citizens? When we have one that replaces the free press with corporate or government press? When we have one that denies portions of it citizens the same rights that others have? When we have one where certain people cannot hold office because of religious or non-religious affiliations? When our democracy creates an intolerant society? When democracy creates a system by which only the wealthy can hold office? When democracy enables and markets entertainment and pleasures over reason and rational thought? Do we have democracy in this democratic (or republic) society?

42. *We have coercion created by the failure of our political writers.* William Godwin wrote of political writers, "Nothing can be of more importance, than to separate prejudice and mistake on the one hand, from reason and demonstration on the other. Wherever they have been confounded, the cause of truth must necessarily be the sufferer." (33, III.ch1, p187)

43. *Our truth suffered from the effect of power and corruption on the free will of people.* The truth has suffered, and for so long of a time. Our true ultimate end did not hide. It has been before our eyes day after day. It has been clear

and plain, as you will see. I cannot accept that we have never seen it. Why then had it not surfaced? Had the obstructions that William Godwin stated above been that strong for so long? Had other systems of thought seized this position to manipulate to their own personal form of false-reality desires? Did power corrupt our collective free will and created within us a grouped adhesive framed-reference to bend our sight of understanding?

44. *Our history of ideas has not been from a correct vantage point of view.* If we know that the historical positions of ideas about our end goal as human beings, or what some call our ultimate end, had been from an egocentric view, that which came from our own reflections, then what is the correct vantage point?

45. *Under thesisism, we must apply feedback to our physical world to achieve our correct vantage point of view.* We must measure our ideas to our physical world to determine where we can and cannot place the sliver idea of reality. We must measure all ideas against this backdrop. We obtain our equations to balance our actions. If we measure ourselves in terms of what is our ultimate end or pursuit in life, we must not look at our emotions and thoughts, but ask what is our relationship to our physical world? Ask yourself, what is the interaction between you and the physical world in its most basic form?

46. *Existence arrives by the action of physical existence.* What is our relationship between our physical world and ourselves? In part, the answer resides in the question. The physical world is the action of the physical material. It is in constant motion around us. We experience it. We feel both the pleasure and terror from it under its terms in relation to ourselves, and we respond to the physical events that occur around us. We build homes to protect ourselves from bad weather. We build places outside to enjoy the weather when it is pleasant. We initially wore clothing for protection from the elements. At the time of this writing, we drive automobiles. This brings us the comfort of convenience to long journeys. We no longer have to toughen up our feet or pick up horse plops, although we now have a new a plop in our atmosphere. We can fly to far destinations quickly. We can obtain food ready for consumption quickly. What then are all these activities?

47. *To manipulate physical existence is not our end.* Is our ultimate end the manipulation of physical existence? If we stop there, we continue to maintain our egocentric focus on ourselves, as this is a one-way view that ignores the same physical world we wish to manipulate. We ignore the relational aspects. In this view, we have the one-way relationship of what is there in the physical world for me. This is how we operate currently. We backdrop our justifications against our internal desires irrespective to what we relationally engaged in. It provides many manufactured-based justifications to capitalism, religion, to many of our scientists and to all of us. It allows us to do simply what

we want without regard to the required accountability to thought with the connections to the physical kept, as well as, the appropriate idea categorization that determines our code of conduct of action between us.

48. *We need to look at the relationship between humankind and our physical-world creation.* To understand our ultimate end of pursuit by human beings involves our relationship to physical existence and our maintaining the physical connection in a continuous state. Under this view, the human being and the physical world is a handshake. We see that it is about the interaction between the physical world and ourselves and with each in their movement. The physical world in its movement is overpowering to human beings, but in our lives, as we learn to live within it. We seek control of it. Nevertheless, control is egocentric. We should seek a relationship to our physical world; therefore, to begin to understand our ultimate end is to evaluate to stabilize ourselves in our physical existence and not our physical existence destabilizing us.

49. *Our ultimate end given:* Our ultimate end is our evaluate-to-balance to our physical reality through an open free will and done so individually and over all individuals. We then have our accurate assessment and understanding to reality and our physically connected and thesis-based justifications to our action or inaction. We then know what justified coercion is and what unjustified coercion is. We then can distinguish between an arbitrary will of another and a non-arbitrary will of another. We then can release our freedom and liberty. Our ultimate end is ultimate in that it involves the continuance of humankind for as long as physical existence provides us a home without our interference of immoral action. Our ultimate end involves our relationship to our physical world, which is our creation and creator, to which we achieve the maximum degree of life and liberty in it while maintaining our code of conduct that our physical world provides. Our provided code of conduct from physical existence is all encompassing in that it involves a code of conduct that is between physical existence and us. Since physical existence made all of us from the same source—physical existence, this includes a code of conduct between ourselves.

50. *Pursuit of happiness is only one part of human existence.* Happiness does not maintain a continued relationship, as happiness in a continued state saturates our brains chemically. As we experience and pursue a state of constant happiness, we seek more and greater happiness to offset the natural saturation, and this in the end brings us frustration and unhappiness. Happiness as the pursuit of material things involves the same problem. We find sources to our happiness differently between people, thus it could never be the ultimate and unifying aspects of human beings. Boethius referred to the variety of desires human beings have as the "sum of happiness." He wrote, "Therefore

happiness is by no means to be sought in these things, which are believed to provide each desirable thing separately?" (40, III.IX.71, p269) While the religious transferred the sliver idea of happiness to their manufactured higher authority, as seen with Thomas Aquinas, our Boethius did too, for he wrote, "therefore, true happiness must reside in the most high God." (40, III.X.36, p277) What our religions had always given us was happiness tied to god-ideas. We had a false reality tied to human emotions. If we replace god-ideas with physical existence, we move closer. Nevertheless, we currently pair happiness with thought existence where it contains no accountability to morality. Our secular side fairs poorly too. What our historical philosophers had always given us were individual ends, which were not in relation to all individuals and with commonality to every person. The never-ending and individual differentiation provided us our biggest clue that it could not be our ultimate end. Think about it, the question involved the ultimate end for *Human Beings*, which encompassed all human beings, yet everyone sought their own specific happiness, thus the quest for the ultimate end mixed an all-individuals idea to an individual idea, or our equal-to-us with our unequal-to-us.

51. *We can reinterpret the ideas of Thomas Aquinas under thesisism to what he considered not to be the ultimate end to happiness.* In this respect, when Thomas Aquinas stated what our ultimate happiness was not, he was correct. We do not find our ultimate end of happiness unified between each individual mental existence. Rather, our personal concept of happiness varies from person to person. Thomas Aquinas said that our ultimate "felicity" was not found in having glory, being rich, having world power, health, sense enjoyment, being moral, being prudent, in our arts, and so on. (37, III.29-36)

52. *Our ultimate end involves our finite existence against an infinite existence.* These items listed by Thomas Aquinas were narrowband aspects of human beings and they involved finite consumption. We have a relationship between the physical world and ourselves, individually and as all individuals, and the relationship to move toward a thesis evaluation of stability and freedom is the understanding and seeking the balance to our life individually and over all individuals. Our ultimate end is in this balance with our creation, that is, our physical world and ourselves. We need *actions* to occur to achieve this *balance*, however, the *actions* themselves, although could bring moments of happiness, were not the enduring state to achieve, as it was finite, whereas, our *balance* is in relation to our infinite physical existence and the duration of ones life.

53. *The ultimate end in thesisism is enduring.* Thomas Aquinas placed our felicity into his manufactured idea about a higher consciousness. This moved us away from our creation and into our thought existence that sought the pleasant emotion of love, which too was finite. When we balance to

our creation, the physical world, we balance to the infinite existence of the physical world and to the entire time of our lives. This makes it enduring. This also allows us to reach our greatest potential for an open free will, and in turn, to love, as we are connecting our parts of life, individuals between all individuals, in equal terms.[33] This love is not the emotional consumptive love, but the enduring love that comes from this achievement of connecting to the eternal-like aspects of physical existence and the life-long aspects of human physical design.

54. *When our handshake with physical existence is broken, our ultimate end is not achievable.* Thesisism is different from learning to manipulate the physical world. It differs because it is not a relationship of *what can this do for me*, but applies all aspects of the physical world in relation to all aspects of ourselves, at the all-individuals level and at the individual level. We cannot maintain our purpose if we do not maintain our sliver idea of reality to our creator, physical existence. Thesisism is an evaluation of physical existence to our morality equations.

55. *We must maintain our handshake with physical existence.* Thesisism is also different from anything presented in that it involves the constant handshake between human beings and the physical world in total. We must maintain a relationship between our thought existence and our physical world. This means we not only have a flow of ideas when we engage in mental animations, but the flow must relate back to our physical existence. This measures reality against the physical world and not to the random animations of human thought. It is a relationship where we ask, what does this mean I do.

56. *Individual ultimate ends achieved individually come at the expense of all individuals and is immoral.* Wealth can contribute to our lives to adjust those things around us to make our individual *sense* of happiness. Nevertheless, we are a group of individuals. When we create our individual happiness as an ultimate end, we create a manufactured idea that can lead to justifications to have those around ourselves to achieve our self-interest individual happiness independent to moral considerations. We see our historical justifications for slavery or to indenture, or to create false freedom, and thus our sense of individual happiness as an ultimate end comes at the expense of others. We become immoral, as our manufactured balance violates the equal-to-us aspects of our common human consciousness. It is our responsibility, both individually and as a group of individuals, to seek this moral balance, not only individually, but also with all individuals as well.

---

33 "Equal terms" here involves the expression of both our equal thesis-morality and unequal thesis-morality.

57. *Our ultimate end requires more than just our thought existence; we require our thought existence to be in a state of free will in relation to the physical world.* Our relationship between the physical world and ourselves, and between us collectively and the physical world, is not a *spiritual* plane to obtain the power of balance to life. This is the thinking of other systems of thought. We achieve our purpose by the experience of our relationship and balance position to our physical world. This involves oneself, your community, land, air, water and all its living creatures. To reach this means we have to set aside personal desires during evaluation. We create our free-flow framed-reference to achieve our free will. Then we can achieve our ultimate end, to evaluate-to-balance our reality relationally to ourselves individually, to humankind and to physical existence.

58. *Historically, we have valued our adhesive framed-references, which led us away from truth.* We have greatly valued our various adhesive framed-references that hold our false-reality desires. We market to them, create economies on them, and develop power from them. Nevertheless, only a few benefit. This small percent of people can achieve a state where they can affect life and life cannot affect them. Nevertheless, it comes at the cost of immoral behavior that results in a high percent of lives with human consciousness manipulated and controlled. We can see this in the extended order of capitalism when F. A. Hayek wrote apologetically for capitalistic invasion and the use of others resources. Hayek wrote, "In some places invaded, as it were, by the extended order, those following new practices, who could extract more from the given land, would often be able to offer other occupants, in return for access to their land (without the occupants having to do any work at all, and without the 'invaders' having to use force), nearly as much as, and sometimes even more than, these occupants had obtained by hard toil." (41, p121) The assumption here was that his use of resources without ideas of balance was superior. The American Indian had understood that we must balance to our physical existence.

59. *Achieving free will does not mean to eliminate personal desires, but knowing when we need to have our free will.* This does not mean we live without desires, but with the ability to achieve our free will as needed. We need the ability to see and recognize our personal desires and to set them aside. We need the ability to recognize the structure of our nature and to operate within its limits. We need the ability to recognize our physical existence in nature as human beings and the physical nature around and within us. Cicero wrote of Cato saying, "It is of the essence of virtue that one makes choices among the things that are in accordance with nature." (35, III.12) What was the "essence of virtue … in accordance with nature" the Stoic referred too? Did they know to what they spoke?

60. *We achieve our ultimate end not by individual method only.* If our ultimate end requires a state of relationship that consists of actions between others, the physical world and ourselves in such a way we each mutually interact with life, how can we achieve this? If we approach in the individual person mode only, which follows our differences and unequal-to-us aspect of our moral model based in human structure, we end striving for specific forms of happiness, pleasure, glory and more. We strive as individual pursuits without regard to our full human nature. Therefore, the "essence of virtue" that Cato spoke of "in accordance to nature" came the closest that I could find to a thesisist outlook. Nevertheless, it is in his "nature" that our physical existence resides. Our "nature" is one source to two expressions. Unless we acknowledge both, we amputate half of existence. The question to ask, when we pull in thesisism, is how does our ultimate end translate into a method to which we can bring accountability to our ultimate end?

61. *We can achieve our ultimate end with the accountability method of thesisism.* We have an accountability method that we can use to move ourselves toward the achievement of our ultimate end as human beings. Our method involves our measurement of ideas against our human structure in physical existence. From our human structure, we discover our morality model. Our code of conduct and moral expression derive from our requirements to equal thesis-morality and unequal thesis-morality. Until we have a moral system of thought with accountability, arbitrary coercion will prevail. Morality and virtue has been an important part of the human fabric. Virtue was important to the Stoics, and they presented it as the only good. Cato said, "Morality alone is the one thing which you call virtuous, right, praiseworthy and decent. So I ask you, if that is the only good, what else is there to pursue? On the other side, if the only evil is what is base, vicious, indecent, corrupt and foul, what else will you say should be avoided?" (35, III.14)

62. *A thesis ultimate end serves improvement of humankind.* There appears to be a "general consensus" that we each have the right to attempt the pursuit of our ultimate end, and our personal desires motivate us. This is fine for others, as it involves their own interpretations without accountability. There appears also a "general consensus" to attempt to accept virtue and moral behavior for their own sake. Again, Cicero wrote of Cato, "The starting-point, therefore, is that things in accordance with nature are to be adopted for their own sake, and their contraries are likewise to be rejected." (35, III.20) Cicero wrote, "The view that anything moral is to be sought for its own sake is one we share with many other philosophers. ... [T]his is the position universally maintained, in particular of course by those who held that nothing else counts as a good except morality." (35, III.36) Thesisism demonstrates with our humanness model of morality that when we measure off our physical world,

we should not only adopt morality for its own sake, but also that it serves as our method to achieve our ultimate end. It brings us our ultimate individual and all-individuals goal of quality human life. Our universal end serves all of us between all individuals and individually. Therefore, the achievement of our ultimate end, our state of balance, to express and seek those of individual nature while in an all-individuals existence, comes from the pursuit of morality and our code of conduct measured off our physical world. Thesisism provides us our accountability method and a way to get there.

63. *Our divine law and natural law division led us to confusion.* John Locke faired well under civil ideas and less under moral ideas. We can see why this is when we read what Montesquieu had to say in his *The Spirit of the Laws.* First published in 1748, in his 1757 edition the author wrote in his forward, "one must note that what I call virtue in a republic is love of the homeland, that is, love of equality. It is not a moral virtue or a Christian virtue, it is political virtue, and this is the spring that makes a republican government move." (42, pxli) He placed virtue into the political arena and into civil law. Now we are blurring the distinction between divine law and natural law, not because Montesquieu was blurring it, but because of acknowledging that virtue exists beyond divine law. He further wrote in his forward, "Finally, the good man discussed … is not the Christian good man but the political good man, who has the political virtue I have mentioned." (42, pxli)

64. *During the eighteenth century, people struggled to move our system of human thought to accountability.* People were struggling at this moment in time with three problems not in their consciousness. One was that morality, which is physically based and has one source but with two expressions, was *sensed,* yet remained unseen by them. Another was how religion moved morality away from our physical creation, making it difficult to see our humanness model. The third was that unaccountable ideas resulted in numerous power seeking organizations and churches. Thomas Jefferson wrote in his autobiography, "an amendment was proposed, by inserting the word 'Jesus Christ,' so that it should read, 'a departure from the plan of Jesus Christ, the holy author of our religion;' the insertion was rejected by a great majority, in proof that they meant to comprehend, within the mantle of its protection, the Jew and the Gentile, the Christian and Mahometan, the Hindoo, and Infidel of every denomination." (43, p40-41)

65. *The split between divine law and natural law took its toll.* In our historical inability to measure against the physical world, which started with our ancient philosophers, like Aristotle and Pythagoras, we had split morality into two distinct areas of natural law and divine law. This resulted in the US Constitution having ideas such as "We the people" tied to natural law and to Montesquieu-like ideas of their time to "love of equality." We see it

clearly with our Bill of Rights and the separation of church (divine laws) and state (natural laws). Montesquieu distinguished the morals of religion and the morals of the political, that they were indeed two different and distinct entities. From a thesisist's point of view, the distinction ran between false-reality and reality-based ideas. The separation between divine law and natural law obscured that morality really was one source, two expressions and tied to the physical world.

66. *Divine law took natural law and removed it from the eternal-like characteristic of physical existence.* Our confusion between divine law and natural law came when we put the eternal qualities of physical existence into an animated idea of a conscious creator that knew and manipulated our existence. We had removed our eternal aspects of morality from natural law, which moved us away from our creation, and placed morality into our thought existence only, where we could then animate anything we desired regardless to the sliver idea of reality.

67. *Under thesisism, divine law and natural law were from the same source, our physical existence.* So what does this have to do with our ultimate end as human beings? That morality extends throughout our existence to all laws. Therefore, to align our ultimate end, both in individual form and in an all-individuals form, requires the understanding of how we arrive there. Montesquieu wrote, "The principle of democracy is corrupted not only when the spirit of equality is lost, but also when the spirit of extreme equality is taken up and each one wants to be the equal of those chosen to command." (42, 8.2, p112) Here we see the fundamentals of thesisism expressed. In the writing by Montesquieu, he touched on our equal thesis-morality and unequal thesis-morality. The problem was that we have not understood that both of these expressions occur at the same time. We determine our moral actions by which side of physical existence expresses itself.

68. *Montesquieu had a sense of equality and inequality.* He saw equality at birth, and then inequality came with growth. He wrote, "In the state of nature, men are born in equality, but they cannot remain so. Society makes them lose their equality, and they become equal again only through laws." (42, 8.3, p114) He was more correct than incorrect. Our physical world cannot change; therefore, our equality remains. Nevertheless, as a child grows to adulthood, our differences grow and reveal themselves. Society involves a human thought system, and when we allow unaccountable animations of ideas, we can create a society where we need laws to restore what our creation has given us naturally. Montesquieu wrote, "Therefore, democracy has to avoid two excesses, the spirit of inequality, which leads it to aristocracy or to the government of one alone, and the spirit of extreme equality, which leads it to the despotism of one alone, as the despotism of one alone ends

by conquest." (42, 8.2, p112) Until we know our accountability method measured against the physical world, we can only state, as Montesquieu did, what our backdrop of human animations seems to give us as a generalized form of truth. What he wrote was the essence of our humanness model out of balance, our equal thesis-morality and unequal thesis-morality moved to one end or the other. What he had described before their occurrence were socialism—extreme equality, and pure capitalism—extreme inequality. This was extremely insightful!

69. *Our humanness model has one source with two expressions that can lead us to achieving our ultimate end.* Montesquieu understood at some level that there was an equal and unequal aspect to human existence. We can demonstrate this duality in our physically based humanness model and our physically based aspects of equal thesis-morality and unequal thesis-morality. If our ultimate end has the same expression for historical ideas of divine law and natural law, or, divine morality and virtue and political morality and virtue, then we are really experiencing a single common aspect of our human nature. Physical existence expresses this through our creation and us from itself and our two expressions of morality. Our use of the accountability method from thesisism to ideas and morality leads us toward our ultimate end and our well-being in our existence.

70. *Divine law can only bring confusion.* Why animate a manufactured idea about a higher consciousness. In doing this, we separated ourselves from our own creation. It removed us from seeing what we could read from our creator, the physical world. It animated a human character to creation and opened us wide for manipulation by any given self-appointed authority. We could fool ourselves only for so long before our creation—our physical world—would overpower any personally held false-reality desires. Although many offer creation as a mystery, it is not. The mystery attributed to the alleged higher authority was simply the higher authority of physical existence.

71. *We could have limited interactions between thesisism and religion.* Thesisism is not necessarily antagonistic to some segments of the religious. The religious could desire and wish to undertake the accountability method of thesis-morality while resolving their manufactured ideas about a higher consciousness in accepting the physical world as our creator and creation, from which we receive its word. If they wish to provide authorship of the physical world to their higher authority and begin to read our physical existence like people read books, they could come to a reconciliation of sorts. Any thesisist would not begrudge anyone using thesisist accountability methods if it works toward betterment of humankind. Nevertheless, we would have disagreements as to where we could apply the label of thesisist thought. Any assimilation would contain within it expected acknowledgement of thesisism

James S. Serilla

and its accountability methods. Acknowledged violations to thesisism would be required.

72. *Here is a historical summary of our manufactured ideas that led us to our events today and how to move to thesis ideas to correct our amputated reason and rational thought.* We have seen how our historical start had a fundamental flaw, as we did not measure our ideas against physical existence. From this, we declared a long series of manufactured ideas that led us to ideas involving a God giving our planet to humankind, to which we tied our narrow self-interests to the idea of the pursuit of happiness without any accountability to our actions and created the faith-based invisible hand idea of economics. Under thesisism, our ultimate end is in our development of each individual to move toward a non-adhesive framed-reference, consequently having a free will, to bring in the reality around ourselves without bending it by attaching non-original master ideas and in turn evaluate-to-balance to our true existence. The output from this leads us to truth, a moral code of conduct, and our thesis-based justifications; and this demonstrates with certainty our justified coercion, which then releases our true freedom and liberty. The question now is, how are fairing today?

BOOK THREE
REAL-WORLD CIVILIZATION

Thomas Paine and the Moral Flow to Government

1. *Thomas Paine had a balance to his thought on government and society.* I have great admiration for Thomas Paine. His intellect was a genuine friend to humankind. Nevertheless, opinions of Thomas Paine vary. For example, Theodore Roosevelt referred to Thomas Paine as a "dirty little atheist," while Ronald Reagan quoted Thomas Paine during his acceptance speech for his Republican Party presidential nomination. (44, p9 & 335) Thomas Paine was neither an atheist nor a Christian. He was a Deist. Deists varied in how they viewed their idea of a higher authority. When it came to Thomas Paine, he connected his deity to the physical world in a greater degree than other Deists. His directional flow of mental animations was not from his God to humankind, where humankind was some kind of favorite child to all other existence. His God did not give the earth to humankind as an unearned gift to be used in any selfish manor. He did not allow his divine being to be placed into his head and then used the idea to animate any desire he wanted. Thomas Paine understood this disorder. He wrote, "When a set of artful men pretended, through the medium of oracles, to hold intercourse with the Deity, as familiarly as they now march up the backstairs in European courts, the world was completely under the government of superstition. The oracles were consulted, and whatever they were made to say, became the law; and this sort of government lasted as long as this sort of superstition lasted." (45, p54)

2. *Thomas Paine was a Deist with a cause.* Thomas Paine did place reality into a manufactured idea about a higher authority. However, his higher authority played no role. He wrote, "I believe in one God, and no more; and I hope for happiness beyond this life." (46, p21) Since he accepted the existence of only one higher authority, he rejected all else. Although we could

179

say more about what constitutes a Deist, this certainly removed him from being Christian. It is interesting from the position of a thesisist that he wrote, "hope for happiness." His hope implied uncertainty, and it demonstrates that he did not let any of his desires move the sliver idea of reality easily. He wrote, "The only idea man can affix to the name of God, is that of a *first cause*, the cause of all things." (46, p47) With a statement like that, what else could he have said about his higher authority idea? Nevertheless, he connected his manufactured ideas about a higher authority to physical existence. He continued with, "In like manner of reasoning, everything we behold carries in itself the internal evidence that it did not make itself." Since we cannot understand existence before our conscious awareness, we do not have within our grasp an ability to comprehend anything that would create itself. This is true in our time as it was in his time. Nevertheless, we cannot necessarily accept his premise that there was a first cause. The human idea of cause has embedded within it a pre-existent. The moment we subscribe characteristics to first cause or our pre-cause, we are trying to animate our experience into something we do not have view of. What we as humans term origins may not have the same characteristic given to us by our experience. We end back to the self-existent cause by Ethan Allen.

3. *Thomas Paine made admirable statements to his position of belief and duty.* He wrote, "I believe the equality of man, and I believe that religious duties consist in doing justice, loving mercy and endeavoring to make our fellow-creatures happy." (46, p21-22) We have evidence that he understood and responded to our equal thesis-morality. He understood that justice was part of the moral equations. The idea of loving mercy assists us in maintaining the E = E equation of equal thesis-morality that people often want to violate. He had us work toward this equation. Mercy had a tendency to set aside our adhesive framed-reference and open our free will. When we do this, we can evaluate-to-balance to our reality. This moved us toward a reasoned and measured happiness. It was not the narrow or selfish pursuit of our individual happiness. The happiness he sought was to all of existence. Thus it began to align with our ultimate end of our evaluate-to-balance, our open free will and our reality.

4. *Thomas Paine aligned remarkably well with the positions of thesisists.* He placed his measurements against the physical world, although he did not describe it that way. He wrote,

> It is only in the CREATION that all our ideas and conceptions of a *word of God* can unite. The Creation speaketh an universal language, independently of human speech or human language, multiplied and various as they be. It is an ever existing original, which every man

can read. It cannot be forged; it cannot be counterfeited; it cannot be lost; it cannot be altered; it cannot be suppressed. It does not depend upon the will of man whether it shall be published or not; it publishes itself from one end of the earth to the other. It preaches to all nations and to all worlds; and this *word of God* reveals to man all that is necessary for man to know God. (46, p46)

5. *As a thesisist, except for the semantics, there is agreement with Thomas Paine in the above paragraph.* A thesisist places various higher authority and higher creator ideas, especially those that carry the idea of consciousness, to the category of pure-manufactured ideas or theorized-manufactured ideas with an extremely low probability. If Thomas Paine placed the sliver idea of reality to his idea of God, yet provided it with no direct interaction, this then pushed his higher-consciousness idea back in its effect the same or similar to a position of influence a thesisist gives. Thomas Paine gave his idea of creation in a narrowband definition, and it allowed us to see that he and thesisists were near identical in the narrowband master idea of creation. His creation became the same as the creation under thesisism in terms of universal language. That universal language was our physical world. He placed his word of God into it, whereas we acknowledge that we are created from physical existence, therefore, physical existence is both our creation and creator to which we measure against.

6. *Thomas Paine took the time to narrowband his ideas.* He did so with his statement that "all our ideas and conceptions" are only from creation. When we realize his *"word of God"* and our position to physical existence under thesisism was that both are *creator and creation*, we find that we have measured our ideas in a remarkably similar fashion. He recognized that measurement against the physical existence of creation removed the human being from the equation to determine truth. He had come essentially to the same conclusions we have. Truth becomes universal to all human beings on earth. Truth dose not live by our rules, we live by its rules. Truth to ideas has a process. We must understand the process to ideas on their terms, not ours. We must observe how they create themselves, how they move, and how they exist. Thomas Paine wrote, "It is only by the exercise of reason, that man can discover God." (46, p47) I have two responses to this sentence when we view this God as our physical existence. One is that we discover truth, we do not make it, and thus Thomas Paine was correct. Second, we would require reason to be with accountability by our maintaining where reality applies. We would require reason to apply the seven elements to determine truth that thesisism provides. We would require the sliver idea of reality to remain in its correct position.

7. *Because of the recognition by Thomas Paine of the unaccountable religious thought around him, he gave up many religious ideas except for a core idea of a higher authority.* He wrote, "Under how many subtilties, or absurdities, has the divine right to govern been imposed on the credulity of mankind!" (45, p13) He saw the absurdities in religious writings and the coercive actions of religion justified by the idea of divine right. He wrote,

> Whence arose all the horrid assassinations of whole nations of men, women, and infants, with which the Bible is filled; and the bloody persecutions, and tortures unto death and religious wars, that since that time have laid Europe in blood and ashes; whence arose they but from this impious thing called revealed religion, and this monstrous belief that God has spoken to man? The lies of the Bible have been the cause of the one, and the lies of the Testament [of] the other. (46, p185)

8. *Thomas Paine was a rarity of truth to political systems.* Of politics, he wrote of himself, "When, therefore, I turned my thoughts towards matters of government, I had to form a system for myself, that accorded with the moral and philosophic principles in which I had been educated." (46, p63) We rarely have an individual that dealt with politics display both intelligence and honesty. The contribution by Thomas Paine to the birth and development of the United States of America is under-appreciated and shamefully unknown among the majority of the American people. The "moral and philosophic principles" of Thomas Paine gave him vision to the truth of society and government. Godwin wrote, "The road to the improvement of mankind, is in the utmost degree simple, to speak and act the truth." (39, Book V Chapter XIV, p120) Thomas Paine wrote, "But such is the irresistible nature of truth, that all it asks, and all it wants, is the liberty of appearing." (47, p1) Thomas Paine was a conduit for the irresistible nature of truth, especially concerning issues of government. This speaking of truth connected to nature may be one of the reasons why we, the general population, know little of him.

9. *Shown in his Rights of Man, we have evidence that Thomas Paine moved away from his deity and toward physical existence for a source of measurement.* Thomas Paine wrote in *Rights of Man*, "Though I mean not to touch upon any sectarian principle of religion, yet it may be worth observing, that the genealogy of Christ is traced to Adam. Why then not trace the rights of man to the creation of man? I will answer the question. Because there have been upstart governments, thrusting themselves between, and presumptuously working to *un-make* man." (45, p48-49) He had moved his measurement of the rights of man to the creation of man. The creation of man is physical. He did not say to trace the rights of man to his deity. In the *Rights of Man*,

he moved his deity toward the singularity of man in our physical world. He wrote of religion that, "all agree in establishing one point, *the unity of man*; by which I mean, that men are all of *one degree*, and consequently that all men are born equal, and with equal natural right." (45, p49) Although I do not agree with his premise that "all agree," which meant all religions agree on this point, his thinking had shifted to equality, and that, my friend, was an equation. That equation is our equal thesis-morality, E = E. By tying his ideas to "natural right" and "born equal," we had the move toward physical existence and away from human beings animating anything they wanted in their heads.

10. *We can see my claimed thesis when he spoke of natural and civil rights.* He wrote, "Natural rights are those which appertain to man in right of his existence. Of this kind are all the intellectual rights, or rights of the mind, and also all those rights of acting as an individual for his own comfort and happiness, which are not injurious to the natural rights of others." (45, p52) This was remarkably similar to thesisism. He had made our rights relational to our existence, which included thought and physical existence. He placed rights into our actions in physical existence and made them relational between an individual and all individuals. This fits our physical reality. It was not by accident that he first described intellectual rights and rights of the mind. Our equal thesis-morality is our human consciousness. This was where our similarity resided. He did not specifically connect it to physical existence, but for these rights to exist there had to be the physical existence of the human mind. The fundamental principle was his "equal natural right" in the preceding paragraph. Along with his intellectual rights, he referred to "all those rights of acting as an individual." Here we had unequal thesis-morality. He understood that equal thesis-morality outweighed unequal thesis-morality when he qualified it that it could not be injurious to others. It is important to understand that his "comfort and happiness" was relational to rights, and not to a human end. He made "comfort and happiness" relational to a balance in physical existence by individual actions "not injurious to the natural rights of others." Since he closely tied "natural rights" to physical existence, we have the beginning of alignment to needed thesis justifications for action or inaction.

11. *Allow me to break from standard and say—Thomas Paine was cool.* Thomas Paine was indeed cool. His clarity in vision and writing to the construction of our governing system was such a value to humankind. His vision and contribution was perhaps the most American in nature to anyone up to George Washington. George Washington played his role as a General, and in his actions as a General and as a President, reflected the ideals behind the intent of our Constitution. The service given by Thomas Paine to the revolutionary war of the emerging United States was equally important

from his political writing of *Common Sense* to his writing of the *American Crisis* series. He wrote the three biggest sellers of the eighteenth century. (44, p8) As General George Washington moved the physical components of the revolution, Thomas Paine moved the mental components. Without the inspirational writings of Thomas Paine, some argue George Washington would have lost his troops early in the campaign. Thomas Paine inspired pre-Americans through his writings, both in his *Common Sense* and his *American Crisis* series, which included the famous line, "These are the times that try men's souls," (48, p63) to move a revolution and to keep it going during troubled times. Nevertheless, this was not the only reason why Thomas Paine was cool, he was cool because he was an honest and moral man that stood up and spoke as he saw it. Thomas Paine held the essence of true American ideals.

12. *Since the influence of Thomas Paine was a mix of political and social morals, we need to focus on his view of the moral purpose of government and contrast it with our government as it operates today.* To do this, we need to look at how he saw the role of government, and how it works morally and what happens when it works immorally. We can start with the words of Thomas Paine, how they line up or do not line up with thesis-morality and then view our government today to see if Thomas Paine would be satisfied with the current performance of the United States government.

13. *Thomas Paine knew words could bring confusion and took the time to narrowband his ideas.* He understood that we needed to align our thoughts so that each of us was thinking the same ideas as we discussed them, otherwise only chaos would arise. In 1776, he published *Common Sense*. The first words were, "Some writers have so confounded society with government, as to leave little or no distinction between them; whereas they are not only different, but have different origins. Society is produced by our wants, and government by our wickedness; the former promotes our happiness *positively* by uniting our affections, the latter *negatively* by restraining our vices. The one encourages intercourse, the other creates distinctions. The first is a patron, the last a punisher." (48, p5) His writing reveals two important understandings. He recognized when words became broadband and took the time to narrowband the words so each person was animating the same idea. The second was his recognition of the source of government. He had government produced by our wickedness. If human beings inherently knew the correct code of conduct to display between one another, and inherently engaged in that code of conduct, government would not be necessary. Thomas Paine chose to state what produced government, but what then is the purpose of government in relation to its producer.

14. *If wickedness was the producer of government, then the purpose of government was to preserve the rights of man.* To preserve the rights of humankind, we must operate under a moral code of conduct. Therefore, the purpose of government was to be our conscience at the level of society; that is, our social and moral conscious. Under David Hume, we could not use reason and rational thought to operate society. The extended order of capitalism shouts coercion when we stop and rationally attempt to question them. Adam Smith had us accepting the forward movement of the extended order of capitalism under the idea of faith with his invisible hand idea. Under thesisism, moral ideas must go through the thesis-morality filter (See Diagram 5). How do we control our "wickedness" that comes from the coercive animal? It starts from our physical existence and ends with our moral consciousness as Diagram 5 shows. Our government is our tool to our expression of our moral consciousness because as Paine writes, "Government ... is like the badge of lost innocence...." (48, p5) To be moral under thesisism, our government must maintain the correct flow of conduct as required by equal thesis-morality and unequal thesis-morality. We can see this moral flow in Diagram 4b. As Thomas Paine noted in his statement that society and government were not the same, this diagram shows the position of our government in our society. It shows society and government under thesis-morality and manufactured-morality states. It also shows how government grew out of it into a more complex system. To make sure the extended order of capitalism operates morally, we need our extended order of government and our source to moral expression. Government must operate in the correct flow to our needs from equal and unequal thesis-morality. By our understanding of government provided by Thomas Paine, we can begin to assess under thesisism if our government, the United States government, is operating morally or immorally at any given moment of time.

15. *How Thomas Paine viewed the American government:* Let us review his position on representative government. "But the government of America, which is wholly on the system of representation, is the only real republic in character and in practice, that now exists. Its government has no other object than the public business of the nation, and therefore it is properly a republic; and the Americans have taken care that THIS, and no other, shall always be the object of their government, by their rejecting every thing hereditary, and establishing government on the system of representation only." (47, p30-31) Thomas Paine has given us his view of the United States government. He stated it was wholly a system of representation. Nevertheless, is this true today?

16. *When we grant ourselves equality and individual voting power, can an individual or a subset of individuals subvert our representation?* As citizens of the

United States, we vote for our representatives. Nevertheless, does voting alone assure representation? It can when every individual citizen has the same value of voting power. However, when the value of voting power is corrupted, our representative system fails. The moral code of conduct for government is to follow thesis-morality. Each individual has the equal-to-us conduct that we must follow by the dictates of physical existence, or what Thomas Paine would refer to, as natural law. This physical connection brings a commonality to the actions of all people so that moral issues of conduct that reside in our equal-to-us can arise and be properly maintained. When we implement unequal-to-us to an equal-to-us concern, we have immoral action taking place. When grouped individualistic systems interfere with our representation process, the value of voting power becomes imbalanced. If the pool of representatives for election can only arise with the sanction of grouped individualistic systems, this skews voting power to the individualistic systems. From a viewpoint of moral flow, we lose our *all-individuals* moral flow and we have individual actions going to individual. Diagram 4b shows this construct. Thomas Paine stated that the "government has no other object than the public business of the nation." (47, p30-31) If we engage in our flow of conduct from *individual to individual*, this cannot be the business of the nation as it differentially treats its citizens. Further, individual-to-individual flow is counter to the physical realities of moral conduct. Thomas Paine had upfront experience with individual-to-individual flow when he stated that we Americans reject every thing hereditary. We had rejected hereditary government and chosen a representative government.

17. *For our government to be a representative system, it has to represent everyone and everyone equally.* Thomas Paine brought this to light when he wrote, "Every government that does not act on the principle of a *Republic*, or in other words, that does not make the *res-publica* its whole and sole object, is not a good government. Republican government is no other than government established and conducted for the interest of the public, as well individually and collectively." (47, p30) He had taken the idea of society and stated it was an individualistic and a collective (all-individuals) entity. This fits with the physical realities of human existence. His stated purpose of government was to maintain its relationship with the whole republic and not segments or portions. He had established the moral conditions required of government. He actually met the definition of thesis-morality. We have it represented in the following statements from Thomas Paine. "On the contrary, the representative system is always parallel with the order and immutable laws of nature, and meets the reason of man in every part." (47, p37) He had reason of man connected to the immutable laws of nature. Since his idea of God was distant and his idea of nature was close, this strongly suggests he measured

his ideas against the physical world. He further wrote, "That which is called government, or rather that which we ought to conceive government to be, is no more than some common center, in which all the parts of society unite. This cannot be accomplished by any method so conducive to the various interests of the community, as by the representative system. It concentrates the knowledge necessary to the interest of the parts, and of the whole. It places government in a state of constant maturity." (47, p34) He animated ideas of government as a common center and all of its parts. We have our equal-to-us and our unequal-to-us. We have our all-individuals and individual needs. He stated our government was to know the interest of its parts and of the whole. He said that government was to be knowledge to conduct thesis-morality to all individuals and to the individual. Thomas Paine knew the answers were in the law of nature. The law of nature, to which we measure our ideas against, was our physical existence.

18. *Thomas Paine had insights into various government systems.* I want to contrast his view of hereditary government with thesisism. Then compare how our representational government currently works. In his *Rights of Man, Part the Second,* he wrote,

> Government on the old system, is an assumption of power, for the aggrandisement of itself; on the new, a delegation of power, for the common benefit of society. The former supports itself by keeping up a system of war; the latter promotes a system of peace, as the true means of enriching a nation. The one encourages national prejudices; the other promotes universal society, as the means of universal commerce. The one measures its prosperity, by the quantity of revenue it extorts; the other proves its excellence, by the small quantity of taxes it requires. (47, p19)

He contrasted the old government with the new intended government. The old was the hereditary government of kings and monarchs. The new was the representational republic of the United States.

19. *Does our current government align with the new or the old or to something new to our times?* Are our President, Congress and Supreme Court meeting the standard of "common benefit of society?" For that to happen, we have to have our correct moral flow occurring from our government. Nevertheless, with the intense lobbing, the excessive amounts of money needed for our representatives to run for office, we have our representatives in our society skewed to those with wealth and power only. With our two party system and the monies needed to run for office, the society of these parties only include the individual self-interests that give them the financial means to run. This narrows representation to selected pools of people. We could think

of this as having similarities to kings and monarchs, because these pools of people derive from individualistic sources. We have the lobbing of corporate desires, religious desires and many other self-interest group desires. Under this, our system operates under the "aggrandisement of itself." In fact, not only does capitalistic self-interest operate under this aggrandizement, but also many organizations operate as if our nation is superior in every way rather than operating for the common benefit of society. Corporations and many religious groups naturally gravitate toward narrow contributions to this society rather than operating in the common benefit of our society. They want continued expansion; corporate power in economic profit and religious groups with power placed on the behaviors of human beings. We are seeing an old system rearing up its head in a different form from kings, monarchs. We have the kingship of corporate giants and the evangelical priestcraft with their corporate marketed houses of god. What does their aggrandizement result in? According to Thomas Paine, it results in war and national prejudices. At the time of this writing, we have our war and national prejudices. Have we lost our representational government? Have we acquired a corrupted moral flow in our government and in our own societal thought?

20. *Let us examine some of the statements of hereditary government by Thomas Paine and compare it to our current government. Example 1:* He wrote, "Man has no authority over posterity in matters of personal right; and therefore, no man, or body of men, had, or can have, a right to set up a hereditary government." (47, p20) A hereditary government involves a person acquiring governing authority over others because of birth or entitlement. This meant representational government did not exist. This hereditary-based leader had authority and power arbitrary to natural law. If we find the ideas of hereditary government silly, stupid and not in align to what our physical world displays, we have to assess ourselves and ask if we operate as a representational government or a hereditary government. No one, according to Thomas Paine, had the right to set up a hereditary government, as it conflicted with natural law. A hereditary government could not fulfill the required moral flows, as the king made his individual decisions in relation to both community (equal-to-us) and individual (unequal-to-us) moral questions.

21. *If no one had the right to set up a hereditary government, which results in individual-to-individual moral flow, then any perversion of our government that disrupts our duel flow to thesis-morality to a one-sided flow has set up a hereditary-like government. Example 1 continued:* Because our corporate entities have moved our unequal-to-us evaluations, which are our all-individuals-to-individual flow, to an individual-to-individual flow, it has resulted in a selected segment of society that can influence our thesis-morality equations. They can influence to disrupt our equal-to-us by shifting it to an imbalance

state and influence the value of their mean difference to an imbalanced state by evaluating themselves. This is immoral. All corporations partake in our society. Our society of all-individuals decides their thesis-justifications to actions relational to society, not the corporate individuals or the governmental representatives acting as an individual for the corporate individuals. It is important to note that the flow of actions within the corporations is not in play here. It is actions of corporations within society.

22. *The flow of unequal thesis-morality from all individuals to the individual includes the individual involved.* Edmund Burke, an economist and an intellectual opponent to Thomas Paine, wrote, "One of the first motives to civil society, and which becomes one of its fundamental rules, is, *that no man should be judge in his own cause.*" (49, p88) Nevertheless, this ignores the dual component in our physical existence of both community (all individuals) and the individual. Thomas Paine wrote in response to Mr. Burke,

> A man, by natural right, has a right to judge in his own cause; and so far as the right of the mind is concerned, he never surrenders it: But what availeth it him to judge, if he has not power to redress? He therefore deposits this right in the common stock of society, and takes the arm of society, of which he is part, in preference and in addition to his own. Society *grants* him nothing. Every man is a proprietor in society, and draws on the capital as a matter of right. (45, p53)

Thomas Paine makes the point that even the individual involved in his individual action can judge his own cause while simultaneously it is in the common stock of society. Thomas Paine allowed judgment by all individuals to include the individual with the judged cause. To make the point, an individual-to-individual flow would be to let any car sales man to decide his position to society and change laws to enhance his position to whatever he decides. A corporate executive or a fast food worker each could decide their position to society and change laws to enhance their position to whatever they decide. We have corporations circumventing society to evaluate themselves by themselves to society in terms of no regulations to protect or enhance our society. Although the individual car sales man, corporate executive and fast food worker has their say, it still requires an all-individual-to-individual flow. When they engage in individual-to-individual flow, they are taking what they desire irrelevant to the benefit or destruction of the society. When we operate this way, we have extreme individualistic systems.

23. *Hereditary-like government with corrupted moral flow, example 2:* "Kings succeed each other, not as rationals, but as animals. It signifies not what their mental or moral characters are." (47, p21) This meant that kings had no physically based societal connection to their position. When

it comes to groups that disrupt the interaction of government with society, the question becomes do corporations act as rational entities, or as an animal separate from rational thought. As we are aware, part of the thesis in this book is that we have a flawed form of rational thought because of the amputation of the required connection to physical existence. Under thesisism, this disconnection is reestablished. It becomes the *rational* that Thomas Paine animates above. He had connected it to natural law. Corporate interest does not have its interests connected to the interest of society, nor is it connected to physical existence. They connect to financial gain and profit. The extended order interests are fine as long as they have evaluated the thesis-morality equations and have their thesis-based justifications to their actions. If we do not engage in conduct with thesis-based justifications, our financial gain and profit as our ultimate end does not tie to thesis-morality and its actions can become immoral without understanding or acknowledgement. Therefore, this interference with our government removes the (accountable) rational from our government and it operates to the animal of corporate interest.

24. *Hereditary-like government with corrupted moral flow, example 3:* "in all countries, are below the average of human understanding; that one is a tyrant, another an ideot, a third insane, and some all three together, it is impossible to attach confidence to it, when reason in man has power to act." (47, p22) We do not have any feedback or sanity check by society when corporations or individuals corrupt the moral flow of conduct with our government. It does not matter if global warming is happening and that we need to move to a clean form of energy if our king is an oil baron. Remember, the king is not government, but the force that determines laws and actions of society. If ninety percent of our society members say we need to move to clean energy, it is meaningless if we do not have representation to our ninety-percent. The king is in charge.

25. *Hereditary-like government with corrupted moral flow, example 4:* Thomas Paine quoted Abbé Sieyes. "Hereditaryship is, in this sense, as much an attaint upon principle, as an outrage upon society." (47, p23) If disruption of the moral flow of government is that it mimics hereditary government, then indeed we have an outrage on our society. Corporations that influence government to act as an individual irrespective to the requirement of government and the government then act on the behalf of all individuals in the society, this induces the same disruption to moral flow as a hereditary government. Their interference with the operation of a republic is immoral. Our citizenry ought to be outraged. We have many factors beyond this writing on why this outrage does not happen. Briefly, one is due to the marshaling of the American people. Another is due to the corporate control of media. We have the selling of worker productively levels over family and life quality.

Another involves a form of financial indenturing. Our individualism has led to the individualization of family, which in turn, places immense pressure on the American people in a small core family unit without much external support of any community-based network.

26. *Hereditary-like government with corrupted moral flow, example 5:* "As this is the order of nature, the order of government must necessarily follow it, or government will, as we see it does, degenerate into ignorance." (47, p26) When we have interference of moral flow in our government, we are out of order to nature. Ignorance was valued with the king. Selective training at the expense of creating ignorance is valued with the extended order of capitalism. The oddity is that the same by-product of capitalism, which is consumerism, is in part the mechanism to bring ignorance to the population. Religion and consumerism under broadband interpretations contains many master ideas. Most of these master ideas may maintain thesis-morality. However, religion and consumerism in the narrowband can reveal master ideas where they do not maintain thesis-morality. Religion under extreme dominance can foster ignorance, which leads to apathy of the masses. Extreme consumerism can lead to ignorance and apathy as well.

27. *Hereditary-like government with corrupted moral flow, example 6:* "How irrational then is the hereditary system which establishes channels of power, in company with which wisdom refuses to flow! By continuing this absurdity, man is perpetually in contradiction with himself; he accepts, for a king, or a chief magistrate, or a legislator, a person whom he would not elect for a constable." (47, p27) How irrational then is our corporate system when it establishes channels of power to government to create individual-to-individual flow. We have a form of rational thought with accountability and a form of rational thought without accountability. An unaccountable form of rational thought is irrational thought. Our irrational thought is that corporations decide their wisdom to social interactions, even if we would not elect them for a constable. We see clearly how our representation collapses and begins to mimic a monarchy or an aristocracy.

28. *Hereditary-like government with corrupted moral flow, example 7:* "As to the aristocratical form, it has the same vices and defects with the monarchical, except that the chance of abilities is better from the proportion of numbers, but there is still no security for the right use and application of them." (47, p32) Is corporate power that runs government an aristocracy? If so, then would not this statement by Thomas Paine hold true today?

29. *Hereditary-like government with corrupted moral flow, example 8:* "When the mind of a nation is bowed down by any political superstition in its government, such as hereditary succession is, it loses a considerable portion of its powers on all other subjects and objects." (47, p28) Political superstition

in relation to corporations is the idea that interference by corporation to determine its own individually based moral standards imposed on society is either acceptable, as they are the special makers of existence, or that corporate run government always has the mutual-benefit idea to society in place. Friedman and Hayek pushed individualism with ideas of self-interest and mutual benefit paired with freedom and liberty. They tied all of it together and injected it into our government. They are unquestionably accepting it as fact when the physical reality is that it is only true with a government that operates under thesis-morality equations. The truth is that their political superstition does destroy power to many portions of society.

30. *Hereditary-like government with corrupted moral flow, example 9:* "Retaining, then, democracy as the ground, and rejecting the corrupt systems of monarchy and aristocracy, the representative system naturally presents itself; remedying at once the defects of the simple democracy as to form, and the incapacity of the other two with respect to knowledge. (47, p33) This is an interesting statement. In effect, he is saying that monarchy, aristocracy and corporate aristocracy[34] cannot follow nature as they cannot follow and connect to knowledge that comes from nature.

31. *Although corporate interference to government creates a hereditary-like government by its creation of the individual-to-individual flow, it does not dismiss that our representatives in government interfere too with the correct moral flow.* Our representatives operate with corrupt moral flow. The reason they do is that government members operate under unaccountable systems of thought. Capitalists complain they have to interfere with government due to improper actions by the government officials. Many government officials have different religious and rational ideologies to which they operate. This means government representatives and capitalistic ideology have problems. Government cannot properly act until its members understand thesis-morality. It also means we cannot demand proper actions from our representatives until we too understand thesis-morality.

32. *Despite the vision of Thomas Paine and his contributions to the American Revolution and to the development of the United States of America, Thomas Paine had many critics.* Nevertheless, the same criticisms of Thomas Paine often ended in support of his intellect and accuracy. Unfortunately, on his attempt to further Deism by his attempt to diminish Christianity, many have overlooked his accomplishments in favor of defending their theology. Even previous friends turned against Thomas Paine. One turned friend was James Cheetham. He went and published an unfavorable narrative of his old friend. Nevertheless, some of the criticisms offered by Cheetham fall short

---

34 Corporate aristocracy does not extend to all corporations. It applies to only those corporations that interfere with our moral flow through our government.

as criticisms today. Cheetham wrote in reference to the *Rights of Man* by Thomas Paine,

> The miscellaneous chapter was peculiarly intended to make the soldiery and the poor eager for a revolution, by holding out to them suitable rewards. It proposes, on the supposition of a new government being established, an augmentation of the pay of the army—a national gift to new married people—a premium to parents for children—a fund for the poor and the aged—for men out of work, and for the education of a million and a half of children. Did we not know that his object was to assort and to organize all the means of national destruction, we might dignify his project with the epithet of chimerical. (50, p146-147)

Today we recognize our support for higher pay and good benefits for our soldiers, tax breaks for married people, tax breaks for those with children, our social security system and unemployment benefits and our public school systems that we have. When we read the words of Cheetham today, his criticisms of Thomas Paine have certainly paled.

33. *Thomas Paine understood that the education of our country's children was important.* The idea of education to all involved a fundamental shift in thought over previous viewed ideas. In order for life, liberty and the pursuit of happiness to prevail under the new United States of America, the governing power of the people must be made available to them not only in declaration, but in preparation as well. The prevalent idea during the time of American Revolution was that governing wisdom resided only in aristocrats. This idea resided in their history. In 1672, Sir William Temple wrote,

> Wisdom is that which makes men judge what are the best ends, and what the best means to attain them; and gives a man advantage among the weak and the ignorant, as sight among the blind; which is that of counsel and direction: this gives authority to age among the younger, till these being at certain years change their opinion of the old, and of themselves. This gives it more absolute to a pilot at sea, whom all the passengers suffer to steer them as he pleases. (51, I, p35)

We all have differences in intellectual abilities. Nevertheless, wisdom is not the acquisition of all knowledge or understanding. Even Hume, Smith and Hayek agree by their own presentation. We acquire through acquisition of knowledge our individual wisdom specific to our experience and our individual wisdom specific to our experience of governing. We acquire our individual knowledge through experience. We learn from our experience and we can transfer learned ideas through education.

34. *If our New World experiment in populace authority was to work, we needed education for the populace.* Nevertheless, the view of the common person was low. Sir William Temper further wrote,

> And, where ambition and avarice have made no entrance, the desire of leisure is much more natural, than of business and care: besides, men conversing all their lives with the woods and the fields, and the herds, more than with one another, come to know as little as they desire; use their senses a great deal more than their reason; examine not the nature or the tenure of power and authority; find only they are fit to obey, because they are not fit to govern; and so come to submit to the will of him they found in power, as they do to the will of heaven, and consider all changes of conditions, that happen to them under good and bad Princes, like good or ill seasons, that happen in the weather and the air. (51, I, p33)

Without education, the populace would not have the needed skills to participate in their governing duty. The statements by Sir William Temple are accurate assessments of his experience. The idea of mass education, beyond religious education, was non-existent. Nevertheless, the same lack of education of the populace led Sir William Temple to animate in his mind that the educated was to have god-like power over ordinary people. He does not see the need to balance the equation $E = E$, but the natural tendency for the educated to do what they will and the uneducated must submit. We then have our $E = E$ replaced with $\bar{E} = U \pm D$. This allows people to view themselves superior in all areas of existence.

35. *This dismissal and at times contempt the educated commonly held against the uneducated during the time of Thomas Paine reflected in their self-proclaimed superiority.* The idea of self-subscribe genetic superiority was common among the ruling and upper classes. Edmund Burke wrote regarding hereditary government and democracy, "These old fanatics of single arbitrary power dogmatized as if hereditary royalty was the only lawful government in the world, just as our new fanatics of popular arbitrary law, maintained that a popular election is the sole lawful source of authority." (49, p37) Here Edmund Burke criticizes both Kings and the populace. Only the aristocrats, who possess superior intellect, ought to be the rulers and deciders. Without high quality and reality-based education across the complete population, we cannot have a fully functioning republic and our required participation in our thesis-morality equations.

36. *As we can see, the ideas of Thomas Paine are as relevant today as when the United States of America began.* His words continue to speak to us today in ways we do not realize. For example, Thomas Paine coined the following set of words, *The United States of America.* (44, p8) He had a remarkable understanding of the underlying moral obligations and actions needed for a republic. Our government is our attempt to counter our "wickedness" by becoming our moral voice. To do that, we must measure ourselves against our physical existence, to our thesis-morality, and importantly, we must maintain our correct moral flow of actions to and from our representation. When this does not happen, we the people have the right to rebel and demand our freedom, liberty and our pursuit of happiness that we reasonably measure against accountability. When all people are empowered with freedom and liberty, we have the ideal of the American Revolution expressed in a society that generates health, intelligence and a balanced pursuit of happiness and actions.

Evangelical Capitalism and Milton Friedman

1. *In recent history, we have entered emotion into our discussion of capitalism.* We have had a ridged defense of capitalism for some time. The United States of America had inherited this individualistic system from its inception. In our current times, and certainly in recent history, socialism and communism have been hot-button issues. However, since the fall of the Soviet Union, we have had an evangelical form of capitalism spring forth like a released racehorse. We have a brand of capitalists that validated themselves more than winners, but also as champions of truth and justice. They view the collapse of communism as empirical evidence that their moral standing was correct and without flaw. The idea that the communists and socialists had been shown to be wrong somehow translated to be the same that they, the capitalists, had been shown to be right. They often validate themselves by the negation of other ideas rather than on validating their own merits. This recent history along with our long philosophical history has opened a downhill path to extreme individualism.

2. *In the last sixty years, a ridged authoritative form of capitalism has arisen.* They pontificate with the same type of self-appointed authorities that we see come from groups that hold manufactured ideas about a higher authority. Part of the ridged ideology represents itself in the lobbyists we have had in our government for a long time. The contention lobbyists brings is a valid topic of discussion. Nevertheless, we have had a change in our nature of discussion about capitalism. We have allowed capitalism to undermine our open and free discussion of it on many fronts. For one, capitalists have altered

their capitalistic-based presentation of political reporting and its interactive programming of free discussion. Milton Friedman wrote of free discussion, "There is no formula that can tell us where to stop. We must rely on our fallible judgment and, having reached a judgment, on our ability to persuade our fellow men that it is a correct judgment, or their ability to persuade us to modify our views. We must put our faith, here as elsewhere, in a consensus reached by imperfect and biased men through free discussion and trial and error." (52, p34) This idea goes back to the "general consensus" idea of John Locke. Since we had no system of accountability, the best we could do was "general consensus." However, we had in the recent past engaged in an interactive discussion that led to this "general consensus." We have replaced the style of debate[35] where different opinions are involved centrally over a few channels and switched to marketing strong personalities that start with the same sense of an all-knowing preacher on a soapbox. Minuet discussions occur in short periods, where the strong personalities have charge, emulating an authoritative stance. This assessment is a broadband thesis presentation, and therefore holds narrowband exceptions.

3. *We have also entered religion into the discussion of capitalism.* Historically, we always have had a blend of capitalism and religion that wavered and varied. Currently, we have the rise of Christian preachers that preach an idea that their manufactured idea about a higher consciousness decides if we are to have money or not. Moreover, if we have money, then this entity gave it to us. If it gave it to us, we owe nothing back to society. If other people or you do not have money, it is because this higher authority does not want them or you to have it. Conveniently, we have no responsibility to our society whatsoever. This thinking and similar thinking is emboldening a callous and selfish fabric in this country. In the free market, we hear talk about the free exchange of mutual benefit. What does the free exchange of mutual benefit mean? A preacher sells us an idea that allows us to think that when we have money it is because an invisible and an all-empowered entity have given it to us. For those that do not have it, it is because our invisible and all-empowered entity does not want them to have it. This allows the buyer of this manufactured idea to forgo any moral obligations to his fellow human beings. The preacher marketed and sold you a product—*a manufactured moral equation!*

4. *What the preacher did, and those who bought his preached product, was to seize one of our two moral equations, unequal-to-us, and moved it to all*

---

35 The style of debate here refers not to the era of John Locke. The debate during the time of John Locke involved only the wealthy and those selected to be educated. Rather, it refers to the opening of modern media of the 1950s through the 1980s. It was during this time that media spoke to the American people to a greater degree as a whole group. Our expansion of media changed this relationship.

situations: We no longer have our two equations, E = E and Ē = U ± D that our physical existence provides us. We only have our Ē = U ± D. Because they use the god-idea to act as justification to remove our differences (D), we have "god justification" equals plus or minus our differences, GJ = ±D. This leads us to a false equation of Ē = U ± D ± GJ, or Ē = U since ± D ± GJ cancels each other out. This in reality becomes $E_{BUYER} > E_{OTHERS}$, which ends in a sold false-reality equation of E > E. When we have this mismatch to physical existence, we can justify with a false reality our self-absorbed, self-indulgent and narcissistic behaviors.

5. *When we do not measure our discussion of capitalism against our physical world, we move to a manufactured form of capitalism.* Capitalism is a tool. It is an individualistic system. It is a human created system. Nevertheless, when it begins to acquire power in a way that it crosses into equal-to-us situations, we create manufactured ideas that can only reside in the minds of people. Exchange of goods has its connections to physical existence. Capitalism is a complex expression of this simple physical-world connection. Before I get into the discussion of the problems of capitalism, allow me to make definitive statements concerning capitalism, government and religion.

6. *Capitalism does not have a component of thesis-morality as part of its system of thought.* Mercantilism, the simple exchange of goods, involves the idea of fair exchange. With fair exchange comes the idea of justice within the exchange. It has this moral implication because at this level it is a direct connection to the physical world. Although capitalism states to have a moral component of mutual benefit and fair exchange, we will show that its primary directive is profit that is independent of any system with accountability to moral considerations.

7. *We will not be arguing the mechanics of capitalism.* The mechanics of capitalism involve the human-generated rules of the extended order. We will examine how ideas presented as moral justifications to capitalist' actions relate to the physical world, or not. We will not concern ourselves with whether this or that tariff interferes with capitalism. We will not concern ourselves whether the government interferes with, or not, free trade ideas. The mechanics of capitalism involve a different set of ideas based in economics and not in morality. When anyone animates economic ideas to our arguments of required moral justifications to capitalism, we have attempts to narrowband and to move away from our moral argument because of the difficulties in defending false-reality ideas.

8. *Government does not have a component of thesis-morality as part of its system of thought.* Although our United States government has a setup for the correct moral flow to occur, it does not operate to its original intention. This is part of our discussion here as well. We outlined our required moral flow of

government in the chapter on Thomas Paine. We have a visual representation shown in Diagram 4b. Before our discussion of capitalism can occur, we have to know what required moral actions our government is to engage in. Because capitalism strongly argues against government and points out many of its shortcomings, many of which are indeed correct, they use these shortcomings to justify their own position. In discussing capitalism, it no way implies that government is not without needed discussion and correction as well.

9. *Current religions do not have a component of thesis-morality as part of its system of thought.* Although religion is suppose to be our source to moral understanding, because of its unaccountable measurement against the chaos of the human mind, it has corrupted the process to reach moral conclusions consistently. We can see this in its tendency to have moral cancellations. We can attribute these moral cancellations to human beings being able to animate reality to anything and thus come to different and conflicting conclusions. An example of moral cancellation was the issue of slavery. Religious people can state with absolute certitude their moral position. However, when conflict occurs, there are no methods to address this conflict. At least they have no method that starts with an agreement on how to bring accountability to their ideas.

10. *All three of these social entities are morally deficient.* Capitalism measures against the individual types of self-interest profit and finance only. Government measures against serving specific individual interests. They do not measure against our thesis-morality and its correct flow of behavior. Religion cannot conclusively focus on the correct moral code of conduct as it measures against the human mind. In our discussion on evangelical capitalism, we will eliminate religion and replace it with thesisism. We will attempt to correct the manufactured thought that presents itself in the ideas given by the capitalists. Additionally, we will acknowledge the immoral actions of government that capitalists point to, yet we will point to a different reason why the government is acting immorally as well.

11. *Adam Smith is the core to which all discussion of modern capitalism seems to have its starting point.* Therefore, I will start with Adam Smith. He was born in Kirkcaldy, Scotland on June 5, 1723. He published his *Theory of the Moral Sentiments* in 1759 and his *Wealth of Nations* in 1776. The economic philosophy that Adam Smith wrote about was prior to the creation of the United States. It does not hold the ideals set forth in our *Declaration of Independence* that "we are all created equal." Aristocracy, plutocracy and hereditary systems were the institutions prevalent during the time of Adam Smith. Arguments concerning the beginning of the United States involved who should have power to run government. It was widely accepted that only landowners had voting power. It was widely accepted that people were

born into position by hereditary lineage. Thomas Paine had argued against this idea. For many during this time, the idea of "we are all created equal" meant that a manufactured higher authority, their God, held this existing equality of humankind. Nevertheless, it did not apply to interactions between human beings with human beings. In turn, this entity gave unequal attributes between human beings. Those that deemed themselves superior empowered themselves by animating that their manufactured entity had given them dominion.

12. *We have these elitists of that time even now.* We have frequent articulation today that this divine entity gives capitalists absolute authority. They provide themselves self-assigned power by selected narrowband ideas of absolute freedom to mean they have the god-given right to move forward in anything they desire without evaluation to our realities. The problem is that with their false-reality ideas we have responsibility and moral obligations without accountability. They assigned themselves the authority of a god rather than humbling themselves to their God. Unaccountable moral ideas lead to manufactured-based justifications of supreme power to engage in coercion. When anyone presents a code of conduct that provides opposition to their actions, they claim coercion to their liberty by their measurement to unaccountable ideas. In their idea of no coercion, it contains no firm statement to morality. In fact, they claim that it is the moral obligation of everyone else to give them what they deem as justice. Their justice is to give them complete freedom to engage in anything they want. We have the religious who can animate anything they want under their rules of thought. The evangelical capitalist can animate anything they want under their rules of thought as well. That is because they break the connections to our physical existence. We can easily demonstrate their breaking from reality.

13. *Our evangelical capitalists frequently refer to Adam Smith.* They frequently refer to the following passage as justification to their unquestionable right to no responsibility and moral obligations. Adam Smith wrote,

> All systems either of preference or of restraint, therefore, being thus completely taken away, the obvious and simple system of natural liberty establishes itself of its own accord. Every man, as long as he does not violate the laws of justice, is left perfectly free to pursue his own interests his own way, and to bring both his industry and capital into competition with those of any other man, or order of men. The sovereign is completely discharged from a duty, in the attempting to perform which he must always be exposed to innumerable delusions, and for the proper performance of which no human wisdom or knowledge could ever be sufficient; the duty of superintending the

industry of private people, and of directing it toward the employments most suitable to the interest of the society. According to the system of natural liberty, the sovereign has only three duties to attend to; three duties of great importance, indeed, but plain and intelligible to common understanding; first, the duty of protecting the society from the violence and invasion of other independent societies; secondly, the duty of protecting, as far as possible, every member of the society from the injustice or oppression of every other member of it, or the duty of establishing an exact administration of justice; and, thirdly, the duty of erecting and maintaining certain public works and certain public institutions, which it can never be for the interest of any individual or small number of individuals, though it may frequently do much more than repay it to a great society. (1, p445-446 Book IV, Chap. IX)

14. *Evangelical capitalists quickly grab two of the three duties from Adam Smith.* Milton Friedman in his book, *Free to Choose*, (53, p29) pointed to the first two, protection from violence and invasion by other countries, and protection from injustice and oppression from within our society. Both of these are broadband in that they imply protection to every member of the society. It involved an idea in the negative, and that idea was *no coercion*. For the protection from within our society, Friedman gave the *armed robber* example. (53, p29) He animated correctly that robbery was wrong. Although robbery involves the action of one individual to another individual, it is wrong because we have an individual acting to shift the $\bar{E}$ (mean equal) by altering the correct $\pm D$ (plus or minus the difference,) which we then end with an unbalance equation, $\bar{E} \neq U \pm D$. This is true even though it involves unequal thesis-morality. Ownership of things involves the expression of our differences. Nevertheless, unequal-to-us when violated relates back to our mean equal. Why? Instead of $(\bar{E} = U_{victim} \pm D) = (\bar{E} = U_{robber} \pm D)$, the robber changed the equation to $(\bar{E} = U_{victim} \pm D) < (\bar{E} = U_{robber} \pm D)$. He is making this shift in the equations by shifting the difference (D). Notice that the first equation is actually $\bar{E} = \bar{E}$ and is functionally the same as our E = E.[36] Based on this, we see that the second equation is actually $E \neq E$. This assumes that within the narrowband definition of robbery we are talking about, it is taking from others without any thesis-based justifications and that the first equations were accurate to start with. It is a moral violation to unbalance the E = E or the $\bar{E} = \bar{E}$ equation.

---

36 For the fundamental difference between E = E and $\bar{E} = \bar{E}$, see paragraph 17 of this chapter.

15. *The duty of protection from injustice and oppression from within continued:* Friedman wrote, "Unless there is such protection, we are not really free to choose." (53, p29) Nevertheless, protection is not about freedom to choose. We seek protection to prevent actions by others that violate our equal-to-us equation, $E = E$, or our unequal-to-us equation, $\bar{E} = \bar{E}$. *This protection is to maintain our moral balance of activity within our society.* We impose protection to maintain our obligations to both all-individuals and individual freedoms. When we want "free to choose," it involves movement to some desired or wanted action. This makes it an individualistic action. Free chosen and individual movement without evaluations to our thesis equations ignores our accountability equations. Our free chosen and individual movement can only occur within the justifications provided in the moral equations. Friedman presented his robber idea as an infraction only against the individual victim when it really was a violation across all human beings. Robbery is not just a violation against any immediate victim; rather, robbery is a violation that applies to all people. It applies to our $\bar{E} = \bar{E}$ equation, which involves our unequal thesis-morality across all people. He then formulated the idea "*not to rob*" his individual to create his idea that all individuals had a right to "*free to choose.*" There was no consequential follow here. "*Not to rob*" is not equal to "*free to choose.*" The protection from robbers involves coercion to stop action, whereas freedom to choose involves no coercion to action to all actions, including the robber's actions! The idea went from a universally accepted idea of proper use of coercion, as thesis-based justification follows the use of coercion against robbers, to an idea that any universal coercion violates freedom to choose. The idea of protection from robbers does not equal freedom to choose. Freedom to choose is restricted to anything that does not violate thesis-morality. Robbery violates thesis-morality. However, robbery is only one of many things that may violate thesis-morality.

16. *Friedman confused business ideology with immoral action.* Friedman wrote, "The armed robber's 'Your money or you life' offers me a choice, but no one would describe it as a free choice or the subsequent exchange as voluntary." (53, p29) When he used the word "choice," he never defined it in any narrowband way. This left the door open for people to plug stealthily or unknowingly the idea of freedom into his first use of the word "choice." He narrowed the word "choice" later as it not being "free choice." Nevertheless, he never defined his broadband word "choice" at the beginning of his sentence. He never does because his first use of "choice" was not about freedom. Business actions have choice. Under robbery, we have no choice because there is no freedom. Instead, the victim has coerced decisions. Concerning his first use of the word "choice," another narrowband idea of choice is opportunity to more than one decision. This narrowband idea of choice has nothing to do

with freedom, as we can see with coerced decisions. He could have written, "The armed robber's 'Your money or you life' offers me no choice." The use of "choice" here involves no idea of embedded freedom. Nevertheless, he could not do that because he wanted to mix business action with the sliver idea of morality. The physical-world reality was that his robber was engaging in a violation that was against not just the victim, but to all individuals. This makes it a moral issue. He did not tie this violation to code of conduct in relation to morality, but transferred it to an individualistic economic code of conduct to market exchange. Friedman wanted to mix thesis-morality actions with market actions to bring a "higher" legitimacy to his position. However, the two are not the same. He was animating as if the robber was engaging in a business action with another individual and moving the sliver idea of morality to his business actions. This fundamental flaw of transferring the idea of morality to non-morality type of economic actions is how Friedman ignores morality and acts as if his economic activity is moral activity.

17. *He had used a broadband idea of an individual action with violations against all individuals and moved it to a narrowband idea of one individual engaging in a business deal with another individual.* In the first, the violation against thesis-morality we can connect to our physical-world realities of our human being structure. We see this in our moral equations. We have $E = E$ and $\bar{E} = \bar{E}$. Business action is individual with individual. Robbery is not business action, but a violation of a moral code of conduct. The two are mutually exclusive. The business violation of Friedman was an idea that broke this connection to our physical-world realities and thus it moved to a manufactured idea that could only exist in his mind. A robber is taking something without thesis-based justification and his actions are immoral. Our moral and immoral actions are always relational to all people. We always operate relationally to our E or our $\bar{E}$. Business actions may be moral or immoral depending if it violates or maintains thesis-justified actions. To animate moral action and business action as the same was to create an idea that could only exist in the human mind. It was an attempt to move the sliver idea of robbery as being immoral and attach that sliver idea to other ideas to justify his false-reality desires.

18. *Friedman gave blind thought to the third duty by Adam Smith of maintaining certain public works.* The first words from Friedman to the third duty by Adam Smith were, "Adam Smith's third duty raises the most troublesome issues." (53, p30) Until this, Friedman clearly understood the writings of Adam Smith. He followed with a quick sentence of "He himself regarded it as having a narrow application." (53, p30) This suggests to me that Friedman did not like the third duty by Adam Smith. Nevertheless, Friedman showed no reference to back up his "narrow application" statement.

Therefore, it was only a statement by Friedman. Then something odd happened. Suddenly, he had the third duty by Adam Smith wrongly used by many "to justify an extremely wide range of government activities." (53, p30) He acknowledged that this third duty was to "preserving and strengthening a free society." (53, p30) Nevertheless, he followed with a warning that it "can also be interpreted to justify unlimited extensions of government power." (53, p30) Finally, Friedman spiraled into a discourse about "third parties" and "dirty shirt collars." (53, p30-31) Friedman never addressed the third duty by Adam Smith.

19. *Adam Smith was clear to what he perceived as his third duty.* Adam Smith continued with discussion pertaining to his third duty in his book only pages afterwards. He wrote,

> After the public institutions and public works necessary for the defence of the society, and for the administration of justice, both of which have already been mentioned, the other works and institutions of this kind are chiefly those for facilitating the commerce of the society, and those for promoting the instruction of the people. The institutions for instruction are of two kinds; those for the education of the youth, and those for the instruction of people of all ages. The consideration of the manner in which the expense of those different sorts of public works and institutions may be most properly defrayed, will divide this third part of the present chapter into three different articles. (1, p453, BV, Chap. I, PIII)

20. *The third duty by Adam Smith reflected his eighteenth century and pre-United States view.* In Article I, he wrote of the physical realities of roads, of bridges, and of tax. (1, p453) In Article II, he wrote of the expense to educate the youth. He did not mention if he meant a selection of youth nor did he reference all youth. However, since youth in its definition includes all of itself, it seems he was referring to all youth. He was recognizing the all-individuals aspect of society, something the evangelical capitalists ignored. (1, p463) In Article III, he wrote, "The institutions for the instruction of people of all ages are chiefly those for religious instruction." (1, p464) This definitely conflicts with our separation of church and state. I would offer that during his time, people viewed religious education as education for the common people. Therefore, the third duty involved not only our society to educate our youth, but to expand the quality of life to people of all ages by education. This quality of life we view differently today. We may argue that religious instruction of adults was a way to keep working class compliant to false-reality desires of hereditary plutocrats. Despite the right or wrong of it, education was an idea based on all-individuals.

21. *Why Friedman did not properly reference the third duty of Adam Smith appears unclear until we consider how an adhesive framed-reference can bend incoming ideas.* When he went from vague references of roads to dirty shirt collars, this was disingenuous to the position of Adam Smith. The reverence Friedman had for Adam Smith gave the impression that Adam Smith was some ultimate authority. When that ultimate authority failed or contradicted the preconceived ideas of reality Friedman had, rather than acknowledging the realities of the thought during the time of Adam Smith, a mental drop occurred, much like religious people trying to make their manufactured ideas fit the claimed reality of their particular book. What we have is an example of an adhesive framed-reference that bent ideas by attaching sliver ideas to move them to a desired false-reality master idea.

22. *Friedman cherry picked what fit his desired position to his extended order of capitalism.* He selected ideas like not to rob, which is to seize property without thesis-based justification and a universal moral idea, and placed the universal moral idea into limited economic ideas, as if robbery was economic activity. In transferring immoral action to economic action, he gave people false-reality ideas that in turn create ideas that to pay taxes was the same as robbery. He cherry picked his predetermined position that individualism was universal and began to force fit reality to fit his manufactured reality. When it was convenient to grab onto the father of finance, Adam Smith, he did so. Nevertheless, when it was not convenient to grab onto the father of finance, he in turn dropped Adam Smith as soon as a contraction to his predetermined ideology occurred. He chose not to evaluate his own ideas or even stand up and challenge his father of finance. Rather, he collapsed into narrowband dribble about dirty shirt collars.

Insect Capitalism and F. A. Hayek

1. *F. A. Hayek was an influential thinker that continues in our current thought about capitalism.* Hayek had written numerous books on this subject. He had used the term *extended order* when referring to capitalism. This extended order was the change from primitive and small civilizations to our current complex civilization. Extended order implies an order that came from an already existing order. His extended order of capitalism was the outgrowth of a part of the original order. Capitalism, like an extended order of socialism, is the extension of one side of our thesis-morality while it amputated the other side. Hayek knew the limitations of unaccountable reason and rational thought. Either he knowingly used it or he unwittingly fell into a desired position of being able to bring no accountability to capitalism. Hayek had reasoned that science and the use of reason and rational thought could not

explain or predict the actions of the extended order of capitalism. More importantly, that rational thought could not provide any justifications to limit their actions. He wrote,

> The reason for the difficulty which the natural scientist experiences in admitting the existence of such an order in social phenomena is that these orders cannot be stated in physical term, that if we define the elements in physical terms no such order is visible, and that the units which show an orderly arrangement do not (or at least need not) have any physical properties in common (except that men react to them in the "same" way—although the "sameness" of different people's reactions will again, as a rule, not be definable in physical terms). (54, p69)

Capitalism is the action of people, which has a physical component. Nevertheless, the question becomes, is capitalism a human-made system where the product of physical actions are beyond our ability to see or did Hayek automatically accepts the amputation of physical existence from reason and rational thought.

2. *The influence of David Hume showed in Hayek concerning individual reason to social structure.* Hayek accepted the view that no individual could reason coherently a social order. He wrote,

> But it is merely one aspect of an even wider difference between a view which in general rates rather low the place which reason plays into human affairs, which contends that man has achieved what he has in spite of the fact that he is only partly guided by reason, and that his individual reason is very limited and imperfect, and a view which assumes that Reason, with a capital R, is always fully and equally available to all humans and that everything which man achieves is the direct result of, and therefore subject to, the control of individual reason. (55, p8)

Bear in mind that Hayek was correct. Our problem with Hayek is that he only deals partially with full human existence. He is correct that we guide ourselves only partly by reason when we consider that we allow *sensing* truth. In this sensed truth, we allow ourselves to measure against the chaos of the human mind. My argument with Hayek is the abandonment of rational thought to a faith-based system of thought. It does not follow that because no single individual can comprehend or understand all things to act as a conscious guide to social order, we cannot apply at the individual level a system of thought with accountability that would translate up as his extended order does currently. We can measure our ideas and ideas of morality against our physical existence as human beings. This provides the commonality and accountability to move from partial reason to full reason. His statement about the assumption of reason being available to all is a reference to the requirement of education from our equal thesis-morality that is based in physical existence. This then leads us indeed to have "everything which man achieves" under "the control of individual reason." This individual reason nevertheless is across all individuals, which he references as "with a capital R."

3. *Adam Smith too influenced Hayek.* Hayek, like others, found Adam Smith to be one of the firsts to stake out the extended order. He had associated many of his ideas to the "invisible hand" of Adam Smith. Hayek wrote, "Economics has from its origins been concerned with how an extended order of human interactions comes into existence through a process of variation, winnowing and sifting far surpassing our vision or our capacity to design." (41, p14) He then followed by referencing the "invisible hand" by Adam Smith. He wrote, "His 'invisible hand' had perhaps better have been described as an invisible or unsurveyable pattern." (41, p14) Hayek was saying that capitalism was so much an individualistic action, and with so many people engaging in individualistic actions, we could not understand it or pull patterns from it. He followed with, "Information-gathering institutions such as the market enabled us to use such dispersed and unsurveyable knowledge to form super-individual patterns." (41, p15) Although he did not say this, it is my interpretation that super-individual patterns were surveyed-unsurveyable knowledge boiled down to interpreted acts of all individuals as if it was one individual. Corporations or large businesses then are super-individual conglomerations engaged in the unknowable. Nevertheless, what is the difference between *unsurveyable* patterns and *unsurveyable* knowledge he claimed above?

4. *Hayek was saying that markets could pull from the chaos of capitalism to make patterns knowable for corporations or large business to operate.* However, if reason and rational thought could not comprehend capitalism, what was it that the marketers used to market? It seemed that he found the use of reason valid to marketing, but not to any thesis-morality flows, such as an individual-to-all-individuals or all-individuals-to-individual flow for anyone else to make statements about capitalism. If we indeed have super-individual patterns, then would we not have super-all-individuals patterns? The fact that Hayek at one points claims "unsurveyable pattern" and then claims "super-individual patterns" contradicts his claim that the *extended order of human interactions far surpasses our vision and our capacity to design.* Is not then marketing a "socialist" action of stripping away our individuality to fit an all-individuals product to varying individuals? If so, then Hayek has not placed everything on the table. This is because he, as well as Friedman, only deals

with individual-to-individual flows, which ignores morality. Not only is he ignoring our equality, but our individuality as well.

5. *More influence from Adam Smith:* Hayek wrote, "Man's knowledge, as Smith knew, is dispersed. As he wrote, 'What is the species of domestic industry his capital can employ, and of which the produce is likely to be of the greatest value, every individual, it is evident, in his local situation, judges much better than any statesman or lawgiver can do for him.'" (41, p14) We can begin to see the focus on unequal thesis-morality. The job of the lawgiver is to maintain thesis-morality and to do this requires us to balance thesis equations. Individuals in local industry made judgements to the ends of their business. The two do not have the same objectives. The statement by Adam Smith, especially under "domestic industry," he made during the time of indentured servants and slavery. Recognition that equal thesis-morality overrode unequal thesis-morality eventually had overturned these institutions of the local industry. You cannot own people as this violates equal thesis-morality—a physically based reality strong enough that even the "general consent" idea of John Locke eventually *sensed it* repugnant. We no longer remove any equal-to-us aspects of a person in relation to labor. In this, we freed the indentured servant as well.

6. *We can begin to view the capitalism of Hayek through thesisism.* Human ideas are a product of our human brain. The interactions between our human brain with our physical world and subsequent experiential existence involve our mental animations and the movement of sliver ideas between ideas. As we know, our human brain can animate ideas and move sliver ideas around to create ideas that can only exist in the mind of human beings. To understand the limitation and potential suffering inherent in the thinking of Hayek, we have to have a clear understanding of thesisism. It is important to understand that we also have a lack of accountability in our use of thought in our government and social science. We must understand this, as Hayek often points to their flaws to justify his arguments. When you accept the tradition to which ideas and words have come to mean, it hides and obscures our underlying real-world realities. Tradition is repetition of ideas that are independent to any requirement of accountability. We have an abundance of broadband and narrowband animations filled with manufactured ideas.

7. *Part of the response by Hayek was in relation to socialist ideas.* Thesisism is neither capitalistic nor socialistic. It is action in relation to what our physical world resulted in. Therefore, capitalists and socialists have their ideas of what are actions of an individual and the actions of all individuals. They each have their view of what is social morality and individual morality. The ideas used by Hayek reflected the traditional ideas that surrounded him. In thesisism, the

ideas of community and individual are not the same as how Hayek animated. We must address this difficulty first.

8. *We need to define the differences between the view of morality held by Hayek and the view of morality through thesisism.* We need to start with individual verses all-individuals ideas and to what they mean, relate and contribute to human mental animation. Although Hayek saw the benefit that came from individual action, he could only animate ideas in relation to the systems of thought that was around him. These systems of thought, using traditional language, were religious thought, scientific thought and rational thought. Scientific thought, as used here, refers to hard science and their relational and required connections to physical existence in terms of cause and effect. Rational thought does not have the same rigid requirements to maintain its ideas connected to physical existence. This was due to a history where people used rational thought measured against preconceived manufactured ideas.

9. *Hayek had an understanding that two different systems existed.* He wrote, "If we were to apply the unmodified, uncurbed, rules of the micro-cosmos (i.e., of the small band or troop, or of, say, our families) to the macro-cosmos (our wider civilisation), as our instincts and sentimental yearnings often make us wish to do, *we would destroy it.* Yet if we were always to apply the rules of the extended order to our more intimate groupings, *we would crush them.* So we must learn to live in two sorts of world at once." (41, p18) The position by Hayek was that on one hand our altruism, solidarity and collective tradition destroys capitalism, and on the other hand, if we applied the individualistic system of capitalism to small units such as families, it would destroy families. Did his collectivism and individualism mean the same thing as equal thesis-morality and unequal thesis-morality? Under thesisism, we must measure all ideas against the physical world and then classified them to their truth position. Remember that truth position is not the same as complete match to reality, but our best assessment at that given moment. When we measure our reality against our physical existence, we enhance our assessment of reality.

10. *One characteristic of thesis-morality is that it can exhibit two expressions, that of universal thesis-morality and limited thesis-morality.* Certain moral statements are universal. Not to murder is an example of this. Murder is killing without thesis-based justification. We have the physical reality of our equal-to-us that applies to all situations. Each situation is not unique. Certain moral statements are limited. When to help a person in need is an example of this. Each situation of need is unique. We have a limited number of situations out of all situations of need that moral obligation applies. We have to evaluate each situation to know if we have a moral situation or not. Our physical-world realities of human commonality and differences dictate this. Within our assessment against our physical world for our moral code of conduct,

we have these two physical-world considerations to make in relation to our equal thesis-morality and unequal thesis-morality. When dealing with Hayek and understanding how thesisism differs from traditional thought, we have to accept this physically connected expression in play to determine our code of conduct.

11. *Hayek gave examples of the two different moralities he perceived.* He wrote, "there are at least two other possible sources of morality. There is, first, as we saw, the innate morality, so-called, of our instincts (solidarity, altruism, group decision, and such like), the practices flowing from which are not sufficient to sustain our present extended order and its population." (41, p70) The second source of morality by Hayek we will review after evaluation of his first. He used the word instincts to refer to what he perceived as socialistic ideas. He related these instincts to the evolution of humankind and their existence in small groups. This regulating instinct toward intrinsic community ideas while not acknowledging our instincts toward acknowledging our individuality was not explained. He simply stated it as some kind of fact. This was a subtle attempt to make it appear that when we regulate human behavior toward our equally, we were engaged in human development that was less advanced, which implied a less intelligent position. This was disingenuous.

12. *The first innate morality Hayek presented was solidarity.* In relation to our physical world, is solidarity universal or limited in characteristic? Does solidarity require an absolute statement like not to murder, or is solidarity in relation to each situation? If we apply it as universal moral idea, we are saying that solidarity applies as a code of conduct to all situations. This would lock us into a constant state of solidarity, as by definition, we would not have any situations in physical existence that would be limited solidarity. Nevertheless, there is. If we applied universal thesis-morality to the idea of solidarity, we have locked ourselves in having to stand for every position, even if that solidarity meant to wear purple ties because someone called for the position of solidarity for purple ties. Many different positions of solidarity or perceived solidarity have no connection to moral code of conduct. Welfare suffered this misapplication of universal application to determined needs rather than applying limited possibilities to each specific need of the person on welfare. Solidarity is a limited moral idea. The application of a moral form of solidarity requires us to evaluate each situation. Hayek himself admitted that during times of war, our reverting to this instinct would be needed and desired. What this translates to is this. We evoke solidarity only when we have thesis-based justifications. The reference to the needed solidarity by Hayek during war acknowledged that a physically connected reason had to exist before we could evoke solidarity.

13. *Let us look at his second and third given instinct.* His second instinct was altruism. Again, we have to ask if altruism is a universal or a limited moral idea. If we were to apply it as if it were a universal moral idea, then we would have to be unselfish to every situation, as absolute would cast over all potential situations. Therefore, Hayek would be correct, as only chaos could arrive from this. Nevertheless, altruism is not universal as Hayek presented, but is limited. Altruism would require a thesis-based justification before it would be a moral consideration. Concerning his third example, if "group decision" was required for all decisions, then we have applied an idea universally when it was limited in character. It must be in relation to thesis-morality. Nevertheless, not all our decisions are thesis-morality situations. Group decisions would be necessary for unequal-to-us moral flow, as we need the (complete) group to determine the value to the mean equal between people. Nevertheless, we cannot make our group decisions to equal-to-us situations. We have no difference to evaluate. Equality exist, thus all moral responses from all individuals would be the same. It appears that his given instinctual or collectivism moral code of conduct that Hayek provided as examples were limited moral evaluations, yet he applied them as universal moral evolution.

14. *If Hayek gave ideas of instinctual morals that were limited morals, can we animate an instinctual and universal moral?* Could we provide an example of a universal moral idea and in turn show how it would affect the conclusions of Hayek? For a moral to be absolute in nature, it must apply to all people rather than against each situation. Capitalists place the idea of self-interest as a basic component of capitalism. If self-interest is part of the extended order of capitalism, then we have an extended order that requires cognition. Self-interest in this extended order requires the understanding of the extended order and the world we live in. If we leave people on their own devices and provide them no education, we would have them placed into the extended order by Hayek under *his* idea of instinctual mode. The truth is that each primitive society provided education. Since each person has human consciousness the same as all others, this sameness places a moral code of conduct to provide the equal opportunity to develop and express ones individual differences. Education then becomes an instinctual and universal moral. Nevertheless, education is a universal moral idea in both the pre and post extended order because we have to learn how to work within our environment, regardless if it is physical existence or human created systems.

15. *In the extended order of capitalism by Hayek, capitalism claimed its prime directive of individual self-interest.* Nevertheless, Hayek ignored self-interests of all individuals while focusing on individual self-interests. His egocentric view of modern economic man or woman as superior to older societies

allowed him simply to ignore self-interests of all individuals as primitive and instinctual. This allowed him to move the sliver idea of superiority to his individual type of self-interests ideas that broke our connections to physical existence and no longer reflected our physical realities. He removed our universal self-interests, which ties to our equal-to-us morality. All references to our reduced universal and equal-to-us morality he abandoned to vague statements of no coercion and no harm to others. This view in the extended order of capitalism came from the singular-individual type of self-interest philosophy by people with self-granted superior position. John Locke provided self-fulfilling philosophical ideas to the landowners and special gentlemen of superior breeding that were mental animations separate from physical existence. Like religious manufactured ideas, they then compound onto themselves to allow the modern view of capitalism to be what it is today. Arose from the philosophy of John Locke, David Hume, Adam Smith and more were self-fulfilling views that fit their individual self-interests, not truth to reality. When you move the idea of no coercion to self-interests from a limited idea to a universal idea, you allow false justifications to engage in false freedom and false liberty. False freedom and false liberty is coercion. No coercion to all individuals involves our equal thesis-morality, whereas, no coercion to individuals involves our unequal thesis-morality. You cannot apply the "no coercion" idea universally to any single individual. If we do, we have a god and a King.

16. *The importance of education in the extended order shows itself with the wealthiest sending their children to Ivy League schools.* Hayek wrote regarding education, "There is not much reason to believe that, if at any one time the best of knowledge which some possess were made available to all, the result would be a much better society." (2, p378) Knowledge itself means nothing if it is the parroting of the best unaccountable ideas continually to serve individual self-interests to their ends. Then indeed this idea serves those in power to remain in power and provides justification not to bring education to all. Hayek further wrote, "It is a different matter, however, to assume that all who are intellectually capable of acquiring a higher education have a claim to it. That it is in the general interest to enable all the specially intelligent to become learned is by no means evident or that all of them would materially profit by such an advanced education, or even that such an education should be restricted to those who have an unquestionable capacity for it and be made the normal or perhaps the exclusive path to higher positions." (2, p383) Physical reality provides us a universal idea that we all have equal right to the opportunity to display our differences. We cannot confuse $E = E$ with $\bar{E} = \bar{E}$. With $E = E$, we have no difference to display. Equal education is about maintaining our $\bar{E} = \bar{E}$, or $\bar{E} = U \pm D$, which are the same. Equal education

does not mean making all E = E, as Hayek attempted. Rather, Hayek provided an apology to change the difference (±D) in the equation for unequal thesis-morality that made our Ē go out of balance. The extended order continually claims individual rights to freedom. Nevertheless, this statement by Hayek provided the tinkering of the plus and minus the difference that the best-qualified person doses not necessarily have a right to it. When we limit our thinking to economics only, we are now measuring against a human created system and not the physical world. When we limit our thinking to economics that came out of the western thought of John Locke to present, we measure against ideas with false justification of nepotism within the ruling class. Nevertheless, a human created system like our current extended order can change the physical-world conditions so that equal education can create problems. However, this does not change the physical existence of our human structure and our thesis-morality equations.

17. *In not maintaining accountability to our ideas, we create mismatches in our human created system to our equations given by physical existence.* A fear held by the extended order of capitalism showed itself when Hayek wrote, "a much sharper division between classes might come to exist, and the less fortunate might become seriously neglected, if all the more intelligent were deliberately and successfully brought into the wealthy group and it became not only a general presumption but a universal fact that the relatively poor were less intelligent." (2, p383) Hayek is saying we need intelligent people to be in with the poor. Whom does it serve to have intelligent people with the poor?[37] If we have intelligent people choosing to be with the poor, fine. If we have a human system that chooses the intelligent to be with the poor by the random placement of birth, we have manipulation to the self-interest of other individuals. The later is an attempt to ignore our Ē = Ē. Hayek followed shortly with, "There are a few greater dangers to political stability than the existence of an intellectual proletariat who find no outlet for their learning." (2, 383) The more we educate people the more there is potential for people to challenge the extended order. Challenges do arise, such as, when we narrow our social structure to economic activity only, we cannot move to our ultimate end of free will and balance to our creation. Certainly, in the *amoral economic* context that Hayek was writing, his statements have legitimacy. Under our current human-created social systems of economics, having an equal opportunity to education can create the problems as Hayek claims. Nevertheless, our moral equations from physical existence remains E = E and Ē = Ē. Despite claims

---

37 Arguments about the poor and the extended order of capitalism involve a deeper economic dissertation than can be present in this publication. Capitalism can and does provide wealth. Distribution arguments, education and a balance to resources have to engage with thesis-morality.

by capitalists, as well as Hayek here, that in the natural nature of things, no actual equal opportunity exists, or equal opportunity creates problems, only serves to bypass a required moral obligation and our search for solutions to it. Our physical world, as an acting creator, has no moral obligations to human beings. However, human beings, as human beings, do have moral obligations between human beings. Our creator—physical existence—displays this moral obligation to us in our thesis-morality equations.

18. *To have cognition of self-interest in the extended order of capitalism, we must have equal educational opportunities for all persons to understand their self-interest and to develop and express their individual difference.* Education then has a universal nature, as does not to murder, that we then express across all people. This is not the same as requiring all people to become a Ph.D., as I suspect Hayek would counter against this argument. Rather, an existence that allows all human beings, regardless of where they were born, the ability to acquire education so to be able to express their individual differences. If not, then the whole idea of self-interest only belongs to a power group that cycles its advantages within it own closed group. This is not to say we are required immediately to have the perfect answer and perfect system in place, and that if any of our attempts fails, then this is a failure to the truth and reality that education is a universal moral requirement. We must conduct our individualism to the physical-world realities that we have one source but two expressions of moral code of conduct to our individualistic behaviors. When we have individual actions and do not understand thesis-morality, we end with the chaos of manufactured types of individual actions. The mental animations by Hayek to the extended order of capitalism seduced that all equal-to-us ideas were instinctual and they destroy our extended society. Because Hayek gave only limited type of moral examples to equal-to-us morals, it suggests selective thought and an adhesive framed-reference to preconceived ideas about individualism applied across only half of physical existence.

19. *Hayek animated anything resembling equal application as socialistic and dangerous.* Despite the wonderful mind of Hayek, which was rich in understanding and conceptual thinking, because of the traditional thought that surrounded him, he did not include the accountability of thesisism. He oversimplified his view of equal application. He wrote, "For those now living within the extended order gain from *not* treating one another as neighbours, and by applying, in their interactions, rules of the extended order—such as those of several property and contract—instead of the rules of solidarity and altruism. An order in which everyone treated his neighbour as himself would be one where comparatively few could be fruitful and multiply." (41, p13) Extending solidarity and altruism to your neighbor would depend on each situation, not across the board that Hayek had animated. It becomes silly to

display constant self-sacrifice to our neighbor. If our neighbor became sick and needed a ride to the hospital, to which his options were limited, here we would have the universal moral of health care kicking in. The religious idea of treating your neighbors as you would treat yourself is an attempt to bring focus to our dual aspects of thesis-morality. We have not presented it clearly in this maxim, as we only *sensed it*, but the statement in its intent absolutely applies both sides of thesis-morality. Nevertheless, Hayek again applied our limited ideas of solidarity and altruism as if they were universal ideas against the idea of simple mutual respect. This is an assault on human dignity.

20. *The dismissal of universal morals by Hayek was the flaw in his thought.* We can debate the arguments about whether we could achieve our universal types of equal thesis-morality through government or by our extended order. It is my personal position that the purpose of our government is to be our reality-based moral conscious for our society. It really ought to be nothing more. If equal opportunity of reality-based education can be achieved by the extended order, then so be it. If the extended order does not want to deal with the moral obligation that comes with it, as any individual self-interest does not pull action to this needed moral obligation, the government can kick in to make it happen. If it were paid through taxes, then so be it. This moral obligation is the cost of doing business in this extended order of business. Any human system we make we cannot allow to act immorally to the whole of society. If equal opportunity of education can be achieve through a combinations of governmental, capitalistic, and even altruistic systems such as religion, then so be it. Pointing out the required moral code of conduct that thesisism uncovers does not make any statement on how we arrive there other than all actions must have thesis-based justifications.

21. *Hayek provided his second moral that came with the extended order of capitalism.* He wrote, "Second, there is the evolved morality (savings, several property, honesty, and so on) that created and sustains the extended order. As we have already seen, this morality stands between instinct and reason, a position that has been obscured by the false dichotomy of instinct verses reason." (41, p70) He was saying that it was a moral right for people to collect and keep money. He was saying that it was a moral right for people to collect as many things as they wanted to collect. Let us hold on honesty for a moment. Under unequal thesis-morality, we have the right to hold anything we have application of self in if no thesis-based justification exists to have the object or thing removed. If someone made a pot, then the person should be able to do whatever he or she wanted with it. If someone made a pot, and for argument, everyone would starve to death without that pot, equal thesis-morality of life would override. The moral obligation to supply the pot would occur. The group should compensate the individual within the operating thesis-based

justifications that may apply. In this narrowband situation, we had equal thesis-morality override unequal thesis-morality, but we did not eliminate the skill of the individual. The mean equal (Ē) remains and the community of all individuals is required to measure and compensate the individual for their individual difference. Now, the community, that is, all individuals, determines the compensation. That compensation to the individual by all individuals, they make relational to available resources.

22. *Therefore, savings and several properties are indeed rights, but are second position moral rights.* These rights are not absolute or universal moral rights. In other words, savings and several properties are limited in nature. Each situation, be it individual, or groups of individuals, have to be examined to the totality of existence. Hayek did not want this totality of existence, as it would place moral obligations on capitalism. He was correct that universal equal-to-us obligations place a weight against individualistic actions. He was correct that limited equal-to-us obligations would also place a weight against individualistic actions. Nevertheless, the weight of the limited moral actions would only become a large weight that would "destroy" capitalism if they were applied in the absolute and universal manner that Hayek described. Socialism did apply these actions in an absolute and universal manner. Hayek was correct that socialism did not serve humankind well in the end. Our equal-to-us and limited moral obligations, such as solidarity during wartime, only kick in under specific and narrow situations. His presentations of limited morals applied universally to the extended order of capitalism were not absolute and they must adhere to our thesis-morality obligations. We cannot ignore our absolute moral obligations, as they come from our creator, our physical-world equations that we must meet. No human-made system can override our physical-world obligations. It is the cost of business to maintain a solid social order for the extended order to operate within. Our higher purpose of a healthy society overrides a narrowband type of self-interest when, and only when, conflict between the two occurs.

23. *Where did the moral of honesty given by Hayek fit in?* Is honesty a universal or a limited type of moral statement? If honesty were a universal code of conduct, then we would have to be honest one hundred percent of the time. We all can think of times when honesty may not be good. In the context of our whole society, or humankind, honesty would be a relative code of conduct to which we would have to examine each situation. We would be required to have a thesis-based justification given if we engaged in dishonesty. In the context of the extended order of capitalism by Hayek, the universal code of conduct of honesty may indeed be an equal application. In all actions of business, honesty would be a requirement. We can make one statement and it applies to all possible capitalist situations. Part of the problem with Hayek

was that he thought of the extended order of capitalism as a being equivalent to society. The two are different. His extended order was only a portion of society. He ignored our physical-world realities and applied ideas that fit his personal false reality. The extended order attempts to use their human created system of business and apply it as if it is social order across all of existence. We have a system that operates inside our social dynamics while operating as if it does not. With Hayek, we could say we have a system that operates within our social dynamics while operating as if it is the only social system in the dynamics. Our social dynamics involves both equal and unequal physical characteristics. It is interesting that he had the ability to perceive a universal form of moral code of conduct with business honesty in the narrowband with his human-made and individualistic system of capitalism, but he did not acknowledge universal forms of moral codes of conduct when it came to human existence.

24. *We can use his words to give demonstration.* He wrote, "The fact that we are constantly choosing between different values without a social code prescribing how we ought to choose does not surprise us and does not suggest to us that our moral code is incomplete." (56, p64) When he said "we," it became all individuals. Nevertheless, the "we" here was the "we" only within his extended order. His idea of the required moral conduct of honesty displayed a "social code" limited to his individualistic system of capitalism. Consequently, in the broadband he was incorrect, since they were constantly choosing between different values using a narrowband idea of a *prescribed sub-social order.* Additionally, his statement was very odd. We can rewrite it as, "The fact that we are constantly choosing moral actions without a moral code measurement does not surprise us and does not suggest our moral conduct is incomplete." We can take out the double negative at the end with "and does suggest our moral conduct is complete." Nevertheless, his morals derived from the unknowable; thus, we could never say it was complete. Here is the flaw in the premise presented by Hayek. For Hayek, capitalism and social code were identical, and social code centered nothing beyond capitalism. This meant his moral code was whatever rules of the game the extended order of capitalism decided. That was how he could conclude his moral conduct was complete. It was an extraordinary amount of hand picking and bending on his part to justify an individualistic system to operate without required accountability.

25. *The system of thought by Hayek was disturbing yet understandable.* It was disturbing in that it was an unnatural progression toward a system of thought to individualism exclusively. With our present movement toward deregulation, this is of concern. It is my theorized-manufactured idea with a good probability and thesis presentation that Hayek had an adhesive framed-reference that prevented him from seeing our true human nature as measured

against physical existence. He eclipsed his free will by the same intellectualism that he reacted against. In his words given in paragraph 21, he said, "morality stands between instinct and reason." (41, p70) The social science of his time influenced his idea of instincts as evolutionary inferior to reason. He then overlaid human progression of civilization on top of older human societies and declared it superior. This aligns with the atheistic ideas of Nietzsche and Ayn Rand who not only presented people with specific differences superior over others, but also presented them as superior across all of existence.

26. *His idea of instincts came from a learned view and his own use of reason and rational thought.* What he said was that morality stood between old social order (instinct) and reason. However, his idea of the old social order was with the use of his own reason and rational thought. In this light, what he said was that morality stood between what he reasoned and what others reasoned. We can see why he dropped discussion of this when he claimed his morality was between instinct and reason. He dropped discussion because he really said nothing. We cannot conveniently push something into the unknown and then justify our unknown position by different narrowband examples, especially when our narrowband examples involve misapplied universal and limited moral ideas that do not fit with physical reality.

27. *Hayek had created a religious-like system of thought.* His economic system took on the traits of religion. The idea behind religion is that despite it being unknowable and non-demonstrable—the self-appointed authorities know the correct way and what they decide we are to follow. Religion claims to be correct by making statements that the unknowable is knowable because of this or that narrowband examples. Examples of this would be our physical world has a natural order, thus it has a humanlike conscious maker. I feel a mental connection to something greater than to myself, thus there is a God. This self-validation by selecting narrowband ideas occurs with the extended order as well. Our knowledge of health care is the highest it ever has been thus capitalism works across all aspects of social existence. Every individual works to their self-interest, therefore morality and the correct code of conduct will automatically arise. It is wrong to rob a person; therefore, taxes are the arbitrary will of government and therefore it is coercion.

28. *Hayek used a faith-based system of thought.* He wrote, "For in fact we are able to bring about an ordering of the unknown *only by causing it to order itself.*" (41, p83) The argument behind this was that the activity of individuals operating in the extended order of capitalism was something that no one individual could comprehend. When it came to capitalistic actions, and the sheer volume it engaged in, sure, his statement was correct. Nevertheless, it does not mean that we could not apply an understood obligatory moral code of conduct. We are talking about moral application and not full

understanding of business activities. He could not apply moral understanding properly because his system of thought came from the unaccountable systems of thought derived from reason and rational thought. Reason and rational thought could *base* itself on manufactured ideas that moved us away from our physical existence. We saw evidence of this in the presentation given by Hayek of only limited forms of moral codes of conduct yet he presented them as universal forms of moral codes of conduct. It seemed to me that Hayek was more than intelligent to know the difference. His silence on universal forms of moral codes of conduct suggests that he held some preconceived ideas and bent his ideas to fit those preconceptions. We can see now that *to sense it* in the act of reason and rational thought was a bleary movement toward the application of thesisism. When alignment to physical existence occurs, we see that thesisism is the mechanism needed to the "causing it to order itself." Our creator is physical existence and the source to reality. Under Hayek, the "causing it to order itself" became the extended order of capitalism by his "we are able to bring about." In this sense, capitalists made themselves creator and god.

29. *Hayek credited religion with the evolution to his extended order of capitalism.* He wrote, "Even those among us, like myself, who are not prepared to accept the anthropomorphic conception of a personal divinity ought to admit that the premature loss of what we regard as nonfactual beliefs would have deprived mankind of a powerful support in the long development of the extended order that we now enjoy, and that even now the loss of these beliefs, whether true or false, creates great difficulties." (41, p137) When he added the words, "premature loss" of religion, it saved his idea. Since we have measured our ideas of morals based not against our physical existence, but against the chaos of our human minds, until we could understand and develop thesisism, our dropping religion prematurely could have had its ramifications. Nevertheless, religion prevented our development of thesisism, which in turn could have prevented development of the extended order to occur sooner and with more accuracy.

30. *The dismissal of rational thought by Hayek was apparent.* He wrote, "The source of order that religion ascribes to a human-like divinity—the map or guide that will show a part successfully how to move within the whole—we now learn to see to be not outside the physical world but one of its characteristics, one far too complex for any of its parts possibly to form an 'image' or 'picture' of it. Thus religious prohibitions against idolatry, against the making of such images, are well taken." (41, p140) Hayek was saying that social order was part of the physical world, but it was too complex for us to understand it. Implied in this was that we ought to not even try, and we ought to let our social order move in its natural unconscious order. This

was a way to say we ought to allow our awareness to move us forward, but we cannot pull it into our consciousness. When it came to social order, the mental animations of humankind historically have been unaccountable, thus the natural order became a manufactured order, as human thought measured against the human mind broke the connection to our physical existence. If we had followed thesisism, maintained our connections to our physical existence, we would have maintained our natural order to our required evaluate-to-balance. Hayek did not want reason and rational thought to make any "image" of capitalism and in turn equated it with the same justification that comes from authoritative religious dogma. He left it to the expert priests and capitalists to determine interpretations of things unknowable. How can we interpret something that is unknowable? This is the contradiction in religion. It is also the contradiction in the extended order of capitalism that Hayek offered.

31. *The extended order often gives false self-justification of themselves by their mere existence.* Sometimes we look around and make leaping interpretations by applying little thought to complex issues. Hayek was terrific in thinking complexly, but decidedly simplistic when it fit his personally held false-reality desires. He wrote, *"But the only religions that have survived are those which support property and the family."*[38] (41, p137) This was a statement of justification for his extended order of capitalism. However, this also was an outrageous and egocentric statement. His religion of property survived because of the active destruction of religions by the religion of property. He justified his extended order under aggression. This was not a natural evolution of the best ideas. They accomplished this with the misguided belief that their God gave special human beings property. This idea of divine gifts provided a manufactured-based justification to seize property. If he credited Christianity with the rise of the extended order, then he credited authoritative dominance and non-free choice as the catalysis to the evolution of modern capitalism. This contradicts the idea of no coercion and individual freedom and liberty. Further, for him to include family was to deny the quality of family life in many other religions. His outrageous statement is especially distasteful to all the religions held by the pre-Christian people in North America through South America. There were numerous religious people with families that his monotheistic European religion of Christianity destroyed by their slash and burn of these families and religions.

32. *Let us move the position of Hayek to its end.* If we have an extended order that operated in the unknown to human reason and understanding, and that we ought to allow its progression forward to use our resources as determined by the self-interests of every individual, what would be our result? According

---

38 Note: The italics are as written by Hayek.

to Hayek, it would progress humankind into wealth and happiness. Do we have any other systems around us that operate in a similar non-conscious way in the utilization of surrounding resources? We do. We can look at our insect world. When the environment affords resources, such as the results from good rains, each insect operates to its self-interest. Each an every insect uses the surrounding resources to the best of their advantage. Our insects multiply and grow. They achieve their wealth and happiness. However, they operate within these short-term goals, and in a non-conscious amoral fashion, they devourer all their resources. Once this occurs, a collapse follows. Our wealth and happiness turns into suffering and death.

33. *Hayek would dismiss this by the idea of market displacements. Part 1:* The idea was that as one-market dies out, another replaces it. He even reverted to Adam Smith, John Locke and James Sullivan for justification. He cited the words of James Sullivan. "The American historian James Sullivan remarked, as early as 1795, how the native Americans had been displaced by European colonists, and that now five hundred thinking beings could prosper in the same area where previously only a single savage could 'drag out a hungry existence' as a hunter." (41, p120-121) The animation was that we would constantly respond to success because of market needs. However, the savage he referred to was not in his extended order, he was displaced by force. Nor did the Native American necessary accept the idea of taking more than what was available. Rather than his living in the idea of constant economic growth, he lived in a state of environmental balance. We have a double standard here, as the extended order never gave the Native American any *(free) choice*, like the robber example by Friedman.

34. *Hayek would dismiss this by the idea of market displacements. Part 2:* A little further Hayek wrote, "In some places invaded, as it were, by the extended order, those following new practices, who could extract more from the given land, would often be able to offer other occupants, in return for access to their land (without the occupants having to do any work at all, and without the 'invaders' having to use force), nearly as much as, and sometimes even more than, these occupants had obtained by hard toil." (41, p121) This was double talk. He referred to the extended order as invaders without force and concluded that we could seize their land and use it. His justification is contained in the idea that if the original inhabitants did not have to work, as it would save them from hard toil, then this was not only an adequate justification, but a moral justification as well. Hayek reduced the Native American to standing around, and they would like it because they would not have to work. We can now see what he embedded in his argued idea. He held within his idea that the Native American was incapable and lazy. He could not leave his egocentric extended order view to see that the

Native American people were hard working people that maintained a balance between themselves and physical existence. Further, he never acknowledged that they had good and solid families.

35. *Hayek would dismiss this by the idea of market displacement. Part 3:* He did not provide an example of how the use of finite resources could end in an infinite market system of displacement. With unlimited resources, this idea of market displacement could hold. However, like our insect world, we live in the same world of limited resources. One limited resource that we ignore all the time is our planet earth. I think it is a fact that many Native Americans actually had the correct understanding to the idea of infinite resources. The infinite resource idea is striking a balance in a manner that nature continues to replenish and maintains a certain level of human being numbers. Malthus in 1803 wrote in relation to resource utilization, "it is extremely difficult to say when they will reach their limits. That there is, however, a limit which, if the capital and population of a country continue increasing, they must ultimately reach, and cannot pass; and that this limit, upon the principle of private property, must be far short of the utmost power of the earth to produce food." (57, p150) This physically based statement by Malthus understood the finite limitations of physical existence that human beings live in. What does this mean? Hayek chose not to view our physical existence, but acted as if we had unlimited resources. It also means we need to understand how to use our resources with a balance to the environment. The displacement needed is not just about switching from oil to some other form of energy when the price of oil becomes too high. We need to displace the current unaccountable system of capitalistic thought with a thesis-based system of capitalistic thought.

Thesis-Based Coercion: Our Release of Freedom and Liberty
Section 1: Maintaining Our Past

1. *The ideas of freedom, liberty and the pursuit of happiness have been around for a long time.* Although we have discussed the ideas behind each of the three, they remain diffused shadowy ideas. Because these ideas are broadband, it has been the contest of our history to attempt to define them. In these attempts, there appear two spheres of thought. One idea is that we must state all ideas of freedom and liberty that we can think of and the other idea is that we must state all ideas that negate freedom and liberty. Either way, ideas of freedom and liberty are infinite in nature. The task of defining every possibility is daunting in that it goes beyond the comprehension of individual minds when we narrowband.

2. *The "invisible hand" idea by Adam Smith had led people like Friedrich A. Hayek and Milton Friedman to make broadband statements about the elimination of individual human coercion against other individuals.* The extended order of capitalism had to permit its "invisible hand" to move in its mysterious ways, as all economic activity was greater than any individual comprehension. Hayek wrote, "The state in which a man is not subject to coercion by the arbitrary will of another or others is often also distinguished as 'individual' or 'personal' freedom, and whenever we want to remind the reader that it is in this sense that we are using the word 'freedom,' we shall employ that expression." (2, p11) Notice that he viewed freedom in a negative form. His word freedom was inclusive of every possible human act. He defined his word freedom in the negative form of no coercion. He did not define what the non-arbitrary will of another was and when coercion was acceptable.

3. *Hayek understood his position to coercion was in the negative.* He wrote, "It is often objected that our concept of liberty is merely negative. This is true in the sense that peace is also a negative concept or that security or quiet or the absence of any particular impediment or evil is negative. It is to this class of concepts that liberty belongs: it describes the absence of a particular obstacle—coercion by other men." (2, 19) Nevertheless, his examples were not negative concepts. They were broadband words. When we measure the idea of peace against the physical world, we realize that it is as positive as the idea of war. What peace and war are, are states of physically based actions. Peace was not the absence of war. It has its own set of actions. They may be a greater set of actions that go beyond the limit of understanding of any individual; they nevertheless remain a set of positive actions. Security also involves physically based interaction. Quiet was not the absence of noise. Quiet has its physical properties as well. When you measure ideas against the human mind, then you can create ideas that appear negative. Freedom and liberty are ideas that appear to humankind as negative ideas, but they are ideas that base themselves in our physical world. They appear negative in that they are infinite; there are more narrowband possibilities than can be comprehended.

4. *Hayek made a broadband statement about freedom and liberty and had it measured against a broadband idea that human beings could not determine when to apply coercion.* With reason and rational thought thrown out, we left ourselves with a measurement system of no attempt to measurement. Ironically, we have left ourselves with the same "general consensus" that was given to us by John Locke. When Hayek wrote of coercion, it was from the view that we *sense* coercion with our human mind. Nevertheless, anything a human being states as coercion could have the idea of arbitrary place into it by another. When we do not have any accountability system of thought to

measure our ideas, we then can transform the argument of the "arbitrary will of another" into coercion. Since we are without a system of accountability to reason and rational thought, what one person defines as "non-arbitrary," another person can transform into "arbitrary." We can now see we have the same problem that we have with religion. As with religion, we can have moral cancellations with the extended order idea of "no coercion." We have circular logic under the thought systems of religion and the extended order.

5. *To get out of this circular logic, we must understand that the problem does not reside in the idea of coercion.* What we need to do is to move our broadband idea of liberty to a narrowband idea and align people to the same idea. We need to shed ideas of liberty where we measure against false realities. Under thesisism, we must measure liberty against our physical existence. Since liberty is our actions in physical existence, we must address each situation. Liberty remains a universal idea because we are not looking for when it applies, as liberty always applies, but for when conflict occurs within our thesis-morality equations. This means we are looking for when liberty can be limited because of the constraints from our thesis-morality equations derived from physical existence. Thesisism can handle this, as we can expose human coercion by measurement against physical existence to find our requirements to our code of conduct.

6. *Friedman made many broadband statements and followed them with narrowband examples that fit his false-reality desires.* Friedman took Hayek one-step further in that he tended to view any form of government action against the extended order of capitalism as a great infraction. Friedman wrote, "Political freedom means the absence of coercion of a man by his fellow men. The fundamental threat to freedom is power to coerce, be it in the hands of a monarch, a dictator, an oligarchy, or a momentary majority." (52, p15) Friedman was adamant against government control of any kind. Friedman handpicked his arguments by giving narrowband examples. Nevertheless, his narrowband arguments to his broadband idea, when carefully examined against physical existence, revealed its flaws. For example, he wrote, "Fair employment practice commissions that have the task of preventing 'discrimination' in employment by reason of race, color, or religion have been established in a number of states. Such legislation clearly involves interference with the freedom of individuals to enter into voluntary contracts with one another." (52, p111) He continued to give a non-specific example of a storeowner being forced to hire a black clerk when it conflicted with the "transmitting the tastes of the community" to hire a white clerk. (52, p112) According to Friedman, we violated the individual freedom of the storeowner "by a law which prohibits him from engaging in the activity, that is, prohibits him from pandering to the tastes of the community for having

a white rather than a Negro clerk." (52, p112) Of course, in his non-specific example this owner went out of business. Friedman saw this as an arbitrary will and governmental coercion to individual freedom and liberty. How did the position of Friedman stand morally?

7. *Friedman gave this as an example of political coercion against an individual.* To understand his mistake in his given narrowband example, it requires an understanding that morality for Friedman, to find acceptance to his argument, requires an individual-to-individual flow. Individual-to-individual flow is not moral flow. In his presented case, it must be a flow from individual to all individuals, which is community. From the view of a thesisist, by going to an individual-to-individual flow of action, Friedman removed moral considerations from his argument.

8. *When we connect to our physical existence, we find his removal of morality.* Allow me to demonstrate that the extended order of capitalism as presented by Friedman was morally void. We have the following moral components contained within his argument. We have the equal thesis-morality of the black clerk. It is equal thesis-morality because all human beings have an equal-to-us by the physical characteristics of human consciousness. We have the unequal thesis-morality of the storeowner. It is unequal thesis-morality because the storeowner invested his application of self. If we stop here, as many people want to do, we are not dealing with all the players in our physical reality. Many people want to stop here because they can then make false claims that morality is relative. Our forgotten player is the failure of the community. Our community is the collection of all individuals. The community has not met its moral obligations. It may not have met it due to neglect or due to bad thinking. In this occurrence, it was due to bad thinking. Since Friedman measured against the human mind, we can see the relativism of his code of conduct here. Friedman viewed that it was more correct to allow the individual storeowner to serve white bigots than to deal with a larger systemic problem of racism. He was incorrect. Government did not violate the individual freedom and liberty of the storeowner. Rather, it was his community of white bigots that violated the freedom and liberty of the storeowner. They, the community of white bigots, did not allow the storeowner to meet his required physically connected moral obligation. His moral obligations were to hire on merit ($\bar{E}$ = U ± D) and not on race (E > E). The government was bringing the required moral health to its society. We can have further arguments arise about whether the storeowner should receive compensation or relocation assistance. However, this now goes beyond the intention here.

9. *Friedman provided other examples of coercion to individual freedom.* He wrote, "A citizen of the United States who under the laws of various states is not free to follow the occupation of his own choosing unless he can get a

license for it, is likewise being deprived of an essential part of his freedom."
(52, p9) If we had licensing requirements that interfered with free enterprise
due to unreasonable inspections or skill level requirements, we would have an
acceptable argument. Nevertheless, if licensing was how government provided
needed regulation to protect the community of all individuals from bad
individuals, then his argument again became a morally void statement. This
time his individual wanted to do business with all individuals, yet operated as
if he or she did not interface with all individuals.

10. *We can see the effect of ignoring our moral obligations when we have no
regulation.* Recently, I saw on cable television a story from Peru. They were
reporting the dangers of eating at restaurants there by showing testimonies
of hurt people. They had bitten into pieces of metal from deteriorating metal
pots that had made its way to the food. They showed the conditions, which
included pots that looked as if they were melting away, rusty and pitted.
Rivets in the pots came out and ended in the food. Apparently, in Peru,
the government did not require a license, nor were government health
inspections made. Only the local news media provided that altruistic public
service. Here we have an issue of equal thesis-morality to contend with, as
bad food, or food with dangerous objects in it, affect people in the physical.
Pain, suffering and physical damage is something that needs equal protection
between all human beings. Our denied individual freedoms by requiring a
license becomes offset by the moral obligation to ensure the safety, health
and the life of the community of all individuals. In fact, no freedom is denied
when we have requirements to license that have thesis-based justifications
of community protection. This is moral action as it connects to the physical
world and protects our equal thesis-morality. This is where our equal thesis-
morality overrides unequal thesis-morality. Moral considerations are the
reason for regulation. If we have no thesis-based regulation of economic
behaviors, we will all bite on false reality. This false reality will lead to the
hard deterioration of our economy, all the way from restaurants to our stock
markets and to our banks.

11. *We can see this bad thinking when we apply it to other situations.* Under
the thinking of Friedman, we should eliminate the requirement for individuals
to pass automobile driver proficiency tests. If we denied incompetent drives,
it would be a violation against any individual to their freedom and liberty to
drive. Whether an individual was competent, had sufficient vision; or despite
the level of alcohol in the blood of any individual, it becomes irrelevant to
the protection of the community. If at this point you think, does this type of
thought have any traction in our society; know that Margaret Thatcher said
this book by Friedman, *Free to Choose*, was something we all should follow.

12. *Hayek presented his view of what we needed to have in place to prevent coercion.* He presented us a list of rights given to freed slaves to demonstrate what we needed to have to achieve our freedom. He pulled his list from ancient Greece. It was in this movement from slave to free man that he determined his rights of attainment of freedom. He wrote, "This list contains most of what in the eighteenth and nineteenth centuries were regarded as the essential conditions of freedom." His list consisted of four plus one additional item. He wrote, "There were four rights which the attainment of freedom regularly conferred." (2, p19-20) His list consisted of:

- "Legal status as a protected member of the community"

- "Immunity from arbitrary arrest"

- "Right to work at whatever he desires to do"

- "Right to movement according to his own choice"

He stated his fifth right. "It omits the right to own property only because even the slave could do so. With the addition of this right, it contains all the elements required to protect an individual against coercion." (2, p20) Hayek thought that if a human being was legally protected member of the community of all individuals, could not be arrested arbitrarily, was free to work at whatever he may choose, could move according to his choice and own property, he then could not be coerced by other human beings. However, these were broadband statements!

13. *His attainment of freedom list had built-in claims without a method to define when those claims were valid.* The right to work at whatever a person desires assumed that all desired work activity was available, as well as the actions of the person being acceptable to others for that person to engage in. Hayek referenced a finite resource, but treated it as an infinite resource. The right to movement according to his choice assumed all places of his choices were available. In this light, it did not address how a freed slave may desire to move in with the daughter of the king, or with any unwilling partner. It does not address if a freed slave desired to work as the general of the military. These statements were utopian in nature and do not fit our physical realities. Thesisism can bring a realistic focus on the realities of existence from which we can know how to conduct ourselves. However, how did Friedman compare?

14. *Friedman viewed the formula to freedom different.* He wrote, "First, the scope of government must be limited. Its major function must be to protect our freedom both from the enemies outside our gates and from our fellow-citizens: to preserve law and order, to enforce private contracts, to foster competitive markets. Beyond this major function, government may enable us

at times to accomplish jointly what we would find it more difficult or expensive to accomplish severally." (52, p2) His protection from outsiders and insiders was similar to the legal status as a protected member of the community that Hayek had stated. They both probably picked this up from the first two duties stated by Adam Smith. If Friedman was viewing protection against thesis-morality violations, then we had physically based protection. If we had thesis-morality violations committed with manufactured-based justifications, then these manufactured-based justifications do not connect to our physical world, as they measured against the random animations of the human mind. If we had action occur with thesis-based justifications, then we had no moral violation occur. Thesis-based justifications connect to physical existence and to thesis-morality. However, when he wrote "private contracts" and "to foster competitive markets," he aligned his idea of protection to the actions of his extended order of capitalism.

15. *Friedman viewed society as if it was only economic in nature.* Further, when he wrote, "to protect our freedom ... from our fellow-citizens," he openly admitted to government coercion against fellow-citizens. Nevertheless, he never defined when we needed protection from our fellow-citizens. He wrote, "Equally important, the major problem in the United States in the nineteenth and early twentieth century was not to promote diversity but to create the core of common values essential to a stable society." (52, p96) Milton Friedman tied stability with fellow-citizenship and a core of common values. He also wrote, "A stable and democratic society is impossible without a minimum degree of literacy and knowledge on the part of most citizens and without widespread acceptance of some common set of values." (52, p86) Nevertheless, the core of common values Friedman had in mind was economic values. Taken together, this meant that anyone that did not accept the core and common values based in economics derived by the self-interests of individuals in position of power was an enemy and we needed to have protection against them. This kind of thinking is our old brand of evangelical-economic type of philosophical thought that dates back prior to the Declaration of Independence in 1776. Only the self-appointed and the self-selected groups decide the core values of the rules of the game to the extended order of capitalism, to which government is to provide them the law and religion is to provide them a God; both of which becomes the hammer. Friedman treated society as if it was only economics, rather than economics being a part of society.

16. *Friedman not only wanted protection from coercion, but also wanted government to provide him protection applied to his extended order rules.* He made no statement about arbitrary wills of others or arbitrary arrests; rather, government was to preserve his "law and order." He made no statement about

whether he made his "law and order" with or without arbitrary will, nor did he say what this "law and order" was and who received the benefit of it. Friedman voided all moral obligations the government had to its people. Rather, the higher order of concern was to enforce private contracts and to foster competitive markets. He turned the obligation of our government to provide protection into being the authoritative muscle behind business activity. He even made his authoritative muscle to apply self-authored rules against his fellow-citizens. He did not want the government to do anything except provide him power to engage in his individual activity without any accountability to moral obligations. In this light, the government by Friedman under the extended order of capitalism becomes the same as a mobster's thug. To understand that this is not an extreme statement, we can look at Diagram 4b and see that individual-to-individual flow is an immoral flow. It disenfranchises the whole population. Anyone against the immoral individual-to-individual flow was to meet Friedman's thug. This is so because the individual (I) in Diagram 4b is the economic self-interests of a subset of individuals acting independent to all individuals of the society and the required thesis-morality equations.

17. *Friedman further compounded his extended order of capitalism when he wanted a separation of capitalism and government; while at the same time, he wanted his government to provide him with power.* He wrote, "There seems to be something like a fixed total of political power to be distributed. Consequently, if economic power is joined to political power, concentration seems almost inevitable. On the other hand, if economic power is kept in separate hands from political power, it can serve as a check and a counter to political power." (52, p16) These sentences were somewhat comical. If we join economic power to political power, of course it becomes concentrated. It was not "almost inevitable." By the fact that it had "joined," meant that it had become one. We also have here a duality in his thinking. He claimed that we had to keep economic power separate from political power. However, in the paragraph 14 above, we see he claimed government was to foster competitive markets. Either we have government separated or not. Further, would not the fostering of competitive markets by the government mean taking away the individual freedom of one person to have a closed market that came to them by chance or by conscious actions?

18. *Friedman then followed that a separate economic power would provide a check on political power.* What would keep a check on economic power, that is, the extended order of capitalism, especially if we had a weak government? We seem to have an assumption that capitalism would not create a central power, thus it will act morally. This moral action would come about by the invisible hand of Adam Smith. We have the animation that centralized

government and power pockets of capitalism were not the same essence of power. Further, it does not follow that capitalism was good because we know government was bad. This was bad logic. Power is power, whether it was in a centralized government or under the control of a group of people separate from government. We can easily end with a small group of people to the whole population that in turn has centralized characteristics to it.

19. *The same words by Friedman meant that capitalism ought to stop lobbing government and get out of law making.* His argument was that our government itself required the extended order of capitalism to be involved in lobbing our government. This was so, according to Friedman, because government engaged in coercion by interfering with their individual freedom to do what they want. Nevertheless, the restrictions imposed onto the extended order of capitalism were under their own determination as well. What we have missing again from the argument by Friedman was any moral considerations. If the government acted as a power to manipulate economic activity where it had no place, then government was acting immorally to unequal-to-us considerations. If, however, economic power manipulates government to act immorally to our equal-to-us or to unequal-to-us considerations, then it too was a corrupted system. Since our government and capitalists operate without accountability, we have a moral void in our present state of affairs. No matter which philosophical hotpot we jump in, we end burnt.

20. *What we really have is a mess.* What the extended order of capitalism has offered us is capitalism without any moral constraints. It measures itself using broadband ideas against the human mind. We have a government that does not understand its own purpose and allows individual-to-individual flows to occur, resulting in immoral actions. We have moral guidance given by our religions, which are non-reality-based and measured against our human mind. This results in moral chaos, moral relativism and moral cancellation because any individual can animate to their own personally acquired false-reality desires. We have our human codes of conduct in all three areas, economics, government and moral conduct, operating in a *free-for-all*. When we are in a free-for-all, we end with power struggles. We have now reached the start of this book in our question of why we do not act to bring humankind a quality life. We have individual self-interest acting without any accountability requirements.

21. *Our human created mess resides around the world, which makes it difficult to achieve the moral balance our physical world requires.* We have different governments throughout our world that behave differently. We have the extended order of capitalism operating in different places with various levels of moral stability or instability. We have different religions that view their manufactured thought existences as the only moral source and each

advocates their move to supremacy in different ways. Since we have all these variations, it makes it difficult to move governments and the extended order of capitalism to our moral requirements. We have obscured our clear understanding of thesisism because we may have to make our thesis-based justifications in relation to the whole world and not just our surroundings. Thesisism is a movement forward from chaos to a form of rational thought with accountability. Because thesisism involves ideas and their relationship with our physical world, it becomes the same measured source for all people around the globe. That is the good news in mist of our chaos. Since thesisism is a movement forward, we then have a history.

22. *Human history provides us an understanding how we came to our current society.* Throughout our human history, we have had many people claim to find the right path for humankind to follow. Theocracies, monarchs, plutocracies and more have arisen and fallen. With monarchs and kings, we had one individual determining humankind code of conduct. If the monarch had an understanding of equal thesis-morality, they made good decisions to equal-to-us situations. If monarch did not, then they were a tyrant. This system did not allow the required flow of unequal thesis-morality from all individuals to a person. Instead, it reversed our requirement from unequal thesis-morality, as it was individual-to-all-individuals flow. We eventually have failure because power prevents our movement to the required balance of thesis-morality. When we use religion as a carpenter's ruler, it involves thought with manufactured ideas. We immediately have placed measurement of ideas against the human mind. A singular religion may maintain itself, but only under authoritative actions. Once our authoritative hold drops, we burst into numerous religions, each person animating anything they wish. This leads us to moral cancellation and making religion even more ineffective. In the singular mode, it too is ineffective, as it becomes the will of a few and it could only survive by coercion. This aspect led our American revolutionaries to create the separation of church and state. We have in our history the collaboration of both kings and religion. The role of religion became whatever the individuals with the religious power decided they could do within the limits of their power. The role of the king or queen became whatever he or she decided they could do within the limits of their power. In either situation, when we have no measurement occurring to thesis-morality requirements, bizarre and horrific events occur. Human society was only as good as the random alignment to thesis-morality. Since we did not measure against physical existence, we had atrocities occur. The push and pull of the king or queen and the church depended on the dynamics of the individuals involved and none of it we measured against the physical world.

23. *In the eighteenth century, we had our aristocracy rising to power without religion or any previous or established government imposition.* It was during this time that our landowners and aristocrats had free opportunity to construct a capitalistic system concurrently with an emerging new social order. Our extended order of capitalism arose, along with the specific philosophical ideas of David Hume, that the use of reason was invalid coupled with the narrow self-interests of many to adopt the "invisible hand" idea from Adam Smith. This was the beginning of a movement toward all individuals, but not inclusive of all individuals. Our statement that "all men are created equal" was not just a statement of our equal-to-us, but that each individual had say to all others as well. They may have meant this *all individuals to each individual* only belonged to a selected group of landowners or aristocrats, but in the end, it moved the new country to a different relational position to our ideas that had never occurred before in written history. We now had a new relational measurement system closer to reality applied to the extended order that could begin to show what it could do when coercion was limited. Not only could our science move us forward, but also people with a pertinacity toward using resources that could take advantage of these scientific advances, as well as resources. This led some people to focus on this aspect alone and then drew conclusions to self-interest.

24. *The extended order of capitalism points to itself as the source for moral justifications because they are the self-proclaimed answer to all things.* Friedman wrote, "History suggests only that capitalism is a necessary condition for political freedom." (52, p10) Our economic behavior is not the sole necessary condition for political freedom. Rather, our political freedom is that we can engage in behavior without manufactured restrictions. It is a mistake to accept the claims by Hayek and Friedman that the activity of all individuals with unfettered freedom as being only economics. Our freedom and liberty is the ability to engage in any activity that does not violate thesis-morality. We measure thesis-morality from our physical world. Our freedom and liberty is not simply the negation of human coercion. Friedman pointed out that capitalism coexisted with Fascism and with the czarist Russia. He wrote, "It is therefore clearly possible to have economic arrangements that are fundamentally capitalist and political arrangements that are not free." (52, p10) He provided us an example that the extended order of capitalism operated without moral requirements. If our government acts outside of thesis-morality, capitalism will align. He side stepped his problem by saying "fundamentally capitalist," yet did not reason to the deficiency in capitalism to explain this alignment. All Friedman did was to take the amoral system of capitalism and claim any political system that allowed the extended order to determine their rules to their narrow self-interests would provide a condition necessary for a politically

free government. When we have political arrangements that are completely free, we would have no government at all. Friedman again confused moral code of conduct with economic code of conduct. This explains why many of us confuse our government with business. For Hayek, he left moral ideas to evolution, the shift from instincts to an extended order.

25. *Hayek assumed only one course of evolutionary path existed and that was to pure capitalism.* Hayek thought morality that developed in small groups did not translate to larger civilizations. Why would our natural morality in small groups not translate to large civilizations? Evolution captures the paths afforded to it. We have different outcomes of species demonstrated by the large variety of life we have on our planet. Why then do we treat the extended order of capitalism as if it is the only possible evolutionary outcome of human activity? In fact, evolution involves the unconscious actions of the physical world. Applying the word evolution to human activity does not account for thought evolution, which resides under different requirements. We can trace capitalistic history to the idea of personal pursuit of happiness as a human end that had overridden other forms of pursuit of happiness or purpose in life. We had large civilizations that existed in North and South America prior to the invasion of Europeans. When we apply unaccountable and human-generated standards of progress based on production and narrow self-interest, we create a *"them and us"* looking glass by ignoring our equal-to-us equation. Capitalists often tout in defense of production and consumer capitalism with strides in health and education. Nevertheless, did not our developments in science involve individuals that worked with our equal-to-us aspects in mind? Did not physical science develop health and education with reason and rational thought that entertained a system of thought with accountability that people, especially in early times, worked on in altruistic ways? They were altruistic in that they had nothing to do with production and profit. They had to do with individuals wanting to know reality. Their pay off was the contribution to civilization. They recognized our equal-ness and wanted to assist in the improved life of all human consciousness, as we, all human consciousness, experience not only pleasure, and pleasure of happiness, but pain as well. For people that are extreme in individualism, it appears difficult for them to see and understand the other source to our moral code of conduct.

26. *The extended order of capitalism has created a set of moral codes of conduct for itself.* Capitalists do not view themselves as morally void. They do have a code of conduct. Friedman wrote, "The existence of a free market does not of course eliminate the need for government. On the contrary, government is essential both as a forum for determining the "rules of the game" and as an umpire to interpret and enforce the rules decided on. What the market does is to reduce greatly the range of issues that must be decided through

political means, and thereby to minimize the extent to which government need participate directly in the game." (52, p15) When we talk of games, we talk of a human created extended order, be it football or capitalism. Friedman spoke that government was to protect us from outside violence and internal violence, thus we can see from his own position that we had a moral duty to keep our thesis-morality equations balanced. Nevertheless, our thesis-morality requirements reside and extend into the extended order of capitalism as well. Any "rules of the game" must comply with thesis-morality and not to the whim of any individual or an individual with power over others. If we do not do this, we are back to our kings and landowners. If we do not comply with thesis-morality, we will have people engage in mental animations that they are greater over other people over all areas of physical existence. Moreover, we would swing the mean equal to a misappropriated amount of difference to unequal thesis-morality and to an unbalance value. If capitalists determined the rules of the game, then we have a specific narrowband view of self-interests, which leads us to all the current problems capitalism exhibits today. When capitalists alone determine the rules of the game, it becomes individual-to-individual flow. We need the participation of all people for moral justification to unequal-to-us activities.

27. *Under all individuals, how are we to determine the rules of the game.* We have attempts made to give the appearance that we, as all individuals, were involved with the rules of the game. Friedman wrote, "The great advantage of the market, on the other hand, is that it permits wide diversity. It is, in political terms, a system of proportional representation. Each man can vote, as it were, for the color of tie he wants and get it; he does not have to see what color the majority wants and then, if he is in the minority, submit." (52, p15) They often refer to this as economic freedom. The actions of individuals will indeed lead to diversity. We have to remember that freedom is larger or more broadband than market actions and that the purpose of voting is different from market actions. He selected the narrowband idea of freedom to markets, which by the market's nature brings diversity, as it is the expression of individuals. Markets can make purple ties. If no one but a few buys them, even they in the end will not be able to buy more. When we associate the two actions of voting with buying a tie, we set up a false reality and authoritative relationship to economic action. The purpose of government is to be our moral consciousness. Voting is part of expressing our social and moral convictions. Buying is an individual economic action. Voting for a "purple tie" implies the purple tie is to engage in the job of some moral and social action across all people. We can see that he mixed two different actions and created a manufactured idea. The tie cannot engage in any moral action or social job function like an individual can. Here he took the word *vote* to a

perverse state. He was attempting to give the extended order of capitalism a *moral power* in the *mere act of buying a tie.*

28. *Friedman moved between broadband and narrowband ideas.* His proportional representation reference above was saying that everyone was equal in his or her consumer desires. Everyone was free to choose whatever consumer item offered. Certainly choosing a purple tie when many other kinds are available involves free action in choice. Nevertheless, we are not free to choose any thing the market offers if it involves thesis-morality violations. Nor is the market free to offer anything it finds in its self-interest. Self-interest is a limited activity. Self-interest in the narrowband, meaning in relation to one individual, or a subset group of individuals, may not be in agreement with the broadband self-interest of humankind. The broadband self-interest of humankind, since it affects everyone one, would override any individual self-interest.

29. *Friedman made diminutive remarks about not committing injustice against others, and he did not define his broadband view of self-interest.* In fact, he wrote, "Indeed, a major source of objection to a free economy is precisely that it does this task so well. It gives people what they want instead of what a particular group thinks they ought to want. Underlying most arguments against the free market is a lack of belief in freedom itself." (52, p15) In the narrowband, you can say his statement was true. Markets do give people what they want, like this or that food, or this or that style of cloths, different games or technical devices or for that matter, pornography. Nevertheless, the idea from Friedman that the free market gives people what they want is a narrowband animation of a broadband idea. Free economy is motivated to profit, and if giving people what they want results in profit, then it indeed does happen. If it does not generate profit, then people do not get what they want. A true statement would be that a free economy gives people what they want provided they can make a profit. Nevertheless, marketing can also manipulate what individuals in the end may want.

30. *Marketing is the science, if I may use that word science in the broadband sense, where they give people what they want and what they make people think they ought to want.* Under his broadband definition of self-interest, his market driven societies can and does exactly this. It operates in two different flows. One flow being markets give people what they want and need as Friedman presents. The other flow has the new extended order of capitalists creating markets. This group decides products and then market to people what they want to market, not what people initially wanted or needed. This contradicts his statement about a particular group giving what they think you ought to want. What we have is thesis-based and manufactured-based marketing. In the first, people move the markets. In the second, the markets move the people.

If we operated under thesisism, this really would not make any difference. Nevertheless, under our current and dominant unaccountable systems of thought, it does. If we moved the markets to our needs, we may move with thesis-based or manufactured-based justifications. If the market moved us, we too may move with thesis-based or manufactured-based justifications. Under thesisism, people could only move markets with thesis-based justifications. Markets could only move people with thesis-based justification.

31. *To work against coercion, we must understand that our physical world has one source to morality with two expressions that we must follow.* We have our human existence. We are our one source. We have our two expressions that come from this physical reality and they are equal thesis-morality and unequal thesis-morality. Like all humans in history, we tend to move to one side or the other, or we deliberately engage in a corrupted flow of activity. We cannot do this without moral violations. Nevertheless, this is what the extended order of capitalism is doing. Friedman wrote, "As liberals, we take freedom of the individual, or perhaps the family, as our ultimate goal in judging social arrangements."[39] (52, p12) Was his "freedom of the individual" as the "ultimate goal in judging social arrangement" a contradiction? Since he used a singular form of the word "individual" and moved the idea to measure against "judging social arrangements," we then have a problem. Note that the "we take freedom of the individual" is the same as individual despite the "we" in the sentence. He made the flow of one individual to judging social arrangement the same as his dreaded socialism. He had his judging social arrangements going back to an individual and applied it to his extended order of capitalism. We must have individual-to-all-individuals flow tied to equal-to-us situations. The perversion is that individual-to-all-individuals flow is equal thesis-morality while he applied it under unequal thesis-morality. This leads to a reversed flow to judgement. He gave one individual ultimate power over all other individuals. Any one individual cannot have ultimate power over all other individuals. This is a moral impossibility in physical existence. He has made one person a god. If he had written "As liberals, we take the freedom of *all individuals* as our ultimate goal in judging social arrangements," we would then have the proper flow to our required unequal thesis-morality. It is subtle. Nevertheless, he flipped the moral flow to an immoral flow.

32. *His system of thought led us to false-reality ideas of freedom.* We must maintain our relationship to physical existence. Our judgment of social arrangements must come about by thesis-morality. It must be in relation to our equal-to-us and our unequal-to-us physical existence. Our social arrangements must meet those situations that require our equality in our human structure. This means that the majority, if they think differently, cannot override this.

39 The use of the word *liberal* by Friedman means *conservative*.

Our creator, physical existence, gives us this equality. Our social arrangement must also meet those situations that involve our inequality in our human structure. This means all individuals must be involved, as the judgements must come from everyone. When the majority judges an unequal-to-us situation as being valid, but in doing so, it violates an equal-to-us requirement, the majority loses. If the majority wants to continue using fossil fuel vehicles, but the result will be destruction of our planet, the equal-to-us aspect overrules. Under Friedman and Hayek, this "judging social arrangements" became a point of manipulation on their part and led to creation of manufactured ideas and actions. It was justified by the manufactured idea of *the greatest happiness for the greatest number.* Greatest happiness had nothing to do with survival or moral considerations. *This is an insect mentality.* For our continued progression as a species, we need to make wise and physically based decisions.

33. *We must maintain both sides of morality.* Friedman and Hayek had an understanding of both sides, but not of the required balance. They moved to an extreme form of individualism. Friedman wrote, "To put this in a different and what may seem a more callous way, children are at one and the same time consumer goods and potentially responsible members of society. The freedom of individuals to use their economic resources as they want includes the freedom to use them to have children—to buy, as it were, the services of children as a particular form of consumption. But once this choice is exercised, the children have a value in and of themselves and have a freedom of their own that is not simply an extension of the freedom of the parents." (52, p33) He understood that individual freedom had constraints when it came to children. He had a vague idea that adults could not coerce other adults, but he brought no system of measurement to us to understand what the restrictions were and where they were limited. With children, he was responding to our equal thesis-morality. Just think about what he responded to here. At some level inside him, he made the evaluative judgment that children had an inherent equal-to-us. Parents had to feed their children. Why? Because our physical-world reality is, we die if we do not eat, and children could not undertake this task alone. Parents have to educate their children. Why? Because our children have to interface with the physical world, to which they were born into. Parents have to take care of the health of their children. Why? Because not taking care of the health of children could lead to their physical death. We do not relinquish these physically equal aspects of children at adulthood. We always have these physically based aspects of human beings connected to the physical world and they always affect us. By moving to extreme individualism, we begin to deny the physical realities that affect all human beings. With the extended order of capitalism, we can begin to mitigate physical existence by

acquired wealth, but that does not change our equal-to-us aspects, nor does it justify our not responding to equal-to-us violations.

34. *The extended order of capitalism is weak when it comes to our obligations to equal thesis-morality.* Hayek wrote, "So long as the services of a particular person are not crucial to my existence or the preservation of what I most value, the conditions he exacts for rendering these services cannot properly be called "coercion." (2, p136) He then followed with an example of people selling water from a spring on an island. He assumed that water could be the property of an individual. When we have no equal-to-us violations occurring, the problem does not present itself. If one person becomes the owner and sole supplier of water and he or she denied it despite plenty of water being available, we begin to have our equal-to-us violation. Water is a physically base force that we all need. Interestingly, Hayek never really resolved this issue in his island scenario.

35. *We have somehow developed the idea that since individual human beings could not comprehend everything, it allowed for justifications against acknowledging thesis-morality obligations.* We have ideas that came from John Locke that made happiness an end as well as his big give away of the earth, along with the conclusions of David Hume that reason and rational thought fails, coupled with the "invisible hand" idea from Adam Smith. All of these ideas converged to provide justification to the extended order of capitalism to engage in economic action without clear moral requirements. Hayek wrote, "The first requisite for this is that we become aware of men's necessary ignorance of much that helps him to achieve his aims. Most of the advantages of social life, especially in its more advanced forms which we call "civilization," rest on the fact that the individual benefits from more knowledge than he is aware of." (2, p22) He was saying we were too unsuited to comprehend the advantages that the extended order of capitalism gives to society. The limits of our minds to understand all actions will always kept each individual ignorant of the greatness of capitalism. He used the idea that no one individual could comprehend all that we needed to comprehend to create the dark room of the "invisible hand," and then he slipped in his "rules of the game" as morality. He had made a broadband statement about human ignorance to all things comprehendible and then selected his narrowband idea of ignorance to a selective positive output of the extended order of capitalism. When you narrowband without acknowledgement, you eliminate all other possibilities. As it stands, we could easily turn his argument to say that our "necessary ignorance" could include disadvantages and even movement toward destructive ends. He ignored this and placed faith into the "invisible hand" by Adam Smith that we would engage in more actions of good over bad. In doing this, we had no visible judgment occurring.

36. *Thesisism states that our unequal thesis-morality must flow from all individuals to the individual.* If we were talking about individual freedom as transformed into economic behavior, that individual freedom we have to subject to both sides of thesis-morality. Nevertheless, the judgment comes about by the input of all individuals, that is, our community. He had no flow and left all individual action unguarded. Under thesisism, we have each individual required to follow the equal-to-us flow to all of us, and all the rest of us to follow the unequal-to-us flow to each individual. Remember, each of the *rest of us* is nothing more than all individuals, and thus each individual of all individuals must follow the equal-to-us flow as well. This is how we maintain our moral obligations.

37. *We can see the individual-to-individual flow in the structure of the extended order of capitalism.* Friedman wrote, "In a capitalist society, it is only necessary to convince a few wealthy people to get funds to launch any idea, however strange, and there are many such persons, many independent foci of support. And, indeed, it is not even necessary to persuade people or financial institutions with available funds of the soundness of the ideas to be propagated. It is only necessary to persuade them that the propagation can be financially successful; that the newspaper or magazine or book or other venture will be profitable. (52, p17) When he says that it is "not even necessary to persuade … the soundness of the ideas," it is clear he was referring to the "soundness" of the idea as having no judgment of it, except for profitability. Without some method of measuring the moral state of the idea, we leave ourselves again with liberty as freedom to do what we want except for the limitation the extended order of capitalism has created for us. We do not have any checks or balances to capitalism under both Hayek and Friedman, except for their own developed rules of the game to profit without the "soundness" of the value to society. Without any sound system of moral evaluation, under the presented ideas by Hayek and Friedman, we have our insect capitalism.

38. *Hayek used the broadband idea of human ignorance to justify his narrowband ideas without any definitive measurement to determine justified and non-justified coercion.* He wrote, "It might be said that civilization begins when the individual in the pursuit of his ends can make use of more knowledge than he has himself acquired and when he can transcend the boundaries of his ignorance by profiting from knowledge he does not himself possess. (2, p22) In the narrowband, there is nothing wrong with his statement. Nevertheless, his "profiting from knowledge" makes no statement to any restrictions to the profiting. He made no evaluations to coercion or to no coercion. In doing this, he did not apply his standard of no arbitrary will of another against his own presentation. The importance is that if we have immoral actions, the lack of coercion to protect freedom and liberty can compound them under the

extended order of capitalism. Nevertheless, the position by Hayek on coercion was, "The task of a policy of freedom must therefore be to minimize coercion or its harmful effects, even if it cannot eliminate it completely." (2, p12) It is not adequate to make vague statements about no coercing against the freedom of an individual. He needed to demonstrate how and what is coercing. The point is that neither Hayek nor Friedman made any statement about when it was acceptable to stop someone in his or her action. This is because they made their idea of no coercion undefined and vague, and they allowed the animation of this fuzzy idea to go to a broadband form. Because they did not define the idea, they left people to fill in the blanks, to create narrowband justifications and animate anything they want measured against their own minds. Moreover, in doing so, we end with each individual engaging in their freedom and self-profiting without any accountable type of moral evaluations being applied. This is what insects do when they work their resources. Since human beings are not insects, but have a highly developed type of mental animation ability, we have a percentage of people work resources by engaging in the coercion of others.

39. *We cannot think in the negative form of no coercion and stop there.* When we view the statement by Friedman in paragraph 37 above that ideas only need to be profitable, this meant the publishing of our ideas belong only to the extended order of capitalism. Perhaps an argument back would be that his statement was only in relation to economic behaviors. Nevertheless, the extended order does not act in a social vacuum. When the extended order of capitalism becomes the dominant source to publish ideas, or the only source, we begin once again to move to our individual-to-individual flow. We could not surface any counter ideas nor needed criticisms of the capitalistic system and their resulting actions. This would mean we could not express certain ideas, as we would deem them unprofitable, or even anti-profitable. Under our current conditions where we have so much media, not only do we have the marketing of ideas taking place, but we have the anti-marketing of ideas to conflicting self-interest and mutually exclusive ideas that work against pockets of economic or social power. The free enterprise that Friedman animated included the free marketing of social ideas, not under consistent individual moral flow discussion, but to marketing strategies that move populations by small groups of self-interest. Therefore, the extended order of capitalism is not the convenient and simple idea of exchanging a product for money, but it moves and shapes our social culture. Here we had Friedman move his narrowband idea into broadband conceptualizations. This continues to leave us with no moral obligations and insect capitalism. The idea of no coercion leaves no room for acceptable moments of conflict between an individual, who believes he is free to do something, yet cannot do so because of the

conflict with the society of all individuals. We need a positive statement to when an individual cannot act, and not a negative statement that we cannot coerce an individual against their will, with the word "coerced" defined by them as stopping their vague and arbitrary "rules of the game."

Section 2: Breaking from Our Past

40. *We need to have a system of thought and measurement to moral ideas that can make positive statements when an individual can and cannot pursue an idea.* Any system of thought must measure against an authority that is higher than and independent to human beings. It must be an authority to the reality of our human existence. It must be an authority than can override any personally held false-reality desires by any human being. It must be simple, easily understood and common to all people of this earth. This authority cannot give any one or group of individuals any special powers or position. Finally, this authority need not be a conscious authority.

41. *We do have a system of thought and measurement to moral ideas where we can make positive statements when an individual can and cannot pursue an idea.* We meet all the above requirements with thesisism. Our higher authority is our physical existence. Our physical existence is our creator and our creation. We are not separate, but relational to it. It is in human being terms our eternal and non-changing existence. It holds the structure to which we live in. It is within this structure that physical existence has moved that has created our reality of human existence. It has ultimate authority on our continued existence. We are the result of the movement of physical existence, and our measurement of our ideas and ideas of morality we make against it. Physical existence overrides any mentally animated idea that breaks from its physical foundation. It overrides our personal desires. Physical existence is the same for all people around our earth and beyond. Our measurement against this higher authority is the same for all human beings on this planet. Our morality measures against this higher authority, and our physical existence has created an equal-to-us and an unequal-to-us.

42. *These are the products of our physical structure as human beings and to which we measure against for our moral ideas.* This physical existence to our human structure is the same for all human beings. This is simple and does not give any individual or groups of individuals any special powers or authority. Physical existence is without consciousness. Human beings have evolved that we have consciousness and can reflect back the reality of the physical world. It is in maintaining this relational aspect between our thought existence and physical existence that we can achieve our success and our highest level as a living animal through observing, acknowledging and acting on the moral

obligations that arrive to us through our reflection. Using this simple tool of thesisism as a measurement to our ideas and actions taken, we can make positive statements to individual activity without infringing or coercing individual freedom and liberty. Individual freedom and liberty is all minus our thesis-morality obligations derived from our physical existence. Never would an individual restrict an individual. Physical existence may restrict an individual, but physical existence is our higher authority and physical existence removes us from the equation to avoid human coercion.

43. *The call to thesisism by Friedman, part 1:* Friedman and Hayek, like all other human beings, had rudimentary understanding to thesisism. They skewed their ideas toward unequal thesis-morality. Nevertheless, they had some understanding of thesisism without knowing it in clarity. Friedman wrote, "There are thus two sets of values that a liberal will emphases—the values that are relevant to relations among people, which is the context in which he assigns first priority to freedom; and the values that are relevant to the individual in the exercise of his freedom, which is the realm of individual ethics and philosophy. (52, p12) Friedman had a vague idea that he must measure against something. He realized that he must make his "values ... relevant to relations among people." He was touching on thesisism. He was touching on the fact of physical existence that we all have a human-conscious structure with a common equality. He was making a weak statement that we had an equal thesis-morality to contend with and it had first priority. However, a spin of sorts occurred here. He realized he had to contend with this "relevant to relations among people," and that it had "first priority." Nevertheless, he did make a correct and positive statement to freedom. It was a spin of sorts in that he did not reference it to coercion as his books dominated in. It was a total miss in that he did not connect his "values" to physical existence, but to the self-interest animations of capitalists. He made a weak statement, especially in light that he acknowledged it as a first priority, but never explained this relational first priority to individual freedom to *all individuals.* It was as close as he would get to thesisism.

44. *The call to thesisism by Friedman, part 2:* When he wrote, "relevant to the individual in the exercise...," it was a strong understanding by Friedman of unequal thesis-morality. He was correct in that it was in "the realm of individual ethics and philosophy," but not the way he viewed it. He distorted his view because he did not measure against the physical world and against our physical human structure. Both Friedman and Hayek correctly recognized that socialist ideas were flawed ideas. Having experienced during their lifetime the governmental actions of the Soviet Union and other socialistic and communistic countries, it had created an adhesive framed-reference to anything that appeared socialistic to be automatically bad. This was simplistic,

but understandable from what was within their reach. Within their reach was destructive socialistic systems and unaccountable rational thought. This unaccountable form of rational thought was not specific to any country, but extended to all rational thought, even to date. When Friedman wrote, "what he [the individual][40] should do with his freedom...," (52, p12) our first step in this action was to understand thesisism and begin to measure ones actions against it. This will keep actions based in reality. It will bring about the best use of resources not only in the short-term, but also in the long term.

45. *The call to thesisism by Friedman, part 3:* Friedman wrote, "there is a broad underlying social consensus. But we cannot rely on custom or on this consensus alone to interpret and to enforce the rules; we need an umpire. These then are the basic roles of government in a free society: to provide a means whereby we can modify the rules, to mediate differences among us on the meaning of the rules, and to enforce compliance with the rules on the part of those few who would otherwise not play the game." (52, p25) Friedman made the government a social and an economic control center. It was a centralization of the activities of all individuals. In the broadband, this idea is fine. However, in the narrowband, government cannot become solely an economic control center. If it does, it is a power source to the extended order of capitalism, and the power pockets created by this extended order of capitalism create an individual-to-individual flow. We see this individual-to-individual flow with his idea of an umpire, as it is one single individual making all the decisions. We end with a moral breakdown. Our government must represent all people and base their decision on thesis-morality. It must represent equal thesis-morality to our equal aspects, thus protecting our minority rights. It must represent unequal thesis-morality to our unequal aspects, thus protecting our application of self. His "umpire" ought to be our tool of thesisism. The "basic roles of government" becomes our thesis-morality and the proper expression of equal and unequal thesis-morality. This means our government becomes our moral consciousness. The *game rules* of the extended order of capitalism must meet thesis-morality and our government must be its check and balance. The only economic influence our government ought to have on our extended order of capitalism is thesis-morality considerations.

46. *The call to thesisism by Friedman, part 4:* Friedman wrote, "The role of government just considered is to do something that the market cannot do for itself, namely, to determine, arbitrate and enforce the rules of the game. (52, p27) Thesisism can determine, arbitrate and enforce the rules of the game. Friedman, however, viewed the government as a power source to protect the (singular) individual freedom and the rules the extended order of capitalism

---

40 The words "the individual" in brackets were added for clarity.

that capitalism had decided for itself. We can insert the reality of thesisism, as a tool, to bring us our moral obligations that are necessary and to avoid any manufactured coercion the extended order of capitalism worries about occurring. Our freedom or liberty can only be freedom or liberty if it meets thesis-morality requirements. If we violate thesis-morality requirements, we create a manufactured form of freedom or liberty that can only exist in the minds of human beings. Slavery was a form of manufactured freedom and liberty from the perspective of the slave owners, as the masters commonly accepted it as lawful and a right to own human beings and to use them in an unrestricted fashion to economic and profit gains.

47. *We can move from a negative idea of coercion to a positive idea of coercion.* We can revisit Hayek's words to the negative idea of coercion. "The task of a policy of freedom must therefore be to minimize coercion or its harmful effects, even if it cannot eliminate it completely. (2, p12) Hayek used the negative aspects of "minimize coercion" to determine freedom. Nevertheless, we can state positively the policy of freedom with thesisism. By his taking the "minimize coercion" stand, he could not distinguish between coercion that was not justified and coercion that was justified in any exact manner. He obscured it by the vague definitions he applied to coercion. To have justified coercion meant that the external source had to have its thesis-based justification, yet with the definition by Hayek, coercion was the arbitrary will of another.[41] The word arbitrary made coercion relative to each individual. Nevertheless, we determine coercion by its relationship to physical existence, not the human mind. Thesisism eliminates the human mind as the source to measurement and in turn eliminates manufactured ideas. Therefore, when we reflect on our physical existence it provides the arbitrary or non-arbitrary will of another based on our thesis-morality equations to our physical-world realities. This creates an important and necessary feedback to our ideas.

48. *Hayek dismissed science and pulled in the ideas of David Hume that religion and science could not grasp our physical realities.* Hayek had the correct understanding of science, in that it involved the idea of being able to predict events. When it involves the human mind, our social structure and the immense quantity of actions, the ability of science to be able to predict human events falters. This has left us with a gaping hole to which we have struggled to move forward in any reasonable and rational fashion. Friedman and Hayek handle this problem by placing faith into the "invisible hand" by Adam Smith that self-interest actions resulted in both success and detriment, but overall, greater in success. We never measured this self-determined success

---

41 Hayek's idea of coercion was the arbitrary will of another is supported in paragraph 2, section 1, and paragraph 49, section 2 in the chapter titled, *Defined Coercion, Our Release of Freedom and Liberty*.

against thesis-morality, but to ancient philosophical ideas that humankind acts with more good than bad. Nevertheless, our scientific and philosophical thought has faltered when we tried to understand human behavior because we have been measuring our ideas not against our physical existence, but against the chaos of our own minds. No uniformity between people exists as false reality abounds. When the cause and effect idea of science measured against each human thought existence, which included numerous false-reality ideas, the result of various conflicting moral ideas then resulted in ideas of *non-arbitrary will against another*. Ironically, science that measures cause and effect against physical existence, did not understand that human behavior was from a conscious entity with an additional existence—thought existence. Unless there is uniformity in human thought existence in how each individual measures his or her ideas, the cause and effect idea essentially measures against each individual person. This can only result in noise because it is as if each person were a separate universe with its own laws of structure. Although science cannot apply cause and effect to social understanding, it ought to have understood reflection of physical existence and discovered the physically based moral equations.

49. *Articulating the idea that coercion was the arbitrary will of one individual against another individual was not adequate to pull us out of insect capitalism.* Hayek wrote,

> It meant always the possibility of a person's acting according to his own decisions and plans, in contrast to the position of one who was irrevocably subject to the will of another, who by arbitrary decision could coerce him to act or not to act in specific ways.
>
> ...
>
> The time-honored phrase by which this freedom has often been described is therefore "independence of the arbitrary will of another."
>
> ...
>
> but when we consider all the confusion that philosophers have caused by their attempts to refine or improve it, we may do well to accept this description.
>
> ...
>
> In this sense "freedom" refers solely to a relation of men to other men, and the only infringement on it is coercion by men. (2, p12)

When we pull it all together, we realize he never defined the word "arbitrary." His individual freedom and liberty was anything one wants minus general broadband statements about no harm and the adherence to *the rules of the game* defined by those with power in the extended order. If we apply thesisism and connect ourselves back to our physical existence, what does arbitrary will of another mean?

50. *We can replace the undefined idea of no coercion being the existence of no arbitrary will imposed onto another individual with a reality-based, physical-world idea.* If we think in terms of thesis will and manufactured will forced onto the will of another, we quickly see that Friedman and Hayek were talking about manufactured wills. Arbitrary will was another way of saying false-reality will. False-reality will is the will of another that can only exist in the minds of human beings. We can only impose thesis will onto another individual. When we have thesis-based ideas that involves the imposition of one will against another, it is not arbitrary. We have measured it against the physical existence of our human physical structure. When we have manufactured-based ideas that involves the imposition of one will against another, it is arbitrary. We have measured it against the chaos of the human mind. This moves us away from the faith-based idea of the "invisible hand" by Adam Smith to a reality-based idea of thesis-morality measurements by thesisism. This then gives us the needed tool to insert into the actions of people that may indeed be beyond the comprehension of any singular individual. The totality of physical existence is beyond the comprehension of any singular individual. Nevertheless, physical existence is a singularity to humankind. The tool of thesisism serves to direct properly the moral flow of actions from every individual, *thus it directs beyond any individual conceptual understanding,* and we express it properly by measuring against our physical existence. This simple formula and the correct application of flow remove us from our insect capitalism and into a thesis-based capitalism. Thesis-based capitalism is reality-based capitalism. Our historical *"invisible hand"* becomes a *visible and viable hand.*

51. *The application of thesisism into our system of thought aligns with the system of thought by Hayek of how civilization progresses. Part 1:* Hayek asserted that humankind did not make their civilization, but was the result of reacting to our physical existence. He wrote, "This assertion would be justified only if man had deliberately created civilization in full understanding of what he was doing or if he at least clearly knew how it was being maintained. In a sense it is true, of course, that man has made his civilization. It is the product of his actions or, rather, of the action of a few hundred generations. This does not mean, however, that civilization is the product of human design, or even that man knows what its functioning or continued existence depends upon."

245

(2, p23) We do know that our continued existence depends on our physical existence. When we measure against our physical existence rather than our human mind, we realize we succeed when our human design is in relation to physical existence. This means we can say that *real-world civilization would be a product of physical existence designed through individual human evaluations.*

52. *This also means we have appallingly missed when we measure against our finite human happiness as an end:* The progression of our civilization results from our actions to our given actions between one another in relation to our physical existence. When we achieve the balance to our reality, it brings us a contented state. When we maintain the correct relational aspects to our ideas and our physical world, we obtain our required feedback to our own thoughts to our physical realities. This feedback, our maintaining the idea of reality correctly placed to ideas, which include ideas with probable levels of reality, keeps us from swinging wildly with horrendous manufactured ideas flying about. We have seen how society swings itself to one end and then to another displayed in divisions like liberal verses conservative and democratic verses republican. When we do not maintain accountability with our sliver idea of reality, we have oscillations that result in measuring our ideas broken from physical existence and made against our arbitrary minds. We make our evaluate-to-balance in relation to *sensing it* mixed with false-reality ideas that we bounce with a vague understanding between our two expressions of thesis-morality. When we engage in thesisism and maintain accountability to the sliver idea of reality by free will, it keeps us focused. This greatly reduces human suffering and enhances the quality of our lives.

53. *The system of thought by Hayek of how civilization progresses, part 2:* He further wrote, "Man did not simply impose upon the world a pattern created by his mind. His mind is itself a system that constantly changes as a result of his endeavor to adapt himself to his surroundings. It would be an error to believe that, to achieve a higher civilization, we have merely to put into effect the ideas now guiding us. If we are to advance, we must leave room for a continuous revision of our present conceptions and ideals which will be necessitated by further experience." (2, p23) It is interesting how Hayek at one moment viewed our ability to understand the extended order of capitalism as beyond the capacity of any one individual, yet here, spoke of "continuous revision of our present conceptions and ideals." We could never progress because we would not have the capacity to distinguish progression from regression. Nevertheless, we do impose patterns created by our minds. The problem with this statement is that when he used the words "his surroundings," it involved both physical existence and thought existence. Hayek was correct in that to achieve a "higher civilization," we must leave room for revision to our present conceptions and ideals. Nevertheless, how do we direct our revision and to

what? We can continue to fly wildly like a moth at a flame of false reality, or we can measure against reality. This idea of revision aligns well with thesisism because thesisism does not start with our knowing everything. It progresses. Thesisism is not an "impose upon the world a pattern created by his mind." *The human mind allows the physical world to create its pattern within us.* This is our free will and our free-flow framed-reference. The reason the system "constantly changes" is not only attributed to changes in our surroundings, but that we human beings have been measuring our ideas against our own human minds. We have created many manufactured ideas that have created a lot of noise of misunderstanding for humankind.

54. *Although Hayek pointed out the limits of science, he did so without acknowledgment to the limits of religion.* Hayek wrote, "Perhaps it is only natural that the scientists tend to stress what we do know; but in the social field, where what we do not know is often so much more important, the effect of this tendency may be very misleading. Many of the utopian constructions are worthless because they follow the lead of the theorists in assuming that we have perfect knowledge." (2, p23) It is important to acknowledge what we do not know, provided we know enough to know we do not know something. It is important to state that any system of thought that creates a utopian construction and assumes to have perfect knowledge is incorrect. Nevertheless, social science is not the only one that has done this. We have many religions that claim perfect knowledge. They too are limited in their understanding yet do not acknowledge it. They too have contributed to suffering.

55. *Science has its limit in social understanding only in that it has limited its definition.* An attempt to have a scientific type of understanding to social activity to be the wiggle and see what happens is a use of science that does not lend itself to record changes in society. Hayek wrote, "The scientific methods of the search for knowledge are not capable of satisfying all of society's needs for explicit knowledge. Not all the knowledge of the ever-changing particular facts that man continually uses lends itself to organization or systematic exposition; much of it exists only dispersed among countless individuals. (2, p25) This is where thesisism differs from science. Thesisism is not a wiggle and record system. It is the study of ideas and how they relate, or do not relate, to our physical existence. We are not creating an understanding of how things work relationally in physical existence, such as why gunpowder explodes, but that by maintaining our relational requirements of reality to our ideas, we find our code of conduct. Discovering and understanding our human physical structure, our equal and unequal aspects, is like reading a topology map.

56. *Science has one universe whereas thesisism has as many as the human population holds.* The cause and effect works for science because they are dealing

with one physical universe. That one universe holds it system of operation. In thesisism, each human being and their consciousness is a universe. It is the universe of thought existence and it is unique to each person. When we do not have any accountability method to ideas, we cannot have any consistency between people. There will be wild variances in behavioral responses based on whatever individual false reality the person measures against. Thesisism can bring a generalized consistency in that it measures the same across all that partake in accountability of the sliver idea of reality. That consistency is physical existence.

57. *Hayek's justification for unaccountable and vague freedom was to have faith that we would end with good over bad.* With Hayek, he left us with random mental animations to what our code of conduct should be. He wrote, "All that we can know is that the ultimate decision about what is good or bad will be made not by individual human wisdom but by the decline of the groups that have adhered to the 'wrong' beliefs." (2, p36) How are we to know a right belief from a wrong belief? How can we determine what is good or bad if we can animate any idea we want and apply reality to any idea? We have many religions, and each according to the other, contain wrong beliefs. Further, according to the words of Hayek, beliefs that disappear meant they were wrong. If we have the arbitrary will of another in their beliefs, beliefs may stay or go for any number of reasons that have nothing to do with them being good or bad. He further wrote, "It is therefore no argument against individual freedom that it is frequently abused. Freedom necessarily means that many things will be done which we do not like. Our faith in freedom does not rest on the foreseeable results in particular circumstances but on the belief that it will, on balance, release more forces for the good than for the bad. (2, p31) Once again, we return to faith-based freedom and evangelical capitalism. He implied we could never apply answerable measurement and that we progressed by trial an error with no ability to know the difference. We indeed have been progressing by trial and error measured against the arbitrary wills of evangelical and insect capitalism.[42] The irony is that we cannot distinguish when we are correct or in error. This progression is independent to the movement to good. Nevertheless, we do not have to progress this way. We can base ourselves in reality and implement thesisism.

58. *It is not that we ought to leave the problem of limited individual reason open to faith in freedom. Rather we take the individual reason and anchor it into the reality of physical existence.* This provides us the stability and cohesiveness needed for any society. Hayek wrote, "And, while the design theories necessarily lead to the conclusion that social processes can be made to serve

---

42 This statement is made in relation to the subject of morality, government and capitalism. The arbitrary wills from people can come from any source.

human ends only if they are subjected to the control of individual human reason, and thus lead directly to socialism, true individualism believes on the contrary that, if left free, men will often achieve more than individual human reason could design or foresee." (55, p10-11) We can remove the unchecked coercive opportunities from the faith in freedom that Hayek expounds. We maintain our "true individualism" when we eliminate measurement based in the experiential existence of humans and shift it to our physical existence. It is not that any one person dictates thesisism. Instead, we all engage in it. The very nature of measurement against physical existence brings us our clarity and stability. Hayek, Hume, and others are correct that no one individual would hold the "design theories" to a moral society. We would have it surface by the actions and pursuits of all individuals under this measurement system.

Section 3: Our Move to the Future

59. *We have thousands of years of faith-based thought systems to see its results.* We had the hotbed of terror in Europe during the Middle Ages. We had the hotbed of terror in the conquest of North and South America. We have the hotbed of terror and anger in the Middle East. In the broadband, all groups separate themselves from one another and do not recognize or acknowledge their equality in life. These groups live immersed in manufactured ideas. These ideas have resulted in so much suffering and death, yet amazingly, these ideas only exist in the minds of human beings. Our creation around us does not reflect this bizarre mental view. It did result in the brains we so poorly use. Nevertheless, we always jeopardize our world stability with manufactured ideas that exist only in human minds. This is shameful. This is immoral.

60. *The moral corruption of governments is staggering.* We have a long history of government power acting not according to thesis-morality. We see moral corruption in socialism and communism. We see their centralization destroy the individual expressions held by people. Our republic[43] is to reflect our equality in that we all have a common human experience. Our republic is to reflect our individuality while we move within our freedoms and liberty with thesis-based justifications. Nevertheless, we have representatives that do not understand thesis-morality and engage in individual-to-individual actions. We end with our moral equations not matching our physical reality. We end with a moral collapse.

61. *We see the interrupted moral flow from capitalism to government that prevents proper thesis-morality expressions.* We have economic theories that replace thesis-morality with self-generated economic rules of the game. We

---

43 "Our republic" is a reference to the United States of America.

have a long history of violated people under the individualistic pursuit of happiness. We have seen slavery, indenture, child labor, horrific working conditions, pensions lost; Savings and Loans bail outs carried by taxpayers and increased shoddy banking practices and credit lending. We have seen deregulation that placed people into jeopardy, be it financial strain or deregulation on drug studies that aversely affects our population. Wealth and power does not align with intelligence and morality. Bruyère once wrote, "Often when the Rich Man speaks, and speaks of Learning, the Learned Man must be silent, listen and applaud; at least he would pass for one of some Learning." (17, p257-258)

62. *Our move to the future is to determine good over bad definitively.* We can do this by our having a reality-based thought system. Any system of thought would not be good unless it is a system of thought with accountability. We bring ourselves accountability when we remove ourselves from the equation. We move to a higher source and one that is eternal to our lifetime reference. We move to a source of measurement that is the same for all human beings. We do this with thesisism.

63. *When we understand and implement thesisism, we can release freedom and liberty from human coercion.* Thesisism allows us to make positive decisions and statements to what is an arbitrary will of another and what is a non-arbitrary will of another. We can bring a guided course to the actions of all individuals and bring intelligence into the "invisible hand" of Adam Smith and to Friedman and Hayek's vague and cloudy ideas of no coercion by the arbitrary will of others against others. Thesisism is an individual code of conduct measured against the physical world, and it brings us uniformity, consistency and reality to all actions across all people. Our understanding of thesisism is not the comprehension of all things by a single individual, but the comprehension of all individuals to a simple system that we base off reality. This controls human coercion against other human beings. It aligns our ideas against our higher authority, which is our physical existence. It does not require any single person or group of individuals to be masters, or special people with self-given gifts to tell others what is truth. It removes the human being from the code of conduct equations, and the equations only measure against our physical creation. The only blockage that now exists between the control of coercion and the release of our freedom and liberty to all human beings on this earth is the existence of personal desires with false reality. This results in all the developed adhesive framed-references that create manufactured ideas and the denied free will of human beings. Our challenge, if we are to survive, and to survive without human created suffering, is to take a moment to think relationally not against our human minds, but to think relationally against our physical existence. Not only is physical existence where we find our selves

living in, but also where we can actually find ourselves. Bruyère wrote, "If poverty is the Mother of Crimes, want of Sense is the Father." (17, p216)

64. *A new moral revolution against the coercive animal starts with you.* If each individual picks up the tool of thesisism, then we can achieve our freedom and liberty. In our freedom and liberty, we can achieve the balance of life and obtain our meaning in life. In our thesis-based actions, we move to create ourselves to an end where our creator achieves it success. Since we are composed-of and composed-by the creator, we achieve our end too. It is time for a physically based moral system. It is time to let go of all the self-proclaimed authorities and their decrees. It is time for each individual to face their creator, open their free will and take in the reality of our creation. It is time we place ourselves accountable to this creation. In doing so, we liberate ourselves from human coercion and become self-responsible. We can begin to change the course of human existence away from war, torture and human bondage. We can do this. We can begin to change the course of human existence to peace, self-reliance and human expression with harmony. Just as humankind continuously regenerates itself through birth, our movement to freedom and liberty continuously begins anew. It begins with you and me—now and tomorrow. It is time for a new moral revolution.

DIAGRAMS ON THESISISM

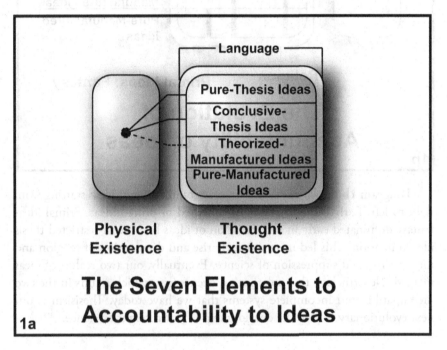

Language

Pure-Thesis Ideas

Conclusive-
Thesis Ideas

Theorized-
Manufactured Ideas

Pure-Manufactured
Ideas

Physical
Existence

Thought
Existence

The Seven Elements to Accountability to Ideas

1a

Diagram 1a shows our four elements in thought existence and their relationship to physical existence and language. Our seven elements to understand truth are physical existence, thought existence, pure-thesis ideas, conclusive-thesis ideas, theorized-manufactured ideas, pure-manufactured ideas, and language use. The lines shown from physical existence to thought existence represent the connections or the lack of connections to physical existence to any given master idea. Pure-manufactured ideas do not have any connections at all. This demonstrated relationship is how we determine accountability to ideas.

James S. Serilla

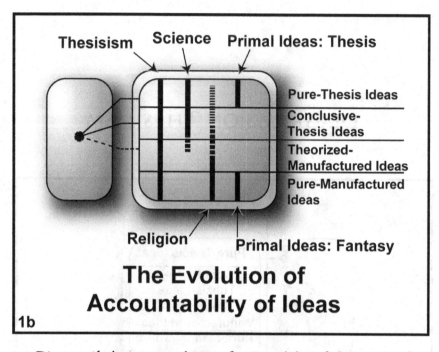

Thesisism **Science** **Primal Ideas: Thesis**

Pure-Thesis Ideas

Conclusive-
Thesis Ideas

Theorized-
Manufactured Ideas

Pure-Manufactured
Ideas

Religion **Primal Ideas: Fantasy**

The Evolution of
Accountability of Ideas

1b

Diagram 1b shows our evolution of accountability of ideas starting from right to left. Early thought existence consisted of primal ideas. Primal ideas fantasy dominated early in the evolution of ideas because of restricted thesis idea animation. This led us to our early rise and domination of religion and the later rise and suppression of science. Eventually, our two realms of ideas merged. Nevertheless, this polarization occurs first, which results in the two incompatible and incomplete systems that we have today. Thesisism is our next evolutionary step in the development of our thought existence.

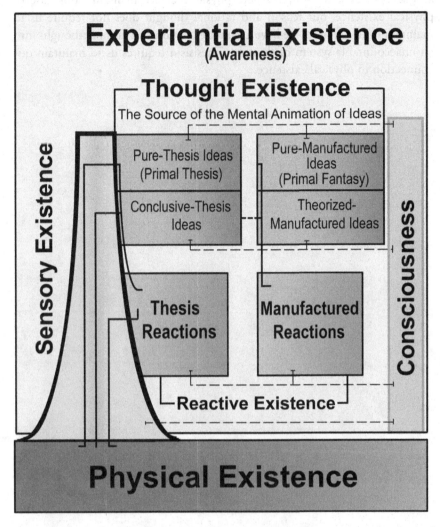

Experiential Existence
(Awareness)

Thought Existence
The Source of the Mental Animation of Ideas

Sensory Existence

Pure-Thesis Ideas
(Primal Thesis)

Pure-Manufactured Ideas
(Primal Fantasy)

Conclusive-Thesis Ideas

Theorized-Manufactured Ideas

Consciousness

Thesis Reactions

Manufactured Reactions

Reactive Existence

Physical Existence

Diagram 2 shows our five existences. *Physical existence* is our physical world. *Sensory existence* is our player to our inputted senses. *Reactive existence* is our source of emotions, as they are the reactive coloring to our reactive perception of the world. *Thought existence* is our ideas. We have the capacity to move sliver ideas into new master ideas by mental animation. Awareness is the combination of sensory, reactive and thought existence. Consciousness is awareness of awareness. *Experiential existence* consists of awareness and consciousness. Traditional philosophers and theologians have amputated our connections with physical existence. We then have our thought measured not against this base of physical existence, but bouncing within thought, reactive and sensory existence only. Where physical science maintains our base to physical existence, our reason and rational thought does not require us to maintain it. In doing so, we have amputated reason and rational thought into an unaccountable system of thought. Thesisism requires us to maintain our connection to physical existence.

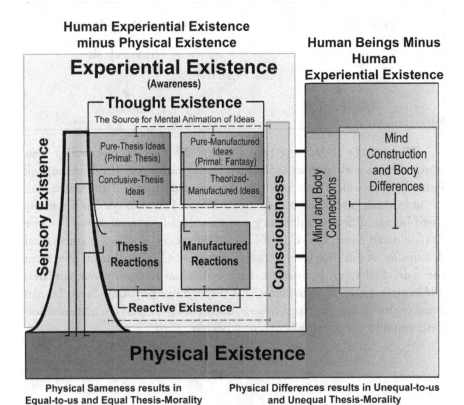

Human Experiential Existence minus Physical Existence

Human Beings Minus Human Experiential Existence

Physical Sameness results in Equal-to-us and Equal Thesis-Morality

Physical Differences results in Unequal-to-us and Unequal Thesis-Morality

Diagram 3 outlines the model of human existence and the sources of equal thesis-morality and unequal thesis-morality from which our code of conduct arises. Experiential existence is the product of the action of the physical. Our equal thesis-morality comes from our experiential existence. Our experiential existence minus physical existence leaves only our ideas, our reactive coloring, and the product of our sensory player. This experiential existence cannot exist without physical existence. The physical generic blueprint of the human brain for experiential existence to operate within is our equality in physical existence. Unequal thesis-morality comes from our physical existence minus any input from experiential existence.

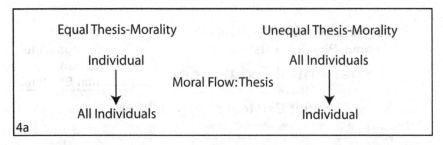

Diagram **4a** shows our two different flows of thesis-morality. Our unequal-to-us goes from all individuals to the individual. This is because all individuals provide a data point to the unequal aspects of the individual. All individuals involve all people, not a subset. It is through our physically based human differences that we get our unequal-to-us equation of $\bar{E} = U \pm D$ ($\bar{E}$ = mean equal, U = Unequal, D = Difference). This is a mathematical description of our inequality between all people. Our equal-to-us goes from the individual to all individuals. Each individual recognizes our sameness and expresses it to all individuals. It is through our physically based human equality that we get our equal-to-us equation of E = E. This is a mathematical description of our equality between all people.

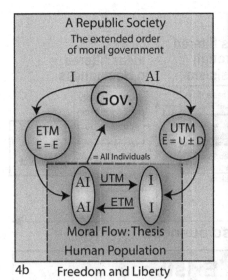

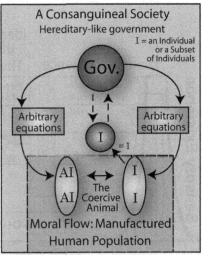

4b   Freedom and Liberty   Arbitrary Will and Arbitrary Coercion

Diagram 4b shows our moral flow through our sociopolitical model that we currently live in. Notice that we can have a moral flow of thesis-morality or a moral flow of manufactured-morality independent to any governmental system.

On the left, we have our correct flow of thesis-morality through our government. We express our unequal thesis-morality theoretically through our elected representatives. For our issues with unequal thesis-morality, the government would express the will of the people under unequal-to-us situations. For our issues with equal thesis-morality, since it is the same for all individuals, theoretically our elected representatives would express equality and minority rights under equal-to-us situations. Note that with all individuals we have contained within it both expressions. Here we can achieve non-arbitrary will and justified coercion. We gain our freedom and liberty.

When we have neither individual-to-all-individuals flow for our equal thesis-morality or our all-individuals-to-individual flow for our unequal thesis-morality, we have individual-to-individual flow. On the right, we have our corrupted moral flow for government. When an individual or a group of individuals determines our equations to self-interest morality, we have a manufactured moral flow. We lose our thesis-morality equations and we operate with arbitrary will and unjustified coercion. Here we lose our freedom and liberty.

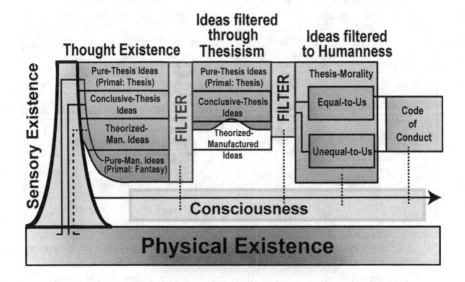

Diagram 5 shows our thesis-morality filter. We first filter our ideas in thought existence through thesisism. Then we filter ideas of morality to our physical humanness, which we show in Diagram 3. Through our humanness, we can determine whether our situation is equal thesis-morality or unequal thesis-morality. With this information, we can know our moral code of conduct between human beings.

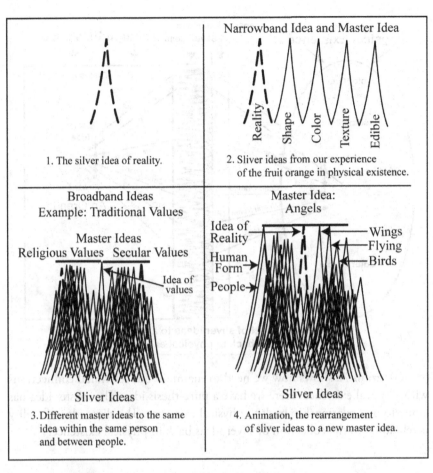

1. The silver idea of reality.

2. Sliver ideas from our experience of the fruit orange in physical existence.

3. Different master ideas to the same idea within the same person and between people.

4. Animation, the rearrangement of sliver ideas to a new master idea.

Diagram 6 shows a representation of the sliver ideas we acquire through our experience of physical existence. Section 1 shows the sliver idea of reality as a singular idea. Because we experience reality largely, we actually come to have a diffuse idea of it. Section 2 shows a small collection of sliver ideas to a master idea. Typically, these are our narrowband ideas. The master idea may or may not connect back to physical existence. In section 3, we have many sliver ideas within ourselves that we can pull together to make any master idea. When we have a large amount of sliver ideas from which we can pull up different master ideas within ourselves or between other people, we have broadband ideas. Section 4 shows how we can pull sliver ideas from different experiences with physical existence to create a new master idea. In the circumstance shown, we falsely attach the sliver idea of reality to a non-reality idea.

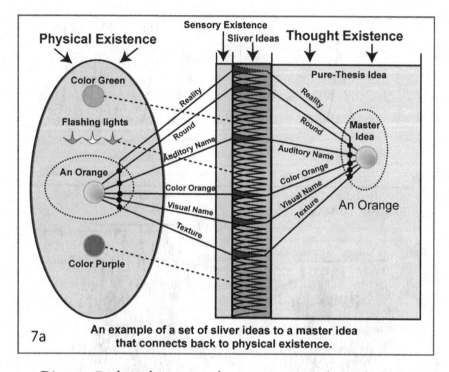

7a **An example of a set of sliver ideas to a master idea that connects back to physical existence.**

Diagram 7a shows how we need to maintain our relational connections with physical existence. Here we have a pure-thesis idea. The master idea has a one to one relationship back to physical existence. The sliver idea of reality is relational to the collection of sliver ideas back to physical existence.

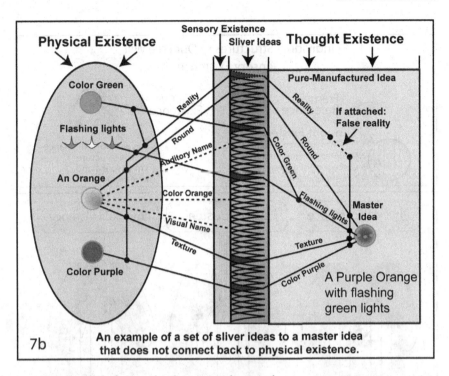

7b — An example of a set of sliver ideas to a master idea that does not connect back to physical existence.

Diagram 7b shows what happens when we do not maintain our connection to physical existence. Here we have movement of sliver ideas to make a pure-manufactured idea. When we pull together separately experienced sliver ideas to new make master ideas, we can have probability levels to reality occur that places them between pure-thesis and pure-manufactured ideas. When we can construe one, two, or more potential alignments with reality to any set of collected sliver ideas, we can begin to categorize them accountably as conclusive-thesis, theorized-manufactured or pure-manufactured ideas.

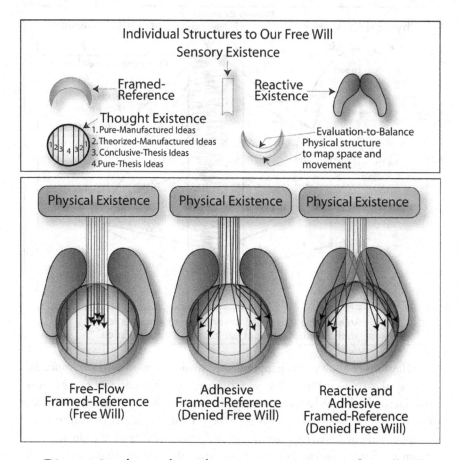

Diagram 8 at the top shows the component parts to our free will. Below we have three constructions. On the left, we have an unrestricted form of free will with our reactive existence not interfering with our incoming information from physical existence. It also has a non-adhesive framed-reference that allows the evaluation of the incoming information in its purest form. In the center, we have an adhesive framed-reference that seizes the incoming information from physical existence and it bends the information by attaching sliver and master ideas. These sliver and master ideas attach to move perception to preconceived and desired master ideas. The far-right side shows the effects of interference from reactive existence and an adhesive framed-reference.

A community is a collection of all individuals (I+I+I...)

—— = Moral Issue   ----- = Not a Moral Issue

Universal Moral Ideas   Limited Moral Ideas

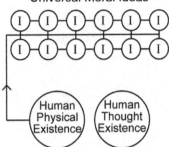
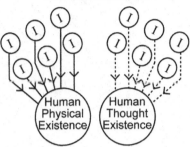

Examples: Not to Murder, Education and Health Care.

Example: Altruism - to help people.
In need of food verses
in need of money for vanity plastic surgery, etc.

Diagram 9 shows the difference between a universal moral and a limited moral idea. The universal moral idea has applicability to all individuals. The limited moral idea has applicability only to specific situations.

GLOSSARY

Adhesive Framed-Reference: An adhesive framed-reference seizes the incoming information from physical existence and bends the information by attaching to them preexisting sliver or master ideas. These new incoming sliver and master ideas attach to move perception to preconceived and desired master ideas. An adhesive framed-reference acts as a net to catch any incoming information from physical existence and moves the information to conform to preconceived master ideas.

Awareness: All activity in experiential existence that is operating in the present.

Broadband Words: When we read or say a word, the person reading or listening has a meaning come into his or her thought existence. A word like morality is broadband because variations of the idea are numerous and different people will think of different ideas of morality. A phrase like *traditional values* is broadband because variations of different ideas would fill the thought existence of people. This then means that people would think of different ideas to the same word or set of words. This can lead us to misunderstandings and miscommunications. Therefore, we must recognize broadband words and reduce the meaning of the word down to its simplest form. This flushes out different meanings to an idea to a common understanding so everyone is animating the same idea. At this point, one can then begin to apply our remaining six elements of understanding truth and to see which category the idea belongs.

Conclusive-Thesis Ideas: When we have a set of direct or implied connections to the physical that creates a consensus among thesisists that it brings a one-conclusion determination, we have a conclusive-thesis idea. Despite the one-conclusion determination, the idea is always open to reexamination.

Consciousness: Consciousness is awareness that is operating in suspension. It has a past, present, and future.

Denied Free Will: When we have a free will that we obstruct with an adhesive framed-reference, we move the incoming physical reality away from our free will and deny ourselves to know this reality.

Equal Thesis-Morality: Our equal thesis-morality comes from the recognition that others physically exist and that they have a consciousness and the physical structures of a human brain the same as oneself. This is our equal between people. This equal-to-us connects us commonly to the physical in physical existence. All issues common to this physical equal-to-us result in a common code of conduct. We express that common code of conduct from each person to all individuals. The expression is from the individual to all individuals because the person holds the recognition and expresses it to all individuals.

Equal Thesis-Morality, Equation: E = E. This is a mathematical description of our equality.

Experiential Existence: The total of thought existence, reactive existence, sensory existence, and consciousness makes for our experiential existence. They all arrive from the physical action of physical existence that results in our brain. Our mind results in an existence that is separate and distinct from physical existence. This existence arrives by the movement of physical existence. Physical existence can be without experiential existence, but experiential existence cannot be without physical existence.

Evaluate-to-balance: Our evaluate-to-balance is the result of evolution concerning our interaction with physical existence. In simple organisms, we have the simple stimulus-response interactions. Physical existence is always in motion. We human beings have constant physical action evaluations of our physical environment as well as internal brain functions to evaluate and determine our actions.

Free-Flow Framed-Reference: When we do not allow our life experience to move or bend our incoming reality, we have a free-flow framed-reference. We then can bring the incoming reality to our proper evaluate-to-balance. We maintain alignment to our physical reality.

Free Will: A will without any impinging forces from self, allowing the will to be in a static state where we can perceive the physical world in its truest sense.

The truest sense comes from the human brain, which then allows its nature to form an understanding of the physical world to which we exist in. A free-flow framed-reference does not interfere with our incoming reality. An adhesive framed-reference by our false-reality desires can impinge on our will to create many animated ideas that move in discord to reality.

Framed-Reference: Our framed-reference involves the initial area of our brain where our incoming reality first arrives. By our life experiences, we build up ideas to which we apply the sliver idea of reality. We may have attached reality accountably or unaccountably. When we allow preconceived ideas of reality to move our incoming reality, we begin to deny our free will. When we allow our framed-reference to contain a free flow to our incoming reality where we do not move our sliver and master ideas with attachment to false reality, we have our free will achieved for proper assessment.

Ideas: We acquire ideas from the input resulting from sensory and reactive existence experiences. They come in as pure-thesis ideas. An idea is not a singular entity. Instead, it is a group of sliver ideas. The volume and complexity of these groups of sliver ideas depends on its original input and any subsequent animation. All sliver ideas—form, color, and activity—contribute to the master idea. We can manipulate them. We can remove any sliver idea. We can add other sliver ideas from other ideas to make a new idea. These animations can lead to ideas that do not exist in the physical world.

Limited Moral Ideas: Certain moral claims are limited in nature and therefore limited in possibilities. The thesis-based justification to any limited moral idea resides with each specific situation. This makes the idea infinite in possible different thesis-based justifications, but there are limited possibilities residing in physical existence to the idea. It is a broadband idea that we have to evaluate to each situation to determine its applications. We can confuse non-moral with moral limited ideas. The idea to help someone in need is an example. Not all situations where someone claims need, is a moral situation. A moral obligation only occurs when a thesis-based justification for the actions exists.

Master Ideas: A master idea is a collection of sliver ideas pooled together to make an idea. We could have a master idea straight from the experience of sensory existence or we could make them by our mental animating abilities to rearrange our sliver ideas into new forms.

Mental Animation: When we think within our thought existence any acquired thesis idea or ideas or any other already animated idea or ideas and we animate changes within our thought existence, we have mental animation. Our animations, since they are in our minds independent to physical existence, can create ideas that do not reside in physical existence. Therefore, we can break any connection to physical existence and create an idea that can exist only in thought existence. We can pass on these animations from person-to-person through language. People can animate the animated ideas even further.

Narrowband Words: When we read or say a word, the person reading or listening has a meaning come into his or her thought existence. A word like apple is a narrowband word because a high percentage of people will think of the apple that you eat, although some may eventually think of a computer or the iPod. A word like orange remains a narrowband word, but a significant percentage of people would split their invoked meaning into two different definitions, the fruit and the color. A word like morality would invoke many different thoughts across people. With narrowband words, we can animate the same idea. When we animate the same idea, we can then begin to apply our remaining six elements of understanding truth and to see which category the idea belongs.

Parallel Existence: Our physical existence exists in parallel. Our incoming experience arrives to us as a collection of information. Our conscious understanding of ideas and thoughts are not singular entities in nature. Rather, we can have many attached ideas, conscious or not, that ride with the idea simultaneously. Ideas are more like a collection of bubbles than a single bubble. For example, the number five by itself is meaningless. Nevertheless, without conscious thought, we animate the attached ideas of quantity, reality in the real world, a spatial component, and even more together to make a master idea.

Personal Desires: We derive this from the spatial aspects of our physical existence that requires the action of thought and its movement from point A to point B. Our historical experiences reside at point A. Part of our historical experiences can be from our personal desires that can alter any perceived idea to attach or delete any sliver ideas to incoming ideas.

Physical Existence: The condition of existence minus consciousness and awareness. It is all that exists minus the product of any experiential existence, human or otherwise. Physical existence is an area, like a theatrical stage, where all physical existence resides and all physical actions occur. Physical existence is our creator and our lived creation.

Primal-Fantasy Ideas: Primal-fantasy ideas references an early evolutionary period where mental animation begins to occur to primal-thesis ideas. Because of lower-level thinking, primal-fantasy ideas tend to dominate over primal-thesis ideas.

Primal-Thesis Ideas: Primal-thesis ideas are similar to thesis ideas except they reference an early evolutionary period where the response by an organism to its environment was in a simple manner.

Pure-Manufactured Ideas: They have no connection to the physical. By mental animation, a person has cut the connection to physical existence. For example, when people animate in their mind the idea of the fruit orange, change its color to purple, and add flashing, green lights to it, they have broken any connections to physical existence.

Pure-Thesis Ideas: They have a direct connection to physical existence. An example would be the experience of the fruit orange. Upon seeing, feeling, smelling, or tasting it, one obtains a memory of it where all the sliver ideas to the master idea connects back to physical existence. Thus, an idea of an orange arises.

Reactive Existence: It is our preverbal system where we evaluate the physical world around ourselves and react to it with a coloring of experience. From these experiences, such as happiness, love, dread and more, comes a coloring of the perception of our world. Our experience of these reactions can turn into ideas.

Sensory Existence: It is our direct senses. It includes sight, sound, taste, touch, and smell. Sensory experience is our player to our world.

Serial Aspects of Language: When we engage in thought of our ideas, we experience them in parallel. However, our output of language is serial in nature. That is why, when we try to speak or write about some idea, we have to create the serial output of that idea. For example, our idea of orange has it as a fruit with a color. We can have that idea in our thought existence in parallel, but when asked to relate the idea, one has to state serially the fruit or color in a serial order. Language cannot output in parallel.

Sliver Ideas: When we experience physical existence through our sensory existence, we have incoming information that occurs in parallel. This collection of information divides into many sliver ideas that then makes the master idea to the original experience. Because we have these master ideas of original experience in a collection of sliver ideas, we can move any sliver idea and rearrange, add or subtract any sliver ideas to make a new collection of sliver ideas to create a new master idea. A sliver idea is one singular aspect of a master idea.

Theorized-Manufactured Ideas: When we have partial or weak connections to the physical that result in at least two possibilities, we have a theorized-manufactured idea. A level of probability arises that can range from very high, yet contains two or more possibilities, to extremely weak connections to the physical with low probability.

Thought Existence: All that exists minus all physical material and the following components of experiential existence, which are sensory and reactive existences. This leaves ideas only.

Unequal Thesis-Morality: Our unequal thesis-morality comes from recognition that we have unequal aspects to our humanness. For example, we have different talents. Unequal thesis-morality is our physical structure minus our experiential existence and our generic pattern to a human mind. This leaves us our differences. Unequal thesis-morality as a code of conduct comes from these differences. Further, unequal thesis-morality goes from all individuals to the individual because it requires the evaluation of others to the individual holding the difference. This is opposite to equal thesis-morality as it goes from individual to all individuals.

Unequal Thesis-Morality, Equation: $\bar{E} = U \pm D$ ($\bar{E}$ = mean equal, U = Unequal, D = Difference). This is a mathematical description of our inequality between people.

Universal Moral Ideas: We can make moral statements that are singular in nature. In this singularity, we have the needed connection with physical existence within its definition. We have our physically based (thesis) justification to the idea within the idea. This makes it finite. An example would be not to murder. It is a universal moral idea. It is immoral to murder, which is killing with manufactured-based justifications. The physical reality of this universal idea resides in the physical equality in every individual. Every situation that brings up this moral idea, the physical connection flows from the idea to physical existence. It is in the flow that the application of it is made. Therefore, we have a universal type of moral flow. We have one idea with one type of evaluation. It applies to all situations where the taking of human life occurs. It is a narrowband idea with a specific master idea that we apply in a broadband manner. Health is something universally needed by all of us. Jeopardizing the health of anyone is universally immoral action. We have an equal-to-us violation. Our thesis-based justification resides in the moral statement.

BIBLIOGRAPHY

1. Smith, Adam. *An Inquiry Into the Nature and Causes of the Wealth of Nations*, Edited by C. J. Bullock, PH.D, Volume 10, The Harvard Classics, Edited by Charles W. Eliot, LL.D., P. F. Collier & Son Company, New York, 1909
2. Hayek, F. A. *The Constitution of Liberty*, The University of Chicago Press, Chicago, 1960-1978
3. Anonymous. (Attributed to George Burhope.), *The Art of Self-Government, in a Moral Essay, In Three Parts, First Written to a Gentleman in the University, and since fitted for Publick Use*, The Second Edition Corrected, London: Printed for W. Taylor, at the Ship in Pater Noster-Row, 1713
4. Sartre, Jean-Paul. *Being and Nothingness, A Phenomenological Essay on Ontology*, Washington Square Press, New York, 1943-1992
5. Anonymous (Attributed to Newcome, Susannah.) *An Enquiry into the Evidence of the Christian Religion*, The Second Edition, with Additions, London, Printed for William Innys, at the West-End of St. Paul's. 1732
6. Volney, M. *The Ruins: or A Survey of the Revolutions of Empires*, Translated from the French, The Third Edition, London, Printed for J. Johnson, St. Paul's Church-Yard, 1796
7. Seneca. *Seneca's Morals By way of Abstract, To which is added, A Discourse, under the Title of An After-Thought*, By Sir Roger L'Estrange, Knt., The Eighth Edition, London, Printed by W. Bowyer, for Jacob Tonson at Grays-Inn-Gate, in Grays-Inn-Lane, 1702
8. Locke, John, Gent. *An Essay Concerning Human Understanding, In Four Books, Volume I*, The Ninth Edition, with large Additions, LONDON, Printed by T. W. for A. Churchill; and Edm. Parker, at the Bible and Crown in Lombardstreet, 1726
9. Hume, David. *A Treatise of Human Nature*, Books 1 and 2 originally published in 1739, Book 3 in 1740, Barnes and Noble, New York, 2005

10. Watts, Isaac. *Logick: Or, The Right Use of Reason in the Enquiry after Truth.* The Fifth Edition, London, Printed for Emanuel Matthews, at the Bible in Paternoster-Row; Richard Ford, at the Angel, and Richard Hett, at the Bible and Crown, both in the Poultry, 1733

11. Freud, Sigmund. *Civilization and Its Discontents,* Translated and Edited by James Strachey, W. W. Norton & Company, New York, London, 1961

12. Freud, Sigmund. *New Introductory Lectures on Psycho-Analysis,* by Sigmund Freud, M.D., LL.D., Translated by W. J. H. Sprott, New York, W. W. Norton & Company, Inc. 1933

13. Leiter, Brian. *Nietzsche on Morality,* Routledge, New York, NY 10001, 2002

14. Nietzsche, Friedrich. *The Genealogy of Morals,* Dover Publications, Inc., Mineola, NY, 2003

15. Locke, John, Gent. *An Essay Concerning Human Understanding, In Four Books, Volume II,* LONDON, Printed by T. W. for A. Churchill; and Edm. Parker, at the Bible and Crown in Lombard-street, 1726

16. Kant, Immanuel. *Fundamental Principles of the Metaphysics of Morals.* Translated by Thomas Kingsmill Abbott. Dover Publications, Inc., Mineola, NY, 2005

17. Bruyère, Jean de La. *Characters: or, the Manners of the Age. with The Moral Characters of Theophrastus,* Printed for E Curell, London, 1709

18. Freud, Sigmund. *The Ego and the ID,* Translated by Joan Riviere, Edited by James Strachey, W. W. Norton & Company, New York, London, 1960

19. Blount, Sir Thomas Pope. *Essays on Several Subjects,* Printed for Richard Bently, in Russel-street in Covent-Garden, London, 1691

20. Nietzsche, Friedrich. *Beyond Good and Evil,* Oxford University Press, New York, 1998

21. Nietzsche, Friedrich. *Ecce Homo,* Penguin Books Ltd., London, England, 1992

22. Allestree, Richard, attrib. *The Government of the Tongue, By the Author of The Whole Duty of Man, &c.,* The Fifth Impression, At the Theater in Oxford, 1693

23. Epicurus. *The Essential Epicurus, Letters, Principal Doctrines, Vatican Sayings, and Fragments,* Translated, with an introduction, by Eugene O'Connor, Prometheus Books, New York, 1993

24. Epictetus. *Epictetus, A Stoic and Socratic Guide to Life,* A. A. Long, Oxford University Press, Oxford, 2002

25. Locke, John. *Essays on the Law of Nature,* edited by W. von Leyden, Oxford University Press, Amen House, London, E. C., 1954

26. Locke, John. *Selected Correspondence*, edited by Mark Goldie, Oxford University Press, Oxford New York, 2002

27. Locke, John. *Two Treatises of Government and A Letter Concerning Toleration*, Yale University Press, New Haven and London, 2003

28. Paine, Thomas. *Agrarian Justice, Opposed to Agrarian Law, and to Agrarian Monopoly*. Albany: Printed by Barber & Southwick, 1797

29. Goodell, William. *Slavery and Anti-Slavery; a History of the Great Struggle in Both Hemispheres; with a view of The Slavery Question in the United States*, New-York: William Harned, 48 Beekman-Street, 1852

30. Ferguson, Adam. *An Essay on the History of Civil Society*, The Fifth Edition., London, Printed for T. Cadell, in the Strand; and W. Creech, and J. Bell, Edinburgh., 1782

31. Vattel, M. De. *The Law of Nations; or, Principle of the Law of Nature; Applied to the Conduct and Affairs of Nations and Sovereigns*, Dublin: Luke White, 1792

32. Allen, Ethan. *Reason the Only Oracle of Man Or A Compendious System of Natural Religion*, Bennington: State of Vermont; Printed by Haswell & Russell, 1784

33. Godwin, William. *Enquiry concerning Political Justice and its Influence on Morals and Happiness*, London, Vol I, Printed for G. G. and J. Robinson, Paternoster-row, 1798

34. Aristotle. *The Nicomachean Ethics*, Translated by J. A. K. Thomson, Penguin Books, 1976, 2004.

35. Cicero. *On Moral Ends*, Edited by Julia Annas, Translated by Raphael Woolf, Cambridge University Press, 2001

36. Erasmus, Desiderius. *Praise of Folly and Letter to Maarten Van Dorp 1515*, Translated by Betty Radice, Penguin Books, 1993

37. Aquinas, Thomas. *The Summa Contra Gentiles*, Translated by Vernon J. Bourke, University of Norte Dame Press. Edition 1975-2001

38. Aquinas, Thomas. *Thomas Aquinas, Selected Writings*, Edited and translated by Ralph McInery, Penguin Books, 1998

39. Godwin, William. *Enquiry concerning Political Justice and its Influence on Morals and Happiness*, London, Vol II, Printed for G. G. and J. Robinson, Paternoster-row, 1798

40. Boethius. *The Theological Tractates, The Consolation of Philosophy*, Harvard University Press, Loeb Classical Library, 1918-2003

41. Hayek, F. A. *The Collected Works of F. A. Hayek, Volume I, The Fatal Conceit, The Errors of Socialism*, Edited by W. W. Bartley III, The University of Chicago Press, Paperback edition, 1991

42. Montesquieu. *The Spirit of the Laws*, Cambridge University Press, New York, 1989-1999

43. Jefferson, Thomas. *Autobiography of Thomas Jefferson*, Dover Publications, Inc., Mineola, New York, 2005

44. Nelson, Craig. *Thomas Paine, Enlightenment, Revolution and the Birth of Modern Nations*, Viking Penguin, 2006

45. Paine, Thomas. *Rights of Man: Being an Answer to Mr. Burke's Attack on the French Revolution*, Third Edition, by Thomas Paine, London, Printed for J. S. Jordan, 1791

46. Paine, Thomas. *The Age of Reason, Being an Investigation of True and Fabulous Theology*, Edited by Moncure Daniel Conway, Dover Publications, Inc. New York, 2004, republication of G. P. Putman's Sons, New York, 1896

47. Paine, Thomas. *Rights of Man. Part the Second. Combining Principle and Practice*, The Second Edition, London, Printed for J. S. Jordan, 1792

48. Paine, Thomas. *Rights of Man, Common Sense and Other Political Writing, Edited with an Introduction and Notes by Mark Philp*, Oxford University Press, 1995

49. Edmund Burke. *Reflections on the Revolution in France, and on the Proceeding in Certain Societies in London Related to that Event. In a Letter Intended to have been Sent to a Gentleman in Paris*, Dublin, Printed for W. Watson, etc.,1790

50. Cheetham, James. *The Life of Thomas Paine, Author of Common Sense, The Crisis, Rights of Man, &c. &c. &c.*, New-York: Printed by Southwick and Pelsue, No. 3, New-Street, 1809

51. Temple, Sir William. *The Works of Sir William Temple Bart, Complete in Four Volumes Octavo, to which is prefixed, The Life and Character of the Author*, A New Edition, London, Printed for J. Clarke, etc., 1757

52. Friedman, Milton. *Capitalism and Freedom*, 40th Anniversary Edition, The University of Chicago Press, Chicago and London, 1962-2002

53. Friedman, Milton & Rose. *Free to Choose*, A Harvest Book, Harcourt, Inc., 1980

54. Hayek, F. A. *The Counter-Revolution of Science, Studies on the Abuse of Reason*, Liberty Fund, Indianapolis, 1979

55. Hayek, F. A. *Individualism and Economic Order*, The University of Chicago Press, Paperback edition, 1980

56. Hayek, F. A. *The Road to Serfdom*, Fiftieth Anniversary Edition with a New Introduction by Milton Friedman, The University of Chicago Press, 1994

57. Malthus, T. R. *An Essay on the Principle of Population*, Cambridge University Press 1992, used text from 1803